COPYRIGHT, CONTRACT, AND VIDEO GAMES

This book uncovers how video game contracts act as monologues of power, moulding players to align with proprietary ideologies.

In the era of interactive technologies, the player emerges as a vital yet curiously overlooked figure. While copyright law governs the creation and distribution of these technologies, it sidesteps the player, leaving private contracts to define their role and obligations. Using video games as a case study, this book fills the gap left by copyright law, offering an innovative socio-legal methodology to interrogate and challenge harmful contractual norms.

By analysing contracts as a form of critical discourse, the book exposes the contradictions and idealisations embedded in these agreements, which often serve to reinforce industry priorities. It is an essential resource for scholars in intellectual property law, video game studies, and socio-legal research, contributing to pressing debates on user rights and the shifting balance of power in interactive industries.

With its fresh perspective on the interplay of copyright, contract and cultural participation, the book redefines the player's role in a rapidly evolving digital landscape, offering new tools to understand and critique the legal frameworks shaping this most interactive of industries.

Copyright, Contract, and Video Games

Terms of Play

Amy Thomas

•HART•

OXFORD • LONDON • NEW YORK • NEW DELHI • SYDNEY

HART PUBLISHING

Bloomsbury Publishing Plc

Kemp House, Chawley Park, Cumnor Hill, Oxford, OX2 9PH, UK

1385 Broadway, New York, NY 10018, USA

Bloomsbury Publishing Ireland Limited, 29 Earlsfort Terrace, Dublin 2, D02 AY28, Ireland

HART PUBLISHING, the Hart/Stag logo, BLOOMSBURY and the Diana logo are trademarks of Bloomsbury Publishing Plc

First published in Great Britain 2026

A catalogue record for this book is available from the British Library.

A catalogue record for this book is available from the Library of Congress.

Library of Congress Control Number: 2026936509

ISBN: HB: 978-1-50998-806-8
ePDF: 978-1-50998-804-4
ePub: 978-1-50998-805-1

Typeset by Compuscript Ltd, Shannon

For product safety related questions contact productsafety@bloomsbury.com

To find out more about our authors and books visit www.hartpublishing.co.uk. Here you will find extracts, author information, details of forthcoming events and the option to sign up for our newsletters.

For Adam.

PATCH NOTES[1]

When reading this book, you might notice a tension between my attempt to make this 'fun' to read (because it is fundamentally about *play*) and the seriousness of law, contracts, and the miles of black and white boilerplate text that now systematically accompany games – which is often not fun at all. I am sure that many scholars who write about games with any attempt at academic rigour have similarly experienced this tension. But in addition to this, I have had the unfortunate meta-task of scrutinising the language of this book – which is itself a book about scrutinising language. One of the fundamental positions of the book is that, when things are written a certain way, they tell you about the values of the person doing the writing. And so, I too must open myself to scrutiny of the deliberateness of my own writing and choice of words. These words will tell you that this is certainly a book about *video games*: you will find 'save points' (rather than summaries), 'levels' (rather than 'parts), and indeed 'patch notes' (rather than a preface). The dogmatic use of 'outwith' can also tell you that I am Scottish, and quite stubborn about it. But I cannot promise that reading the book will always be *fun*, much in the same way there are many games you will also not find fun to play.[2] In fact, I harbour secret hopes that some of these findings may be *so* 'un-fun' as to cause enough dismay to draw attention to some important policy issues and create impetus for change.

In addition to being about games, this book is grounded in law, specifically copyright law. However, it may also be of interest to readers from social sciences, media studies, and game studies, or other disciplines. For this reason, I do not assume a background knowledge in copyright fundamentals, and throughout caution that this is not a 'hardcore doctrinal' law book. Borrowing again on gaming terms, I have tried to configure the difficulty mode for this book as 'casual'. Copyright scholars are nonetheless likely to be the primary audience, and for that reason, it may interest you to know that this book is adapted from my PhD thesis,[3] which was about the copyright *user* more broadly construed. Only a modicum of

[1] Patch notes are summaries of changes made in updates to games, written by the game's developers.

[2] Noting that the assumed relationship between games, fun, and playability are more nuanced than this brief introduction suggests: see eg T Barker, 'Unplayable Games: Time and Digital Culture' 'Unplayable Games: Time and Digital Culture' (2023) 2 *Kunsttexte*.

[3] As an additional note, the thesis this book was based on was largely written during the Covid-19 pandemic in the UK, and in the spirit of scrutinising the language I have used, there is a curious, implicit yearning for physical presence throughout the book. Games are analogised as a space to be inhabited; contracts as a monologue by an imagined orator. Licences – inanimate, black and white documents – are anthropomorphised and given agency as something that 'tells' or 'encourages' the player to behave in a certain way.

reflection was necessary after my defence to realise that instead, it was more clearly about games and the player, hence the rebranding (and rather substantive changes to Chapters 1 and 2). And while I try to never plead the relevance of games as a general rule, nor diminish their importance, the need for 'rebranding' does bely some implications beyond the medium: you may indeed find that many conclusions about the 'player' could apply to many different copyright 'users', of music, art, film, and more.

The 'image' of the player, such as it is, is depicted on the front cover, where they are re-imagined as a pixelated version of DaVinci's Vitruvian man, a famous symbol of the idealised proportions of the human form. But, as is the case in art and anthropology, this book shows that the 'perfect player', like the 'perfect person', also doesn't exist – this image is just an idealised vision of what a player *should* be, as dictated in the various contracts they are exposed, and agree, to: a subject of 'contractual imagination', rather than artistic.

Finally, in this book you will find plenty of scepticism, and criticism, of certain business practices of the modern games industry. But I am not ignorant to the struggles of game production – an increasingly complex, hugely expensive, and lengthy task. Larger productions typically require up to five years of development time, costing tens of millions for their creation, even when excluding marketing expenses. Indeed, at the time of writing, the reality of the difficult working conditions for the people who make games – the crunch time, mass lay-offs, the largest strike in Hollywood history, a huge and controversial merger in the shadow of multiple sexual harassment claims – rightly garner sympathy for those involved in game production. Perhaps it goes without saying, but I also enjoy games, and do hope that they continue to be made – albeit under sustainable working conditions. But I also hope that the people that play them are treated fairly – and this book is, at its core, about that. In sum, I hope readers will agree that it is not incompatible to be supportive of the people who make and play games, while being critical of the system that often exploits them both.

Amy Thomas
November 2025

ACKNOWLEDGEMENTS

My first thanks go to Roberta, and the whole team at Hart, for believing in this project and supporting it throughout.

Second thanks then go to all the kind colleagues who so nobly sacrificed time from their academic summers to review material for this book (in alphabetical order): Magali Eben, Kris Erickson, Ula Furgal, Marta Iljadica, Aline Iramina, and Luis Porangaba. I hope one day to return the favour to you all. Any errors remaining are my own. Thanks also go to my PhD supervisors, Martin Kretschmer and Marta Iljadica, and to my viva examiners, Tanya Aplin and James Meese, all of whose feedback and encouragement on my thesis was instrumental.

I have been fortunate to benefit from generous support, both professional and personal, when writing – and I have the happiness of occasionally being able to blend the two together. This includes the CREATe team at the University of Glasgow – it is my privilege to work with you all – and my fellow academic game enthusiasts in both the Press Start network and Interactive Entertainment Law Review circuits. Jiarong and Sevra deserve many special thanks for their ongoing personal and professional support.

To my friends and family: I hope it goes without saying that you are always the inspiration: Mum; Dad and Sho; Aly and Martin; and all the other Cutts and Garretts, Johnstons and McVeans, Shirkies and Collins, Caldwells and Donnans (the latter of which I am now proudly part). Skye dog, my constant companion throughout, has closely supervised the work.

During writing, and to my delight, the number of my nieces has continued to grow: starting with Isabelle (December 2020) and Lucy (October 2021), and now wee Ellie (August 2025). I hope you all pursue your dreams, whatever they may be. And a special note for Lucy: this is the booky-book I was writing whenever we weren't playing together. In your young wisdom, you said that all good books have pictures and, that preferably, are pink – you were absolutely right of course. It turns out pictures are quite hard to do, but pink is very possible.

CONTENTS

LEVEL 2

LEVEL 3

TABLE OF CASES

Court of Justice of the European Union

Germany

South Africa

United Kingdom

United States

TABLE OF LEGISLATION

International treaties

Canada

European Union

United Kingdom

United States

Introduction

Don't be a rules lawyer.

– Gaming idiom

When we play a game, our first thought is not always about whether it's legal to do so. In fact, our idea of 'play' may even be entirely oppositional to the idea of 'law': frivolity, leisure, and fun, in the face of authority, restriction, and the utmost seriousness. But games are proprietary products that bring us – knowingly or unknowingly – into a dialogue with the law whenever we play them. Games are composed of a multitude of copyright protected audiovisual works and software – the characters, soundtrack, and code – underlying each virtually rendered leaf, brick, flame. And as a proprietary, copyrighted product, our access to games is subject to ongoing, private regulators, some of which are operated by the largest, most powerful tech companies in the world: Apple, Google, Microsoft among many others. In short, play has become 'p/owned',[1] and when we play, we also agree to the legal 'terms of play' set by these powerful actors.

The terms of play are typically laid out as a contract, which can take myriad forms of lengthy, 'black and white' boilerplate: end-user licensing agreements, terms and conditions, terms of service, and usage policies, among others.[2] Ubiquitous to all digital goods, we have largely ritualised clicking the checkbox that confirms we have '(read and) agree' to the terms therein before playing. These strange, legal artefacts are universally disliked, ignored, and largely invisible until litigated. Their ongoing existence also begs explanation. And while these tools have not been immune from the gaze of copyright scholarship,[3] this book argues that contracts have a function *beyond* just a legal text of Levitical rules. Instead, they are imbued with broader social, cultural, and often ideological, meaning – collectively, a kind of 'contractual imagination' of how a player as a good, legal

[1] Here, 'owned' refers to the proprietary, legal ownership of the game itself, whereas 'pwned' – apt gaming slang – refers to the utter domination or defeat of/by another player.

[2] Whether such texts technically meet the legal criteria of 'contracts' (requiring eg offer and acceptance or a 'meeting of minds') is a topic of scholarly debate, especially given that they are typically offered on a non-negotiable 'agree or walk away basis' (see for example N Elkin-Koren, 'Governing Access to Users-Generated-Content: The Changing Nature of Private Ordering in Digital Networks' in E Brousseau et al (eds), *Governance, Regulations and Powers on the Internet* (Cambridge University Press, 2009). It is not the purpose of this book to consider the merits or demerits of this argument, but rather I take an existentialist view: we consider them contracts because we label and treat them as such.

[3] Contract as a form of governance is a central argument for two key texts that inspire this work: L Lessig, *Code: And Other Laws of Cyberspace, Version 2.0* (Basic Books, 2006) and J Cohen, *Configuring the Networked Self* (Yale University Press, 2012).

subject *should* behave in the eyes of a game company.[4] The player, as imagined in contract, is not an inevitable or stable legal subject, nor one that we should passively accept. It shows that the terms of play – and even the manner of *how* they are written and presented to the player – are highly contestable, presenting subjective, industry priorities as commonsensical and '(read and)' agreeable when they are often anything but.

I. 'Rules Lawyering' as a Research Method

As the above paragraphs suggest, this book is not purely about law. Nor is it a book about whether terms of play are strictly legal or not – a matter much better addressed elsewhere.[5] Instead, the legal aspects of this book are better understood as a way of illustrating the *problem* under examination: that copyright gives game companies real, legal entitlements to construct the player in a particular way and in doing so, normalises contestable, imbalanced power relationships through contract. This is a foundational issue in the structure of copyright, with no general doctrine on the relationship between copyright and contract being given at international level.[6] As such, rather than being grounded in a particular jurisdiction, the legal aspects of the book are often discussed illustratively, perhaps inevitably skewing towards the US given its centrality in the early development of game software, and its ongoing significance in the game industry.

Instead, the primary method employed in this book is a form of 'rules lawyering': a gaming idiom for someone who insists on the rules, often at the expense of the spirit, of the game. I examine the contracts that structure terms of play, and follow them to their literal conclusion. I scrutinise the logic of those terms, and interrogate the precise way in which they are written: what do they technically allow or prohibit, and what would be the reason for a game company to do so? Why do these contracts 'speak' in a certain way, employing language that is often an impenetrable wall of 'legalese'? How do they encourage, or discourage, players from engaging with specific terms? And why would those specific terms be important to disguise? How are legal entitlements of the player – given to them by law – subverted or obscured by the contractual text? What is the significance in referring to a player as a 'customer', a 'fan', or even 'you'?

[4] The idea of contract as a text, narrative or tool of subject formation is similarly forwarded in MJ Radin, *Boilerplate: The Fine Print, Vanishing Rights, and the Rule of Law* (Princeton University Press, 2013).

[5] E Derclaye and M Favale, 'Copyright and Contract Law: Regulating User Contracts: The State of the Art and a Research Agenda' (2010) 18(1) *Journal of Intellectual Property Law & Practice* 65.

[6] The most important international agreement here is the Berne Convention (the Berne Convention for the Protection of Literary and Artistic Works (Paris, 4 May 1896), 1161 UNTS 3, entered into force 5 December 1887, as revised at Paris on 24 July 1971, as amended on 28 September 1979), which has 182 signatories as of 2025.

To understand this, I employ Critical Discourse Analysis (CDA), a qualitative research method that examines how language constructs our realities. Through CDA, terms of play become a form of discourse: they tell a *story* about the player as a legal subject, written by an entity with specific, often commercial, interests in mind.[7] As such, the story of the player as a 'customer' – the formal, paying recipient – may be very different from that of the 'fan' – the devout and supportive follower. However, and importantly, I do not claim that any of these are the 'true' identity of the player; this is not an empirical study about how players read, understand and adjust their behaviour in response to this language. Indeed, we should take seriously the well-established research that most people do not read these contracts at all;[8] and it is unlikely that they are actually influential in how players behave in reality. Instead, and ironically, when trying to better understand the player, we often learn more about 'the man behind the curtain': that is, the game company itself (or its representative) that offers those terms. The significance of the difference between the 'customer' and the 'fan' is in the *imagined*, idealised qualities of the player as a legal subject by the game company. The key, in short, is in the *telling*: the player's story is written, unilaterally, by an entity with subjective, commercial priorities. And as players, we don't engage with the shaping of this story. We can't change a contract we are offered, or have a hand in drafting it: it is a monologue we receive.

This book is not an endorsement of this logic. Rather, it is a dismantling of it, with a healthy scepticism of the legal power granted to a games company which made it possible in the first instance. Power is a consistent theme here, whether by scrutinising the *real* power given by copyright law, or the *impression* of power given through contract (the significance of calling 'you' the 'customer' or the 'fan'). This power is even present even where it is largely invisible: disguised, and normalised, hidden systematically behind checkboxes that we click every day. As such, the book has both descriptive and critical dimensions: descriptive in that it identifies and examines the ways in which players are constructed through contract; and critical in that it questions who has a stake in that construction.

In the spirit of rules lawyering, and as a matter of terminology, any rights in a game – whether real, claimed, or imagined – are likely generated by a plethora of different copyright 'authors' – that is, the people who actually make a game – including software developers, graphic artists, sound engineers, performers, and scriptwriters (and many more). Games may be developed over many years, across various jurisdictions, and under varying contractual conditions (employment,

[7] In this book, the contract is often anthropomorphised and given agency, eg 'the contract constructs …'. While there is obviously a human behind this construction, without being able to accurately identify the role of this human (a lawyer? the rightsholder? an automatically generated boilerplate contract?) referring to the contract in this way is more succinct.

[8] See generally Y Bakos et al, 'Does Anyone Read the Fine Print? Testing a Law and Economics Approach to Standard Form Contracts' (2009) Working Papers 09-04, NET Institute; and JA Obar and A Oeldorf-Hirsch, 'The Biggest Lie on the Internet: Ignoring the Privacy Policies and Terms of Service Policies of Social Networking Services' (2008) 23(1) *Information, Communication and Society* 128.

commission) such that the network of authorship is both vast and complex. In most cases, however, *ownership* vests in the entity which brings the game to market – typically a publisher or producer – but an entity which I label vaguely as the 'game company'.[9] The vagueness of this term is deliberate because we cannot make assumptions about authorship and ownership, nor the intentions of the game *creator* in relation to the player, but rather who is in control of a game on the market, and who is actualising the rights they claim through law.[10]

II. Overview of Levels

The book is structured around three 'levels', a reference to the structure of discrete game spaces with set boundaries and different objectives, through which you may progress to completion. Level 1 explains *why* the player is connected to copyright and contract; Level 2 shows *how* the player can be constructed through the terms of play, and; Level 3 shows *what* this means about the player, and the entity that constructs them. By design, this can be read as a narrative that progresses through each level, and to this end each chapter contains 'save points' – summaries which distil the main components to take forward to the next level– and that you can return to if you find you've lost some progression. Some chapters also include 'side quests': these are not central to the main mission of progressing through the level, but include additional information which may improve your experience.

Level 1

Chapter 1 explores the connection between the player and copyright law. It explains how the player has come to be regulated through copyright, as the recipient (user) of a game as a copyrighted work. The chapter also considers that even where players may behave creatively themselves, they have generally not been considered as authors or performers who may own competing rights, but rather makers of 'user-generated content'. The chapter concludes with the impression that the figure of the player in copyright is important, but both opaque and contestable, leaving an empty space for more specific regulation through private contract.

Chapter 2 then introduces 'player contracts' as the main unit of analysis of the book. First, the chapter illustrates the legal interplay between copyright and contract, showing how significant discretion is given to rightsholders (game companies) to re-shape players outwith copyright law. The second part of the

[9] In a limited number of cases, this must also be extended to an individual – for example, the 'one man army' Eric Barone, as sole (human) creator of *Stardew Valley*.

[10] I discuss authorial intent in games in more detail in A Thomas, 'Contested Game Spaces: Romance Modding and Copyright' (2024) 7(2) *Interactive Entertainment Law Review* 55.

chapter is a historic overview of how player contracts have developed in practice, showing how they have been used as a responsive tool, adaptive to the social and cultural needs of game companies at any given time. The construct of the player in contracts is shown to be constantly in flux throughout history, moving from a 'co-creator' to a 'thief', to (now) somewhere in between.

Level 2

Chapter 3 outlines the methodological approach to the research, introducing CDA as the lens through which player contracts are interpreted. This chapter also describes the construction of the dataset of player contracts and explains how contracts are treated as texts that encode social, legal, and cultural meanings which can be codified and interpreted.

Level 3

Level 3 details the research findings, consisting of three chapters, each of which comprises a theme identified from the methodology.

Chapter 4 explores the theme of *Authority*, which shows how the shared regulatory practice of copyright, manifested via player contracts, can be reconfigured to align with the ideological trajectories of specific game industry communities. The chapter shows how copyright, and the authority it bestows, is selectively engaged with by different game industry communities: embraced by some and rejected by others. Regardless of the disparity at industry level, the chapter shows how the player is commonly assumed to be a legal subject who is vaguely *oppositional* of the copyright regime, whether as a suspect actor to be controlled, or a ludic entity who rejects the proprietary vision of game software.

The theme of Chapter 5 – *Access* – represents the most homogenised construct of the player in this research. Contracts emphatically construct the player as both a non-owner and, perhaps more crucially, a non-reseller: they are the endpoint in the transactional chain who is permitted to access the work. However, this designation does not necessarily mean the player is a *consumer*, in the sense of being an owner of a copy of a work. Instead, the qualities of the consumer are reserved only for when commercial interests are at stake, whether in the 'battle' against piracy or the 'war' against a competitor.

The third and final theme is illustrated in Chapter 6 – *Artifice* – which explores how player creativity is mediated through contracts. In the chapter, the player is positioned as a maker of 'user-generated content' only in name, disguising the aspects of authorship or performance in function. These qualities are hidden behind a differentiated discourse, which is outwardly informal, polite, and friendly towards the player, but inwardly controlling and contradictory. Artifice is therefore evident in two respects: in the disguise of authorial or performance qualities; and in the disguise of the contractual language itself.

Should you progress through each level, you will find the conclusion (a kind of 'boss level', in gaming parlance). It ties together key themes from the findings, considering the normative and policy implications arising from the research, and avenues for further enquiry.

Level 1

1

The Player in Copyright Law

I. Introduction

Historically, the player did not have a direct relationship with copyright, a law which has been primarily concerned with the exploitation of creative literary and artistic works in the *public* sphere. Play has been – and continues to be – a mostly private activity taking place in the home or local community that copyright – in principle – should not touch. Older (and even ancient) games may have been regulated by some laws – especially in public-facing competitions – but were not obviously an object of copyright regulation, in the sense that someone would not obviously be interacting with a *creative* work.[1] Even in the early 20th century, when copyright (and other intellectual property rights) began to creep into branded, mass-produced branded board games, copyright's reach beyond the point of purchase remained very limited. Now, with the preponderance of software-based video games, the player is certainly the recipient of a copyright-protected, proprietary product. And as a result, players routinely come into contact with copyright, as well as the interests of the entities who own that copyright, on an ongoing basis.

While the player now has routine interactions with copyright, this chapter shows how they are neither well defined nor understood in law. In part, this is because copyright is technical and economical in nature – it seeks to identify and reward the people who make creative things (the authors, and often the owners), and to define the responsibilities of the people who receive a copy of that thing (the users). In principle, this is a relatively simplistic and binary view of the world, between those who produce and those who consume.[2] But it opens a fundamental, ontological question about *who the player is* for the purposes of copyright. Players can defy these categorisations or have qualities of both. Certainly, a player will buy and use a game. But this is not an entirely passive interaction, despite the popular

[1] Boyden, for example, argues that games have historically been conceptualised as systems or frameworks, inviting interaction rather than creative expression. See BE Boyden, 'Games and Other Uncopyrightable Systems' (2011) 18 *George Mason Law Review* 439.

[2] The existence of the binary is not universally accepted, or rather, has been critically discredited: see C Craig, 'Reconstructing the Author-Self: Some Feminist Lessons for Copyright Law' (2007) 15(2) *Journal of Gender, Social Policy and the Law* 207 at 233: '… The result is a copyright model that forces all intellectual production into doctrinal categories shaped by individualistic assumptions about the authorial ideal, producing the simplifying dichotomies of creation/reproduction, author/user, laborer/free-rider'.

impression of the 'couch potato'. To progress through the rules, processes, challenges and restrictions in a game, the player needs to make choices, develop skills, and actualise those outputs. A player might choose to develop their avatar's skills in a particular attribute – say, their endurance, which impacts their ability to travel further or carry more items in a game – and invest in gathering specific resources to make an object which can help others move over particularly difficult terrain.[3] These are deliberate, sometimes rather clever, and often very time-consuming choices – but are they creative, or purely mechanical? What if, instead, the player uses content from a game to make new things entirely? The phenomenon of the game streamer, personality, or influencer has in effect spawned a new industry in itself which – for a lucky few – can make for a lucrative career in 'playing games'.[4] And how does any of this impact the copyright of the game company?

In sum, finding the line between 'creator' and 'user' is important because where the player falls in this binary will ultimately impact how they are governed and by whom. If a player is – reductively – simply a user of a copyrighted work, then the law leaves a large amount of discretion to the rightsholder (the game company) to determine how that work can be used. If, however, the player is considered as a creator in their own right, they may benefit from their own exclusive rights when they interact with a game, or make new content with it. Omnipresent throughout this chapter is a question about power: who has property, and who is permitted to trespass upon it and under what conditions?

Side quest: copyright in games

It is not the purpose of this book to offer an exhaustive assessment of how copyright attaches to a game – rather, I am concerned with the player interacting with it. But given my assumption that the player is in dialogue with *copyright* when interacting with a game, it is worth briefly addressing. In particular, because there is no subsistence of copyright over *all* aspects of the game, it is an important 'side quest' to be aware of the nuances in relation to this.

Games are complex, multimedia works,[5] meaning they are made up of lots of different creative components, made by multiple different people, over a prolonged period of time. For simplicity, games are composed of two elements: the 'back-end' (what the player can't see) and the 'front-end' (what the player can see).

The back-end of a game includes components which may have different copyright statuses, as illustrated in Table 1. Of primacy is the game code, a series of instructions that determines how the game responds to the player's input. It can determine, for example, how an avatar moves, or how the environment responds to them; if the avatar shoots a gun, will an inanimate object 'collide' with it and be destroyed? If an avatar interacts with an in-game character, how will that character respond based on the avatar's previous actions in the game? Such code – whether object or source code – can

[3] This is a reference to Hideo Kojima's self-conceptualised 'strand' type of game – namely, the *Death Stranding* series.

[4] I Ignatova, 'A £24b Market: Why Do Game Studios Pay Influencers' (*80.lv*, 15 August 2024) https://80.lv/articles/a-usd24b-market-why-do-game-studios-pay-influencers.

[5] T Aplin, *Copyright Law in the Digital Society: The Challenges of Multimedia* (Hart Publishing, 2005).

be protected by copyright as a 'literary work'. This code is the instructional aspect of the game software, which more broadly includes other essential elements for 'running' a game, such as libraries, or game engines. Game software is also usually protectable by copyright.

There is, however, an important – and not altogether obvious – limitation to this protection, illustrated in Table 1. It is a clear principle of copyright law that rules, systems and processes can't be protected.[6] Or rather, while copyright can protect the *expression* of game code and software – the way in which it is written and compiled – it cannot protect the underlying ideas or functions that the software enables. These ideas and functions are usually referred to as 'game mechanics' (the design of challenges, or how outcomes are determined in a game) that structure the 'gameplay' (the way a player experiences a game). For example, the idea of 'jumping' over an obstacle in a game, and that this would result in the award of a 'point', would be an example of one such unprotectable mechanic. The reason for this limitation is largely a matter of public policy, to prevent the monopolisation of overbroad principles of play.[7] Yet, the now broad and unambiguous scope of protection for software means that the systems, rules and processes of games are effectively embedded *within* this, and become protected by proxy.[8] The quality of being able to jump in a game to overcome obstacles *is* a rule, which must – by its nature – be embedded in protectable software. Nonetheless, and in practice, courts have been hesitant to find infringement where a game mechanic is copied, or where there are subsequent similarities in gameplay.[9]

Table 1 Aspects of games and their copyright status

Back-end game element	**Definition**	**Copyright status (generally)**
Game code	Source and object code	Protected
Game software	Includes game code, but also other components, including libraries, game engines etc	Protected
Game mechanics	Rules and systems that structure game play	Not protected
Gameplay	How the player experiences interacting with a game	Not protected

[6] See Boyden (n 1) and A Thomas, 'A Question of (e)Sports: An Answer from Copyright' (2020) 15(12) *Journal of Intellectual Property Law & Practice* 960.

[7] P Samuelson, 'Why Copyright Law Excludes Systems and Processes from the Scope of its Protection' (2007) 85(7) *Texas Law Review* 1921.

[8] This necessarily functional element of software led commentators to conclude that the presumption of software copyrightability should not be so straightforward: see P Samuelson, 'The Uneasy Case for Software Copyrights Revisited' (2011) 79(6) *The George Washington Law Review* 1746.

[9] See *Atari Inc v Amusement World Inc*, 547 FSupp 222 (D Md 1981); *Atari Inc v North American Philips Consumer Electronics Corp*, 672 F2d 607 (7th Cir 1982); *Data East USA Inc v Epyx Inc*, 862 F2d 204 9 UPSPQ2d (BNA) 1322 (9th Cir 1988); *Capcom USA Inc v Data East Corp*, WL 1751482 (ND Cal 1994).

The 'front-end' of games has received more immediate and unequivocal copyright protection.[10] Audio and visual components, or unique choices of character or level design – effectively, the 'wrapping' around the game mechanics – more evidently resemble other types of copyrighted works (like images and music) for the purposes of comparison. Again, however, the clear delineation between audiovisual aspects and back-end materials is contestable in practice. We 'see' our avatar jump in response to the press of a button – an audiovisual aspect actualised by the execution of the code. Throughout this chapter, there is a suggestion that this is an inherited, but imperfect delineation by the courts, which may have served a broader policy purpose in the early days of game development.[11] But in principle, this delineation serves to explain the difference between protecting the yellow hue and V-shaped mouth of *Pac-Man*, and protecting the process or 'play' of being chased by an enemy around a maze.[12]

Some jurisdictions protect the game in its entirety, as a standalone copyrightable work,[13] as an (albeit complex) form of software, or – more rarely – as an audiovisual work.[14] Others look to the constituent, severable parts of the game – its audio or visual components, and underlying software and code, and protect these separately.[15] The differences in the legal treatment of game components may give rise to the concern that different people may own and control different aspects of them – which of them, then, is the relevant 'rightsholder' for the purposes of this research? Game developers may write the code, graphic artists may design the in-game environment, and voice actors may perform the dialogue of the characters. However, as a general rule, rights to these creative components – regardless of *who* made them – flow upwards to the game publisher (an entity referred to in this book as 'the game company'). In larger productions, creators will usually be employees, members of subsidiaries, or commissioned for purpose-specific work. In any case, the routine use of contracts which transfer copyrights to the game company ensures that those rights are consolidated into one contracting entity that can determine how the work is used and distributed – this is the rightsholder that we will study.

Having established who makes and owns the game, and how this is legally treated, we return now to the player. In part, the purpose of illustrating the nuance and ambiguities in copyright subsistence of games is to enable us to reflect on where the player 'lives' in relation to this. Specifically, the player lives in, and interacts with the *gameplay*, the

[10] See decision in favour of the defendants as 'cloners' in *Atari Inc v Amusement World Inc*, 547 F Supp 222 (D Md Nov 27 1981) – in respect of a re-skinning of Atari's *Asteroids*.

[11] Amid ongoing uncertainty about the scope of protection for software (particularly the delineation between protection of object and source code), prioritising audiovisual assets as more obviously 'artistic' works offered some security against 'bad faith' (cloning) actors (with which many of the cases in this chapter are concerned).While formalised in the US in 1980, the aspects of protection were only confirmed in 1983, in *Apple Computer Inc v Franklin Computer Corp*, 714 F2d 1240 (3d Cir 1983).

[12] *Atari Inc v North American Philips Consumer Electronics Corp*, 672 F2d 607 (7th Cir 1982).

[13] Namely in the US, which can protect 'the entire effect of the game as it appears and sounds' (*Tetris Holding LLC v Xio Interactive Inc*, 863 F Supp 2d 394 (DNJ 2012)) and in the EU following Case C-355/12 *Nintendo Co Ltd v PC Box SRL*, EU:C:2014:25.

[14] A Ramos et al, 'The Legal Status of Video Games: Comparative Analysis in National Approaches' (WIPO, 2013).

[15] For example, the UK, which operates with a 'closed-list' of subject-matter does not include video games (see the Copyright, Designs and Patents Act 1988).

actualisation of the protected software and code, and unprotected functions and ideas.[16] The player is the entity that presses the button that 'jumps', or 'shoots'; but it is not clear that jumping or shooting are related to copyright at all – rather only the underlying code, and the visible representation of that jumping and shooting. In the latter chapters of this book, I show how the technical reality of what is defined by law is of little significance in relation to how the player is constructed in contract; what is often more important is what is *claimed* to be real and acted upon by the game company. But for now, it is worth reflecting throughout this chapter on how the ambiguity in protection of the game – its interactive and complex nature – can be mapped onto ambiguity in the status of the player. If we can't claim with certainty to understand the nature of the object in which the copyright subsides – the game – then it is certainly difficult to ascertain the status of the person who interacts with it. This lack of clear definition, I would submit, represents a particular vulnerability for the nascent, legal subject of the player.

II. Player as Creator

Contemporary video games are creative works according to the law, with the award of copyright(s) belonging to the game company. But is the player also a creator? As the introduction to this chapter suggests, there is a logical connection between the player and the things they *create* through play; between the creative choices being made by a player in executing the inputs and generating related outputs. It is the player who, for example, creates a character, makes choices about their appearance and personality, who strategises detailed battle plans, and ultimately abandons them in a dramatic, forward charge stimulated with a stylised battle cry of their own character's name.[17] The player might also make new things with game content, either within the game itself (in-game characters or designs, for example), or outwith the game (game videos, or merchandise, for example). In the legal sense, we are specifically asking whether the player is an *author* or *performer* of a work, which are technical tests with relevant legal criteria to be fulfilled.

A. Player as Author

The author of a copyrighted work is the person(s) who created it. And because games dynamically respond to the player's interaction, determining the pacing or sequencing of the game, and making combinations of unique choices, legal

[16] Noting here that the 'player space' in mechanics may now also enter into dialogue with patent law as game companies increasingly appear to seek protection via these routes (consider the infamous 'Nemesis' system patent: see L Bonk, 'Shadow of Mordor's Innovative Nemesis System Is Locked Behind a Patent until 2036' (*EnGadget*, 26 February 2025) www.engadget.com/gaming/shadow-of-mordors-innovative-nemesis-system-is-locked-behind-a-patent-until-2036-195437208.html).

[17] The reference here is to 'Leeroy Jenkins' – a viral meme in the mid noughties that has subsequently been incorporated into *World of Warcraft* merchandise (see Know Your Meme, 'Leeroy Jenkins' https://knowyourmeme.com/memes/leeroy-jenkins).

questions have arisen about whether this means a player can be an author of their gameplay.[18] Effectively, does our interaction with a game transform it into a new creative work entirely, with a new author?

While we are primarily concerned with the *legal* test of authorship, this question does have prior grounding in game studies, which can help frame the legal analysis that follows. Broadly, there is a tension as to whether games should be understood as ludological or narratological in nature.[19] If a game is ludological, then it is primarily a vessel for the game's mechanics and the player's choices – it is inherently interactive. Under this paradigm, the game is not complete without the player, so someone with a ludological perspective on games might emphasise the player's role in 'making it' when they play it. Such a view would seem to favour player-as-author. However, if a game is narratological, it resembles other works which have a set narrative, like books or films, with a pre-written structure and inevitable progression. More specifically, any outcomes that are *facilitated* by the player are actually pre-determined by the rules of the game – the rules that are written by the game's developers. The narratological perspective would therefore diminish the role of the player's authorial capabilities, with a more straightforward and deterministic view that those capabilities are only possible through the work of the game developer in the first instance. In reality, many games have aspects of both. But these philosophical questions are omnipresent in the judicial reasoning that follows – are players 'creative' with a game, or do they just have the *impression* that they are?

Copyright law has largely taken the position that games are narratological and, as such, that the player is *not* an author of a new work when they play or 'create' with a game. The legal argumentation that tested this proposition has mostly been used as an unsuccessful defence strategy by defendants attempting to deflect responsibility for any infringing similarities with a pre-existing game onto the player. In particular, these arguments were tested in an early spate of game 'cloning'[20] cases where defendants disputed the copyright of the pre-existing game due to its lack of fixation (games being variable and responsive rather than 'stable'), and because it was the *player* who made the infringing similarities – the audiovisual similarities – appear on a screen, not the developer themselves. In essence, these arguments (paradoxically perhaps) contended that the pre-existing game had no copyright capable of being infringed *because* of the interactive role of the player in actualising and varying the game – but without contending that the player has actually authored anything in doing so.

[18] Particularly *Atari Games Corp v Oman*, 979 F2d 242 (DC Cir 1992) where the US Copyright Office initially denied registration of a game in part because the audiovisual components were 'created randomly by the player and not the author of the video game'. This was reversed on appeal.

[19] For an excellent overview, see G Lastowka, 'Copyright Law and Video Games: A Brief History of an Interactive Medium' (*SSRN*, 2013) https://papers.ssrn.com/sol3/papers.cfm?abstract_id=2321424.

[20] See also the analysis on 'cloning' discourses in C Katzenbach et al, 'Copies, Clones and Genre Building: Discourses on Imitation and Innovation in Digital Games' (2016) 10 *International Journal of Communication* 838.

At its initial outing in the US in 1981, the argument that games were 'mere ephemeral projections' of a player's reactions (and thus not copyrightable) was dismissed out of hand ('without merit').[21] The possibility was then considered in more detail in *Stern Electronics v Kaufman*,[22] a case concerning a clone of the arcade game *Scramble*, a side-scrolling shooter game with futuristic aircrafts. The defendant – Omni – had developed a game with similar sights, sounds and mechanics, rather transparently branded as *Scramble 2*. In this case, Omni submitted that the audiovisual outputs of *Scramble* lacked sufficient fixation to attract copyright protection in the first instance – in effect, as no copyright existed in the underlying material, then no infringement had taken place when *Scramble 2* was made. Rather, Omni argued, it is the *player* who controls the outputs of a game by determining the similarities in the sequencing of game events through their own choices – in this case, if they 'fail to destroy enough fuel depots his spaceship will crash' or 'if he succeeds in destroying missile sites and enemy planes'.[23] Note that Omni did not use this line of reasoning to suggest that it should be the player that has title to litigate rather than the plaintiff at hand (Stern), but rather a suggestion that the game is in an 'ownerless' state, similar to the traditional understanding of game copyright illustrated above (or rather, a ludological interpretation). The court was unpersuaded by this reasoning, concluding that the player only generated a *variation* of a fixed, audiovisual output that was ultimately pre-determined by the game developer. Because the games at hand had a minimal element of constancy in terms of their appearance – in this case, the shape, colour or size of a spaceship for example, or the terrain in which it flies – then 'the player's participation does not withdraw the audiovisual work from copyright eligibility'.[24] This is so even if that pre-determination exists only in theory rather than reality: in principle, every possible permutation of game outputs is stabilised in some form in the game memory, even if they are not retrievable in practice.[25] For the court in *Stern*, the mere *capacity* for repetition of effects and the constancy of them within a game was sufficient to make *Scramble* a fixed original expression of the game developer – not of the player. This case was subsequently relied on to refuse a claim of player *co*-authorship in the US,[26] with similar reasoning being considered persuasive in a later case in South Africa.[27]

Further litigation nonetheless resumed in the US, with similar facts being explored in *Midway Mfg Co v Artic*. This case likewise concerned an alleged 'clone' of the iconic *Pac-Man*, as well as a circuit board which increased the speed of

[21] *Midway Mfg v Dirkschneider*, 543 F Supp 466 (D Neb 1981).
[22] *Stern Electronics Inc v Kaufman*, 669 F2d 852 (2d Cir 1982).
[23] ibid 638.
[24] ibid 856.
[25] Described in the case as 'imprinting' (ibid 856).
[26] *William Electronics Inc v Artic Intern*, 685 F2d 870 (3d Cir 1982). The characteristics of co-authorship have been exhaustively researched in D Simone, *Copyright and Collective Authorship: Locating the Authors of Collaborative Work* (Cambridge University Press, 2019).
[27] *Golden China TV Game Centre and Others v Nintendo Co Ltd* [1996] 4 All SA 667.

gameplay of *Galaxian*, another popular arcade title.[28] As in *Stern Electronics*, the defendant (Artic) again submitted that the plaintiff (Midway) had no copyright interest in the underlying games – *Pac-Man* and *Galaxian* – for its clone to infringe. Again, it contended that the plaintiff was not responsible for the choices and arrangements of outputs happening on a game screen, but rather it was the player that made these creative decisions by determining, for example, the speed and route of the gameplay (again, implying a sort of 'ownerless' game state). However, the possibility that the player was the 'true' author of the game-work was ultimately dismissed:[29]

> Playing a video game is more like changing channels on a television than it is like writing a novel or painting a picture … [The player] is unlike a writer or a painter because the video game in effect writes the sentences and paints the painting for him; he merely chooses one of the sentences stored in its memory, one of the paintings stored in its collection.[30]

Here, the narratological thinking of the court is more transparent – there are explicit references to other 'narrative'-based works, like books: a fixed, pre-determined narrative that the player cannot affect, but only follow. The suggestion here is that the player is merely a conduit for the 'guiding hand' of the game creator and that any *impression* of player agency or creative choices is ultimately constrained by rules, systems and restrictions. Largely, this reiterates the precedent in *Stern* – that the capacity for repetition and relatedness in a series of outputs means it is the original creation of the game developer and not the player, who merely follows this system to its natural result.

The capacity for player authorship was not dismissed out of hand in the *Midway* case. Instead, the court suggested, rather ambiguously, that even if a player made creative choices in a game – a novel dodge move against a ghost in *Pac-Man*, or an especially creative arrangement of alien-shooting in *Galaxian* – this would nonetheless be considered an *unauthorised derivative work* because of its close interrelatedness to the pre-existing game-work.[31] In US law, this would be considered an infringing creation to which no copyright would attach – a type of creative, copyright-adjacent activity without the benefits of rights. This was ultimately confirmed in *Micro Star v FormGen*,[32] where the defendant (FormGen) offered for sale a disk comprising player-made maps for *Duke Nukem 3D*, a game owned by the plaintiff (Micro Star). As with *Stern* and *Midway*, FormGen again argued that the Micro Star had no copyright interest to pursue in the first instance, as it was the player who made the maps through their own creative choices. For example, the player would choose the layout of map elements, like walls

[28] *Midway Manufacturing Co v Artic International Inc*, 704 F2d 1009 (7th Cir 1983).
[29] ibid at 1011.
[30] ibid at 1012.
[31] ibid at 1014.
[32] *Micro Star v FormGen Inc*, 154 F3d 1107 (9th Cir 1998).

or obstacles, adding textures to those elements (to make it look like brick, for example), and by placing enemy 'sprites' at strategic places on those maps. FormGen submitted that it was these players that made the infringing outputs – the maps – which were ultimately repackaged and offered for sale (presumably with their consent). The court, however, affirmed the suspicion in *Midway* that these were in fact unauthorised *derivative* works, despite the facilitation (and presumed authorisation) of those creations via an in-game building tool. Lamentably, the court did not consider in detail the degree to which the player's contributions constituted a creative expression; rather, they were treated, by omission, as a natural by-product of following the rules and facilitations of the game (and in any case, an infringement).

Elsewhere, a similar trajectory of judicial opinions is evident in Germany,[33] with early cases considering copyrightability of games taking a more sceptical view of their interactive nature. Surprisingly, the argument was in fact successfully levied as a defence in the 1983 *Donkey Kong Junior* case, holding that games could not be an audiovisual work (capable of being infringed) where the audiovisual component was merely 'an evaluation of reaction and skill of the player'.[34] Likewise, the *Pengo* case then denied copyright protection to the audiovisual components of a game because the interface of play lacked originality – it was 'a simple play activity which requires no more than attention and reflex actions'.[35] Again, note that the courts here do not deem this 'authorship' of the player, but rather the kind of ownerless state originally tested in early US cases, and now – briefly – accepted in Germany. The precedent was eventually reversed, first in the *Puckman* case in 1983[36] and as affirmed in the *Amiga-Club* case in 1992, both of which found the boundaries set by the developer and the minimum repeatability of sequences made games 'comparable to the playing back of individual parts of films'.[37] This reasoning is now similarly matched to the narratological view which has been authoritative in the US.

Finally, the player-as-author has been considered most recently in the UK in the *Nova v Mazooma* case, concerning a 'clone' of a virtual emulation of billiards.[38] In order to determine the similarities between the games in contention, the court first considered the subsistence of the game's graphic works – that is, the individual *frames* of the game that show the balls on a billiard table, or the movement of the cue. This nuance in recognising the 'frame' here is important: the audiovisual output of a game is not a seamless 'film' per se – rather, it is a rapid succession of still images, creating the impression of movement on the screen (hence the

[33] The cases here were determined before the harmonisation of many aspects of EU copyright law (following the implementation of Directive 2001/29/EC of 22 May 2001 on the harmonisation of certain aspects of copyright and related rights in the information society [2001] OJ L 167/10 (the InfoSoc Directive) circa 2002).

[34] Judgment of the Court of Appeals in Frankfurt, [1983] GRUR 757.

[35] Judgment of the Court of Appeals in Frankfurt, 13 June 1983, [1983] GRUR 39.

[36] OLG Hamburg, GRUR 1983, CH Beck, Munich 1983, pp 436–437.

[37] OLG Köln, GRUR 1992, CH Beck, Munich 1992, pp 312–313.

[38] *Nova Productions Ltd v Mazooma Games Ltd & Others* [2007] EWCA Civ 219.

measurement of frames-per-second – FPS[39] – in game hardware to indicate smoothness of a game's appearance). From this very technical level, a game is not a unitary audiovisual work, but rather a series of millions (billions) of individual graphical frames. These frames are, of course, not all hand-curated by an individual, human developer – instead, they are generated by the game software in response to the player prompt. As such, the court was guided by a peculiar, UK-specific legislative provision regulating the authorship of 'computer-generated works' to determine who, in this case, was the author of the work on the screen: the game developer who made it possible, the computer that processed it, or the player who pressed the button?[40] The court concluded that the author in such a case is the 'person who made the arrangements necessary to create the frame images': namely, the *developer* of the game software who made the instructions to show those particular frames. Returning to the theme of determinism or indeterminism, narratology and ludology, the court largely affirmed the opinions of courts around the world: that parameters available to the player – regardless of the *impression* of openness – are ultimately 'a series of pre-defined operations intended to achieve the desired result in response to the requests of a customer'.[41] The court further went on to explicitly reject the role of the player in authoring anything 'original', as an essential pre-requisite of copyright protection:

> … the player is not, however, an author of any of the artistic works created in the successive frame images. His input is not artistic in nature and he has contributed no skill or labour of an artistic kind. Nor has he undertaken any of the arrangements necessary for the creation of the frame images. All he has done is to play the game.[42]

Within this is a suggestion that if a player can make an 'artistic' kind of contribution when they play a game (rather than, in this case, perhaps simply moving a billiards cue), this could be original and thus potentially grant a copyright interest to the player.[43] But how much artistry is possible within a game, if courts stress that games are inherently bound by rules and limitations? Instead the UK court's suggestion, as the most recent example of player-as-author legal discourse, is that the creative aspect of a game is (counterintuitively) in the *determination* of rules, systems and processes – aspects traditionally outwith the boundaries of copyright – rather than its interaction.[44] Again, we find ourselves in the puzzling place of the

[39] Though, unhelpfully, this acronym can also be mapped onto 'first-person shooter' to describe the genre of a game.

[40] Copyright Designs and Patents Act 1988, s 9(3).

[41] *Navitaire Inc v Easyjet Airline Co and BulletProof Technologies Inc* [2005] ECDR 17.

[42] *Nova Productions Ltd v Mazooma Games Ltd & Others* [2007] EWCA Civ 219, para 106.

[43] While it is beyond the scope of this book to offer a full review of the originality standard across jurisdictions, 'originality' was previously defined in the UK as requiring 'skill, labour and judgement'; in the EU, originality is defined by 'free and creative choices'; and in the US a 'modicum' of creativity is required.

[44] Again, reminiscent of the limitations still observed in respect of sports and copyright protection: see Thomas (n 6).

player in the 'in-between', occupying both property-full, and property-less game space.

The conclusion from the player-as-author legal discourse suggests that courts have found the *playing* of a game as antithetical, indeed oppositional, to the kinds of original, creative expressions that may attract a copyright: these activities are assumed to be, by their nature, different in their purpose. Players might have a degree of *agency* to make choices in a game, but this is not the same as authorship for the purposes of the law. Rather, elements of game interaction are treated as invariable, with fixed components and sequences, and a static range of inputs and outputs. However infinitely variable interactivity may be within a game, the game company's 'guiding hand', and mere capacity for anticipating this, is enough to absorb the player's creative contributions.

B. Player as Performer

While courts have demonstrated little sympathy for the player-as-author concept, this leaves open the possibility that the player can still make choices and evidence skill in a game, even when constrained within a bigger system of rules. This has given rise to metaphors which analogise games as theatre, and the player as an actor (performer) therein.[45] It is possible to connect the actor, charged with interpreting a pre-determined script, and the player of a game who likewise can imaginatively fill unspecified or ambiguous actions or directions.[46] We know we must avoid the ghosts in *Pac-Man*, but *how* we do this is up to us, and will vary from player to player.

Performers' rights are closely related to copyright, and are sometimes referred to as 'neighbouring' rights or 'rights akin to copyright'.[47] They usually subsist when someone makes a performance of literary, dramatic, or musical copyrighted works, but may be more broadly construed.[48] So here, we would be asking first if a game is one of these works (or like one of these works) that is capable of being performed, and what is required for a performance of that game.

However, even more so than the player-as-author argument, it is difficult to find support for the player-as-performer. The argument was acknowledged briefly in the 1989 US case *Red Baron-Franklin v Taito*, concerning the unlicensed public 'performance' of the game *Double Dragon* in an arcade.[49] Here, the court

[45] See JH Murray, *Hamlet on the Holodeck* (MIT Press, 1997); R Bushnell, *Tragic Time in Drama, Film and Videogames* (Palgrave MacMillan, 2016); S Fasciana, 'The Gaming Theatre Company: Players, Gameplay, Performance and the Law' (2022) 5(2) *Interactive Entertainment Law Review* 80.

[46] See L McDonagh, *Performing Copyright: Law, Theatre and Authorship* (Hart Publishing, 2021).

[47] Performers rights are typically conceptualised as a 'neighbouring' right, rather than a 'pure' copyright, and include the rights to make or record their performance, and the right to control the use of those recordings.

[48] See Fasciana (n 45).

[49] *Red Baron-Franklin Park, Inc v Taito Corp*, 883 F2d 275 (4th Cir 1989).

acknowledged that 'performances' of games are dependent on the player's actualisation – that it is the player who presses the buttons that make the avatars punch and kick each other. And indeed, this performance is variable dependent on their skill and personal inputs. However, the capacity for interrelatedness and deterministic sequences of game events (citing *Stern* and *Midway*) meant that, again, the player's 'performance' was still ultimately an interest of the game company, rather than the player. This logic was latterly affirmed in a case concerning public performances of games in cyber cafes as being an activity requiring prior consent of the *game* company, but without necessarily generating a new performance interest for the player.[50] Whether this logic also extends to the public communications/broadcasts of game playthroughs taking place via online platforms has yet to be confirmed.[51]

Again, more recently in the UK, the *Nova* case also acknowledged that the player had a central role in actualising the sequence of game events through their interpretative agency – a role which has characteristics of a quasi-performance:

> Although the game has a set of rules, the particular sequence of images displayed on the screen will depend in very large part on the manner in which it is played. That sequence of images will not be the same from one game to another, even if the game is played by the same individual.[52]

However, the court ultimately found – perhaps paradoxically – that it is precisely because of a game's *lack* of stability that it could not be a 'work of action … capable of being performed'.[53] Instead, the court decided that a game is simply 'a game' – again suggesting that the process of exploring rules and systems is somehow *oppositional* to the creative endeavour of a performer.[54] Readers are welcome to reflect on the adaptability of the 'stability' argument – that the

[50] *Valve Corp v Sierra Entertainment*, 431 FSupp 29 1091 (District Court WD Washington 2004). Of interest, see *Allen v Academic Games League of America, Inc*, 89 F3d 614 (9th Cir 1996). This case concerned playing board games in a public space, which was not considered a performance, thus by extension the people playing those board games were not performers. However, this decision was largely driven on public policy grounds – that one shouldn't get to dictate how and when a game is played.

[51] The only known case was eventually settled outside of court: *Epic Games Inc v Mendes*, Case No 17-cv-06223-LB (2017).

[52] *Nova Productions Ltd v Mazooma Games Ltd & Others* [2007] EWCA Civ 219 at para 116. Note that the *Nova* court's interpretation of 'sufficient unity' was based on *Green v Broadcasting Corporation of New Zealand* [1989] 2 All ER 1056, which suggested that dramatic formats must contain a degree of repeatability from performance to performance. Subsequent developments in *Banner Universal Motion Pictures Ltd v Endemol Shine Group Ltd* [2017] EWHC 2600 (Ch) instead defined unity as requiring more of a baseline framework from which something may be repeated in a recognisable, rather than uniform, fashion. See also *Ukulele Orchestra of Great Britain v Clausen* [2015] EWHC 1772 (IPEC).

[53] *Nova Productions Ltd v Mazooma Games Ltd & Others* [2007] EWCA Civ 219 at para 116.

[54] However, and in any case, the court in *Nova* went on to doubly confirm that even if a game were capable of being performed, a literary work (the underlying component of the game as a computer program) could not simultaneously be a dramatic work.

interrelatedness of video game frames is enough to secure its copyright and minimise the role of the player, but likewise is so lacking stability that the player also cannot perform it.

Arguably, the courts' approaches to the 'player as performer' are even less coherent than the rather emphatic (but consistent) rejection of the 'player as author'. There is throughout an implicit recognition that a player *can* be creative (performative) in making unpredictable choices within a game, yet there is reluctance to classify them as anything more than an *unauthorised* performer, whose activity is but an extension of the game company's initial property interest. The player may have agency in the choices they make, and these may be performative choices, but this is ultimately dampened and distorted by the mere presence of the game company's initial copyright interest and capacity to pre-cognate those choices: essentially, a kind of 'creative rule following'.

III. Player as User

If a player is not an author or a performer for the purposes of copyright, they must instead be a *user* of a game. Unlike the analysis of the player-as-author or performer, this section does not offer counterfactual cases or legislation to affirm this but rather presents it as a diagnosis of exclusion. But what is a 'user'? This is often presented as a self-evident definition, but the term is frustratingly opaque – it simply describes someone who *uses* a copyrighted work without commenting on the quality of that interaction, or the person behind it.[55] So even if we conclude that a player is a copyright user, that is not necessarily a helpful diagnosis – because we don't really know what a user is.

In fact, unlike the designation of author or performer, it is difficult to say that the user is a distinct legal subject in copyright at all. Coined around 1967, the term is instead a migrant from the software industry.[56] It has since – as confirmed by Helberger and Hugenholtz – come to form the exclusive term to designate the recipient of a copyright work.[57] And, indeed, it may be the most accurate term to describe the often impermanent, opportunistic, use-based relationships of the digital era, rather than, for example, the implications of destruction and

[55] See for example Litman, who argues that the category term 'user' should be abandoned in its entirety (J Litman, 'Readers' Copyright' (2011) 58 *Journal of the Copyright Society of the USA* 325).

[56] At the time, the term 'user' differentiated between those who interacted directly with a computer mainframe, usually a programmer, and the 'end user', more analogous to the customer at the end of a transactional chain. Nowadays, the two tend to be subsumed with little credence to the historical distinction, and when the 'user' is invoked, this is often more analogous to the historic 'end user'.

[57] N Helberger and PB Hugenholtz, 'No Place Like Home for Making a Copy: Private Copying in European Copyright Law and Consumer Law' (2007) 22(3) *Berkley Technology Law Journal* 1061.

non-replenishment inherent in 'consume',[58] or the implicit space of the 'public' domain that the user can fall into.[59]

While copyright does not define the user as such, it does define *uses* through copyright 'exceptions'. Copyright exceptions, and related regimes like the fair use doctrine in the US, are legislative carve-outs that designate which uses are permitted in relation to a protected work. It is this *relation* to the protected work – the thing made by the 'author' – that makes the beneficiary of copyright exceptions a 'user'. Copyright exceptions can be about specific uses of a copyrighted work, such as parody, or criticism and review, and a player can be a copyright 'user' when they re-use game content for this purpose. However – and perhaps more saliently – the mere *interaction* with a protected work may implicate copyright exceptions where the user has to make any necessary, temporary copies of a work as part of a technical operation.[60] So when a player acquires a game, they may rely on a copyright exception simply to *use* the game as intended, specifically when they make temporary copies of game software in the hardware's memory (eg the RAM) or on a screen. This rather explicitly situates the player as a user by default – they are the beneficiary of a copyright exception when simply *using* a game. We might surmise then that the broader purpose of the 'user' designation in copyright is to distinguish between uses of works that are lawful and uses that are unlawful.[61] In the former case the player would be a 'user', but in the latter is more likely to be a 'pirate'.[62]

The crucial aspect of this categorisation is that it suggests a symbiotic relationship between the player, the game, and the rightsholder – and it also suggests a hierarchy. A player is a user, because they are (lawfully) using a protected work – the game. The law also makes some allowances for non-infringing uses of a game

[58] The concept of the consumer is arguably much more developed than the user. In the EU, for example, they are recognised as a person who is both 'savvy and susceptible' (LA Heymann, 'The Public's Domain in Trademark Law: A First Amendment Theory of the Consumer' (2009) 43(3) *Georgia Law Review* 651) – 'reasonably well informed and reasonably observant and circumspect' (Case C-210/96 *Gut Springenheide and Tusky* EU:C:1998:69, para 31) and play a critical role as a 'driving force of economic growth' in the internal market (European Commission, Communication from the Commission to the Council, the European Parliament and the European Economic and Social Committee (2007) Empowering consumers, enhancing their welfare, effectively protecting them. EU Consumer Policy strategy 2007–2013, Com(2007)99, Brussels, 2–6). This construction has led to the safeguarding of the – ostensibly vulnerable – consumer through eg consumer protection laws. See also GB Dinwoodie and D Gangjee 'The Image of the Consumer in European Trade Mark Law' in D Leczykiewicz and S Weatherill (eds), *The Image(s) of the Consumer in EU Law* (Hart Publishing, 2015).

[59] J Ginsburg, '"Une Chose Publique"? The Author's Domain and the Public Domain in Early British, French and US Copyright Law' (2006) 65(3) *Cambridge Law Review* 636.

[60] In the EU, embedded in InfoSoc Directive, Art 5(1); in the US, Copyright Act 1976, s 117.

[61] The concept of 'lawfulness' is discussed in more detail in Chapter 2. But broadly, this delineation is important, if leading to a 'circular logic' in EU law: see TE Synodinou, 'Lawfulness for Users in European Copyright Law: Acquis and Perspectives' (2019) 10 *Journal of Intellectual Property, Information Technology and Electronic Commerce Law* 20.

[62] The strategic significance of the 'pirate' designation is discussed in more detail in J Meese, *Authors, Users and Pirates: Copyright Law and Subjectivity* (MIT Press, 2018).

by carving out certain limitations and exceptions. But the game is in turn owned by an entity that has *affirmative* rights in that same law. And as such, the player's interests in using a game must always be contextualised against the rightsholder's, as the entity that creates a space for them to inhabit. In short, the rightsholder of the game is akin to a landlord, and the player their tenant.[63] Continuing this analogy, in Chapter 2, I explore how the 'lease' – the player contract – sets the terms on which a rightsholder can realise those rights, shaping the conditions under which a player is a 'lawful' user.

A. Player as (User-)Generator of Content

As analysed above, players are not considered authors or performers of games as copyrighted works, but there is nonetheless some recognition that they can be *creative* with game content. The categorisation of the player-as-user leaves open the possibility that the creative player can fit within the developing, nebulous legal category of user-generated content (UGC). In principle, this category could apply to any type of content created or uploaded by a user, however it is now routinely applied in discourse – and occasionally legislation[64] – to specifically refer to the re-use of copyrighted works and the creation of derivative works.[65] While UGC is not a new variable in the game industry,[66] it is now certainly among the more prominently discussed legal issues in video game copyright literature.[67] And indeed, on the face of it, this may seem an apt descriptor of eg gameplay where the copyrighted 'space' is provided for by the game rightsholder, but the creative interactions within that space are enacted by the player (forming the basis of the

[63] This postmodernist take on the games as a 'space' to inhabit is discussed in more detail in A Thomas, 'Contested Game Spaces: Romance Modding and Copyright' (2024) 7(2) *Interactive Entertainment Law Review* 55.

[64] 'User-uploaded content' appears explicitly in Directive 2019/790 of 17 April 2019 on copyright and related rights in the Digital Single Market [2019] OJ L 130/92 (CDSM Directive), Art 17; in Canada, the exception for 'non-commercial user-generated content' also appears in the Copyright Act 1985, s 29.21.

[65] The taxonomy of UGC offered by Gervais is a useful interpreter for this: see D Gervais, 'The Tangled Web of UGC: Making Copyright Sense of User-Generated Content' (2009) 11(4) *Vanderbilt Journal of Entertainment and Technology Law* 841.

[66] As early as the 1980s, UGC was prevalent: *Castle Smurfenstein* is for example, a modded (parody) version of *Castle Wolfenstein.*

[67] To name but a few: TD Marcus, 'Fostering Creativity in Virtual Worlds: Easing the Restrictiveness of Copyright for User-Created Content' (2008) 55 *Journal of the Copyright Society of the USA* 67; G Lastowka, 'Minecraft as Web 2.0: Amateur Creativity & Digital Games' (SSRN, 5 October 2011) https://papers.ssrn.com/sol3/papers.cfm?abstract_id=1939241; G Lastowka, 'The Player-Authors Project' (*SSRN*, 2013) https://papers.ssrn.com/sol3/papers.cfm?abstract_id=2361758; M Iljadica, 'User Generated Content and its Authors' in T Aplin (ed), *Research Handbook on Intellectual Property and Digital Technologies* (Edward Elgar, 2020); D Lintaman, 'Unusual Canvasses: Resolving Copyright Infringement through the Lens of Community Customs' (2020) 3(1) *Interactive Entertainment Law Review* 3; Z Deng and Y Li, 'Players' Rights to Game Mods: Towards a More Balanced Copyright Regime' (2021) 43 *Computer Law & Security Review* 105634; A Thomas, 'Merit and Monetisation: A Study of Video Game User-generated Content Policies' (2023) 12(1) *Internet Policy Review.*

judicial decisions outlined in the sections above). It can also be an apt descriptor for the new technologies that offer new opportunities for players to create content both *within* and/or *outwith* the game world. Extensive examples follow for the benefit of the uninitiated.

Within the game, UGC may be implicitly authorised to the player through the availability of in-game creation tools that allow them to customise certain aspects of the game ('painting through pixels').[68] Typical examples include customisable character designs, maps, music, and clothing or environmental textures and patterns. In *Animal Crossing: New Horizons*, for example, players can create 'patterns' which can be applied to clothing, flooring, wallpaper and furniture, as illustrated in Figure 1.[69] Players can then upload this creation to a game server, and share this with others through unique 'custom design' or 'creator' codes, enabling others to apply the pattern in their own game worlds.

Figure 1 *Pixelia* wallpaper – animal crossing: New Horizon's Pattern Maker (author's own)

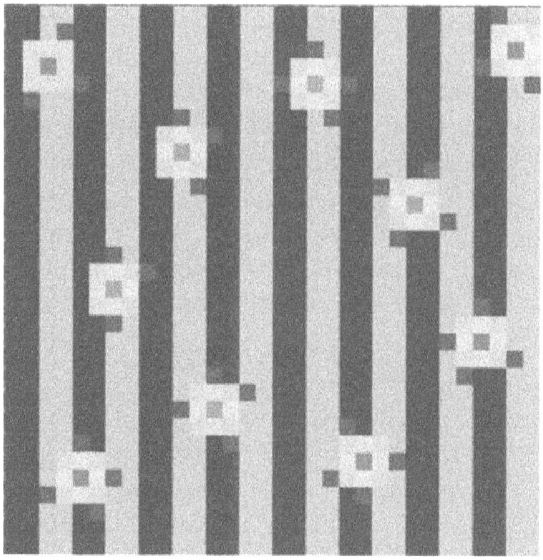

The nature of in-game UGC can be much more substantial where the purpose of the game itself is to *create*. Usually dubbed as a 'sandbox' game, such games have no objectives other than to grant a large degree of creativity to the player. *Minecraft* is the typical example of a successful sandbox, centring around a virtually infinite world made of individual, modifiable 'blocks'. Users can interact with these blocks to influence the shape of the environment (eg using dirt, sand,

[68] WJ Nichols, 'Painting through Pixels: The Case for a Copyright in Videogame Play' (2007) 30(101) *Columbia Journal of Law and the Arts* 117.

[69] Eagle-eyed readers will recognise the similarities between my *Animal Crossing* wallpaper and the disputed wallpaper in *Designer Guild Ltd v Russell Williams (Textiles) Ltd* [2000] UKHL 58.

and granite to build mountains or rivers) and create new objects (eg a castle) at their own pace, with no narrative constrictions. To take an example of the types of worlds that can be created in *Minecraft*, consider the Cairngorms Minecraft Project, a virtual replication of the Cairngorms National Park.[70] Built by members of the Cairngorms Youth Action Team, the Cairngorms Minecraft Project map is scaled to size (approx. 1,700 square miles), so that the player can cover the same amount of ground per in-game day as they could in 'real life'. The map also replicates many of the iconic geographical features in the National Park, including the Cairngorm Plateau and Lake Avon. Such sandbox games can, of course, also be used to emulate 'protected' worlds. *Minecraft*, for example, is also host to *Minecraft Middle Earth*, a like-for-like replication of Tolkien's fictional world from *The Lord of the Rings*.[71]

Perhaps the most well-known example of in-game UGC is the practice of 'modding' (a slang term derived from 'modify'), referring to any player alteration to the game code to make a game perform in a way not originally conceived of by its creators. Mods can constitute minor tweaks that range from the bizarre (eg replacing a *Resident Evil 2* villain with Thomas the Tank Engine)[72] to, essentially, a form of post-release quality assurance (debugging, improving usability, accessibility, gameplay, or graphics).[73] Mods can also be more substantive, major overhauls of a game. Quite famously, *Counter-Strike*, one of the most influential first-person shooter games in history, was initially a mod of its predecessor, *Half-Life*, before it was subsequently acquired by Valve.

Outwith the game world, UGC is more diversified – and difficult to quantify – as it can exist anywhere outside of the game space.[74] The most well-known type of this UGC is game streaming (live, unedited recordings of gameplay) and 'Let's Plays' (non-live, edited recordings of gameplay) which are hosted on online platforms such as YouTube or Twitch. These recordings usually involve a player playing a portion of, or occasionally the whole of, a game, accompanied by their own commentary, which tends to be critical or humorous rather than eg an objective strategy on how to complete the game (though game strategies, walkthroughs and 'speed runs' are also popular). Famous gamer personalities and influencers have arisen from this particular form of UGC, and indeed, it can be a profitable lifestyle for a lucky minority who make their fortunes – in whole or in

[70] Cairngorms National Park, 'Cairngorms Minecraft Project' (Cairngorms National Park, date unknown) https://cairngorms.co.uk/caring-future/education/learning/minecraft/.

[71] Minecraft Middle Earth, 'Minecraft Middle Earth' https://www.mcmiddleearth.com/.

[72] ZombieAli, 'Thomas the Tank Engine over Mr X' (*Nexus Mods*, 3 March 2019) https://www.nexusmods.com/residentevil22019/mods/62.

[73] Recently, and most notoriously, *Cyberpunk 2077's* poor performance was improved substantially by community mods (including 'better vehicle handling' or a 'better mini map' (see 'The Best Cyberpunk 2077 Mods' (*PC Games*, date unknown) https://www.pcgamesn.com/cyberpunk-2077/mods-best).

[74] The most comprehensive assessment to date was undertaken in an impact project developing on the findings of this research, which quantifies different allowances from game end user licensing agreements (see You Can Play, https://www.copyrightevidence.org/ycp/overview).

part – through 'playing games'.[75] With standalone game streaming communities on online platforms, and well-established systems for securing revenue, this type of UGC is perhaps better understood as a player *industry* which can have significant economic benefits for both game publishers and gamer personalities alike.

Other, less common, types of UGC that exist outwith the game space include a new strand of virtual photographers, who use in-game photography tools to capture stills of increasingly beautiful and complex game worlds. Virtual photographers may enhance the game using improved graphics, details, lighting, and reflections and – much like a non-virtual photographer – will similarly spend much time waiting on and constructing the perfect shot. Virtual photographers display their shots in alternative virtual spaces (eg social media) or occasionally in physical formats in galleries. One of the better-known virtual photography series by street photographer Fernando Pereira Gomes replicates this genre of photography in the world of *Grand Theft Auto V*.[76]

Less commonly, and more controversially,[77] UGC outwith the game space also includes user-created *games* based on the original game world (better known as 'fangames'). This may involve one of two possibilities: either using the original game software as a template, with the user's own audiovisual contributions, or using the audiovisual assets of the original game creator, with different software code. Occasionally, and in part contributing to their controversy, fangames may entirely 'clone' the original, generally if the game is no longer accessible (usually due to hardware or software redundancy).[78] As a recent example, user EpicLBPTime recreated the entirety of *P.T.*, a 'playable teaser' of an upcoming *Silent Hill* game. Despite critical acclaim, *P.T.* was subsequently cancelled shortly after the release of the teaser, with the teaser also being removed from download on digital stores. EpicLBPTime thus recreated the game to emulate the now defunct, cult-classic title.[79]

The purpose of illustrating these different types of UGC is twofold. First, there is evident diversity in types of game UGC, which suggests some futility in treating

[75] M Perez, 'Top-Earning Video Gamers: The Ten Highest-Paid Players Pocketed More Than $120 Million in 2019' (*Forbes*, 2020) https://www.forbes.com/sites/mattperez/2020/01/29/top-earning-video-gamers-the-ten-highest-paid-players-pocketed-more-than-120-million-in-2019/.

[76] 'GTA V Player Takes "Street" Photography Using In-game Camera Phone' (*Independent*, 2013) https://www.independent.co.uk/voices/iv-drip/gta-v-player-takes-street-photography-using-game-camera-phone-8879370.html.

[77] Certain game publishers, particularly Nintendo, take a very hostile approach to this. See R Craddock, 'Nintendo Issues Mass DMCA Takedown, 379 Fan-Games Forcibly Removed' (*NintendoLife*, 6 January 2021) https://www.nintendolife.com/news/2021/01/nintendo_issues_mass_dmca_takedown_379_fan-made_games_forcibly_removed.

[78] See T Phillips, '"Don't Clone My Indie Game, Bro": Informal Cultures of Videogame Regulation in the Independent Sector' (2015) 24(2) *Cultural Trends* 143 and C Katzenbach et al, 'Copies, Clones and Genre Building: Discourses on Imitation and Innovation in Digital Games' (2016) 10 *International Journal of Communication* 838.

[79] M Wales, 'Player Takes Impressive Stab at Recreating Cult Corridor Horror PT in Media Molecule's Dreams' (*Eurogamer*, 23 January 2019) https://www.eurogamer.net/articles/2019-01-21-player-takes-impressive-stab-at-recreating-cult-corridor-horror-pt-in-media-molecules-dreams.

this as a category term. The second is more fundamental, because the circumstances in which UGC is made and distributed – and the purpose of its creation – may influence how it is treated in law. For example, some of the activities above may fall within the scope of a purpose-driven exception – say, for example, that a player records themselves playing a game accompanied by an extensive critique. Some jurisdictions also have broader, specific 'UGC' exceptions,[80] or otherwise allowances for 'transformative' uses of copyright works, thus forming a viable – if untested – UGC defence.[81] However, sceptics may point to the trap posed above: courts have been reluctant to acknowledge *any* creative *expression* within the pre-set determination of a game system. This logic would seem to preclude both the authorial interest discussed above, or a defence of UGC: 'transformations' of a game are inherently recognisable as the game itself, and interrelated to the game creator's design. Indeed, many types of UGC – absent an exception (or, as we will see in the chapters that follow, an explicit authorisation by the rightsholder) – may instead simply be infringement. This is, in part, the implication embedded in EU legislation concerning UGC, where it is employed as a descriptor of content which includes (unauthorised) elements of other third-party works.[82] In any case, and as illustrated in Chapter 6, UGC is often *tolerated* infringement. Given the value that can be returned to a game rightsholder where UGC prolongs a game's lifespan, generating ongoing interest in the product and repurposing it for new audiences – and by retaining the goodwill in retaining the esteem of the player community – many will be interested in tolerating these activities, if not outright permitting them.

Regardless of the legal treatment of UGC, readers would be right to find this concept puzzling. Essentially, UGC recognises that there is a creative product, but that this is not quite the same as a new 'copyright' product, despite sharing many of the same characteristics. Like a game rightsholder, the player who 'makes UGC' also makes creative choices in how they interact with a game, or repurpose its content, selectively making decisions that impact its presentation and pacing. For this reason, many critics are sceptical of UGC as a new legal category.[83] Per Gervais, 'there is no such thing as [UGC]';[84] the label of 'user' in lieu of 'author' is merely an underhand means of introducing a new normative vector in copyright. It is an artificial way of delineating 'amateurish' creativity (player-made 'UGC'), made from re-purposed works, from the professional (company made 'games').

[80] See eg the exception for 'non-commercial user-generated content' in the Canadian Copyright Act 1985, s 29.21.

[81] Namely in the US: see Copyright Act 1976, s 107. See Fasciana (n 45); D Hagen, 'Fair Use, Fair Play: Video Game Performances and "Let's Plays" as Transformative Use' (2018) 13(3) *Washington Journal of Law, Technology and Arts* 245; and D Burk, 'Owning eSports: Proprietary Rights in Professional Computer Gaming' (2013) 161 *University of Pennsylvania Law Review* 1535.

[82] Namely, Art 17 of the CDSM Directive.

[83] See particularly C Craig, 'Reconstructing the Author-Self: Some Feminist Lessons for Copyright Law' (2007) 15(2) *Journal of Gender, Social Policy and the Law* 207; Meese (n 62).

[84] D Gervais, 'The Tangled Web of UGC: Making Copyright Sense of User-Generated Content' (2009) 11(4) *Vanderbilt Journal of Entertainment and Technology Law* 841.

While keeping this fundamental conflict in mind – that UGC refers to creative inputs that are not the 'right kind' of creative for a new copyright – for the moment, we should take an existentialist approach – that UGC exists 'because we say it does',[85] if only for the purposes of illustrating the player's legal treatment.

So far, the legal image I have sketched of UGC is patchy – it is something we say exists (legally) and yet is difficult to conceptualise as a stable or standalone category that would help us understand the player in copyright. Indeed, the only consistent conceptualisation of UGC – whether legal, illegal, authorised or unauthorised – is that it is made *non-commercially*, that is to say, not for profit.[86] Indeed, this caveat is explicit in the Canadian 'non-commercial' UGC exception,[87] and many other jurisdictions will be influenced when judging the application of an exception by asking whether the UGC competes in the market with the primary work, or is otherwise used for profit.[88] The suggestion here is that, while a game creator can claim *authorship* via their creativity and exploit their work commercially, when the player is creative and claims *usership*, they are an amateur – quite literally, they must be creative for the *love* of the work, rather than the promise of remuneration.[89] Given that many types of UGC have a commercial characteristic that would generate a player revenue through eg, subscriptions, advertising revenue, or patron platforms – the fabulously wealthy streamer economy is self-evident proof of this – the picture of player-as-user is again imperfect.

On that note, we might conclude that 'UGC' as a label for the creative player is imperfect, though is arguably an imperfect match for an imperfect concept. When we categorise the player as a 'user', we are not saying they cannot be *creative* like an 'author' can be creative; but we are recognising that they cannot be the recipient of the same *rights* as the author. Or rather, while a player can be creative with a game, this is not the same 'kind' of creative as the (copyrightable) creativity of the game company.

IV. Save Point: Chapter Summary

As mentioned at the outset, the point of this chapter is to illustrate the relative absence of the player in copyright doctrine – but more accurately, perhaps,

[85] ibid 843.

[86] While there is no static definition of commerciality in copyright law, the definition given by Creative Commons indicates that this could be 'any manner that is primarily intended for or directed toward commercial advantage or private monetary compensation'. See 'Defining "Noncommercial": A Study of How the Online Population Understands "Noncommercial Use"' (2009) 11.

[87] Copyright Act 1985, s 29.21.

[88] See eg Copyright Act 1976, s 107(4).

[89] Notably, the literal definition of the 'amateur' is explicit in the OECD's authoritative definition: see OECD, 'Participative Web and User-Created Content: Web 2.0, Wikis and Social Networking' (OECD, 2007).

doctrine has *attempted* to wrangle with the player. In doing so, it does offer an imperfect *impression* of them – as if through frosted glass.

First, legal decisions have confirmed – consistently – that a player cannot be an author or a performer of a game. Through an analysis of judicial decision-making in early game copyright litigation, it is evident that courts have adopted a logic whereby the game company is the player's 'guiding hand' – offering creative capabilities to them through the interactive medium, but ultimately constraining them by pre-determined rules, systems and processes.

Second, if a player is not an author or a performer of a work – then they must be a *user* of a game. In offering this diagnosis, I caution that the definition of the user is not self-evident in copyright, but is instead extremely vague. It is a distillation of several complicated and competing legal concepts, implying both consumerist and creative qualities (recreational and *re*-creational) – someone who is entertained, but also engaged and in dialogue with the work. As evidence of this, the chapter introduces the nebulous legal category of UGC, which acknowledges that a player can be creative with a game but again falling short of awarding an authorial interest to them.

In concluding this chapter, there is an impression that the player is a *vulnerable* legal subject, both factually –a player does not have the same affirmative rights as an author – and also in reality, where power imbalances between game companies and players is very real. This theme – that the player is shaped by legal power in property – carries into Chapter 2, where I show how contract has a key role in expressing and realising interests of the game company.

2

The Player in Contract

Copyright gives game companies an important initial award of exclusive legal rights over their games; but it is contract that makes the *realisation* of those rights possible. Contracts are what set the terms on which the player is allowed to play a game, legally.[1] In doing so, companies can construct the player through the range of permissions, and prohibitions, which they have been legally entitled to dictate.

Players have routine interactions with these contracts, even if they are largely invisible – or, rather, deliberately ignored. Indeed, documents which prompt us to 'click to agree to the terms and conditions' have become a prerequisite of almost every interaction with almost every digital product. As a preliminary matter, and as will be illustrated throughout this chapter, whether these documents technically meet the criteria for a legally binding 'contract' continues to be debated,[2] mostly because it is difficult to see any meaningful 'agreement' or 'consent' where a contract is offered on a non-negotiable basis, and *must* be agreed to before accessing the product. Conceptually, this may be closer to a 'statement of terms', rather than a 'meeting of the minds', a common legal test for contract formation.[3] However, for the purposes of this research, I am not concerned with proving that these are valid or enforceable contracts to be *important* to the player. Instead, I focus on showing how contracts are a statement of *intent* by a games company – they tell us about who they think the ideal player is in a particular time, regardless of whether this can be 'legally' realised when tested. The question of enforceability is, however, omnipresent in especially in the overview of doctrine in Section 1, in part because it is a good indicator of understanding the legislator's or judiciary's intent for the law to legitimate, or denounce, a particular activity. And while this chapter describes the qualities of how these contracts are presented to the player in Section 2, they are not analysed for their legal compliance as such.

[1] Per Meese, we might understand contracts as a company's 'own discourse through which to legitimise their activity' (J Meese, *Authors, Users and Pirates: Copyright Law and Subjectivity* (MIT Press, 2018) 98).

[2] See MJ Radin, *Boilerplate: The Fine Print, Vanishing Rights, and the Rule of Law* (Princeton University Press, 2013) and J Cohen, 'Lochner in Cyberspace: The New Economic Orthodoxy of Rights Management' (2019) 97(2) *Michigan Law Review* 462.

[3] Elkin-Koren, for example, suggests these 'contracts' are in fact a unilateral action through which the rightsholder is exercising its property right and confirming the terms of the work's use: N Elkin-Koren, 'Governing Access to Users-Generated-Content: The Changing Nature of Private Ordering in Digital Networks' in E Brousseau et al (eds), *Governance, Regulations and Powers on the Internet* (Cambridge University Press, 2009).

Instead, for the purposes of this research, the branding of the 'contract' (and the assumptions of this definition) is better understood as the wrapper *around* the technical, legal instrument – namely, the copyright *licence*. Technically, it is the licence which creates the relationship between the game company and the player in the first instance, by granting a purpose and/or time-limited permission to use a copy of a game. And while we will see that licensing clauses are often embedded *within* these contracts, the broader context and terms of those contracts are vitally important, such that we can safely consider them the primary object of study, technicalities notwithstanding.

This chapter consists of two sections. Section I outlines the relationship between copyright and user contracts more widely, examining the broader doctrines about contracts made between rightsholders and users in relation to *any* type of copyright works (ie it includes, but is not limited to games). This section considers the subservience of default copyright to contract law, showing how user contracts can encroach upon lawful exceptions, and overreach into the regulation of non-copyright relevant activities. Section II consists of a historical narrative of player contracts more specifically (ie contracts made only in relation to the use of a game) to show how, through doctrine and practice, they have become a tool of broader player regulation. Through each time-period, the distribution method of these contracts and their relationship with copyright are detailed to illustrate how rights in games have come to be realised vis-à-vis players. In doing so, this chapter surmises that the construction of the player through contract is highly strategic and malleable in both law and practice; that, effectively, contracts can shape the player to be whatever a company needs them to be in any given time. And copyright, while seemingly invisible in this abstraction, is nonetheless essential and facilitatory by granting the legal power to do so.

I. Copyright and User Contracts

The norm of using a copyright to contract directly with a user is a relatively recent development. Historically, after the point of sale, a user would not anticipate an *ongoing* relationship with a rightsholder via contract – they could buy a book, and walk away.[4] Likewise, any private or non-commercial uses of that object would not typically have been within the remit of copyright, which has always been more concerned with the *public* exploitation of creative works. Unless you were photocopying that book and selling it on a market, then there would be no room for other enforcement measures. Only in the digital era has it become commonplace for everyday interactions to implicate copyright: namely when we use the (often invisible) underlying, protectable software that populates almost everything we

[4] See L Guibault, *Copyright Exceptions and Contracts. An Analysis of the Contractual Overridability of Limitations on Copyright* (Kluwer Law International, 2002) 3.

consume on a screen. With users now systematically interacting with copyright, so too has this prompted the consideration of user-side contracts. These contracts are typically encountered through a standard form, digitally embedded document, like terms and conditions, terms of service, and end user licensing agreements, where we must 'click to agree' in order to access the product. As noted in the introduction, these contracts usually include copyright *licences*, where the rightsholder will retain their copyright in respect of the work they are distributing, while giving limited *permissions* to the recipient to use a copy of that work.

We might think of these contracts as an *additive* mechanism for regulating copyrighted works. I use the term 'additive', because technically, user contracts are not *essential* for protecting a work; copyright offers baseline protections which would always prevent certain activities like a user copying or distributing a work without permission. For these activities, the rightsholder could be assured that their prevention 'goes without saying'. But if the rightsholder wants to change these baseline protections – whether by asking for more or less, for example – they are usually permitted to do so via contract. Likewise, user contracts are technically not essential for facilitating the sale or distribution of those works, even though we tend to systematically encounter them at the point of sale. But they may have a role in setting the conditions of access, for example, by stipulating that the user pays a monthly subscription fee. In sum, from the user's perspective, copyright and contract are highly interrelated. At the point of access, it is not apparent which is being implicated: the right or the rules. While a user may have a property or consumers' interest in the copy of the work they own, this is muddied by the omnipresence of the copyright, which is retained by the rightsholder. Resultingly, any prior presumptions of a clear distinction between the two are increasingly breaking down.[5]

Complicating this, there is no general rule which addresses the relationship between copyright and contract and which should prevail if there is a conflict between the two – eg if copyright says one thing, and a contract contradicts this. Copyright is largely internationalised, regulated by multi-country treaties, while contract is regulated at national level with rules that vary by country. As a result, in jurisdictions which have a strong freedom of contract ethos – the US or UK for example – there is very little of default copyright law that cannot subsequently be changed by mutual agreement.[6] Or rather, while copyright is the *default* law that protects creative works, many of its provisions only apply absent an agreement to the contrary.[7] Naturally, this may leave the user at a disadvantage if a contract modifies a permission otherwise given to them by copyright law. On this point, the

[5] See J Griffin, 'The Interface between Copyright and Contract: Suggestions for the Future' (2011) 2(1) *European Journal of Law and Technology*.

[6] Noting that some rights are inalienable in certain jurisdictions: for example, moral rights, or certain rights to fair remuneration in much of continental Europe.

[7] M Kretschmer et al, 'The Relationship Between Copyright and Contract Law' (UK Strategic Advisory Board for Intellectual Property Policy, 2010) 106.

following sections consider two important intersections between copyright and user contracts which are relevant for our study of the player: first, to show how contracts can be used as a tool to modify copyright exceptions; and, second, to show how copyright, by giving rightsholders the mandate to define lawful *access* to a work, can act as a proxy for regulating non-copyright matters. The former can be understood as copyright *override*, as it varnishes over the intentions of the legislator, while the latter can be understood as copyright *overreach*, because it extends beyond the remit of copyright, absent a rule to the contrary.

A. Copyright Override: User Contracts and Copyright Exceptions

As illustrated in Chapter 1, the player is largely considered a copyright user, because they are the beneficiary of copyright exceptions. Copyright exceptions might enable the player to repurpose game content for new creative uses – say, a parody – but are also implicated even where a game is simply used, because it necessarily creates transient copies of the protected work in the relevant hardware (in the cache, RAM, or screen display, for example). In either case, exceptions can be understood as an expression by the legislator of its intention for a balance of interests between the rightsholder and the recipient of the work. The rightsholder's interest in their work is, in this sense, not absolute in principle.

Regardless, many exceptions – however limited they may be, and to greater or lesser degrees – can lawfully be overridden by contract. This value is embedded at the 'roots' of copyright in the Berne Convention, where the allowance for exceptions is subservient to ('must not prejudice') the 'legitimate interests' of the rightsholder. Those 'legitimate interests' can be expressed through contract, which may indeed prohibit an activity that is expressly permitted by a copyright exception.[8] This may be specific – for example, by saying that the user cannot use the work for the purposes of making a parody. Or, this may be achieved through the broad reservation of a specific right – for example, by prohibiting the user from 'copying' *anything* without prior authorisation, which would also include any copying for the purposes of making a parody. The latter is particularly important where software is concerned – and games are by their nature underlain with software – as a user contract that prohibits *all* copying could extend to the transient and temporary copies that allow a digital work to be used in the first instance – an issue detailed further below. If a user needs permission to do even this, then it doesn't matter if the law says they *own* a copy of a work when they buy a game: the rightsholder still needs to give them permission to *use* it – and can take that permission away.

[8] For excellent and exhaustive analyses, see Guibault (n 4) and M Senftleben, *Copyright, Limitations and the Three-Step Test* (Wolters Kluwer, 2004).

Contractual overridability of copyright exceptions is one of the main contentious characteristics in categorising them as an affirmative user *right*, an increasingly discussed policy issue.[9] Facially, the distinction between a 'user right' versus a 'user exception' is purely rhetorical, but re-framing our assumptions around copyright exceptions does raise an important conceptual question for our understanding of the player. Copyright exceptions are better understood as the absence of infringement; they are a statement by the legislator that permission is not needed from the rightsholder to do a particular activity with a protected work. In litigation, the absence of infringement can be helpful because it can be a viable defence to using a work lawfully, without the rightsholder's permission under certain circumstances. But exceptions are of little use to a user seeking to rely on them to *demand* the use of a work in the same way an author could demand that someone *stop* using their work. So, for example, if a player wants to access game software for the purposes of making a parody, this is only considered non-infringing in certain circumstances, but there is no corresponding duty on the game company to enable access for this purpose.[10] Certain jurisdictions – particularly the EU and Canada – have re-framed their legislation to more closely resemble a user 'rights' regime by creating affirmative duties on other actors to enable the actioning of an exception. But in terms of broader doctrine, the framing of user exceptions as a limitation to the rightsholder's copyright remains accurate.

Arguably, the high watermark of contractual overridability for copyright exceptions is in the US.[11] In the US, exceptions are implemented via the fair use doctrine, a multifactorial defence allowing for the lawful re-use of a copyrighted work in certain circumstances.[12] While generally considered to be the broader and more forgiving of copyright systems in allowing users to lawfully re-use works more liberally than other jurisdictions, it is also – ironically perhaps – the most susceptible to contractual override. In terms of user contracts, cases concerning uses for the purposes of reverse engineering,[13] quotation[14] and education[15] – activities

[9] It is outwith the scope of this chapter to undertake a full review of the climate or appetite for users' rights, but see excellent full assessments offered in N Helberger and PB Hugenholtz, 'No Place Like Home for Making a Copy: Private Copying in European Copyright Law and Consumer Law' (2007) 22(3) *Berkley Technology Law Journal* 1061; P Chapdelaine, *Copyright User Rights: Contracts and the Erosion of Property* (Oxford University Press, 2017); and C Geiger and BJ Jutte, 'Copyright as an Access Right: Concretizing Positive Obligations for Rightsholders to Ensure the Exercise of User Rights' (2024) 73(11) *GRUR International* 1019.

[10] T Rendas, 'Are Copyright-Permitted Uses "Exceptions", "Limitations" or "User Rights"? The Special Case of Article 17 CDSM Directive' (2022) 17(1) *Journal of Intellectual Property Law & Practice* 54.

[11] See *ProCD Inc v Zeidenberg*, 86 F3d 1447 (7th Cir 1996), and also affirmed where terms are offered via a hyperlink in *Meyer v Uber*, 868 F3d 66 (2d Cir 2017).

[12] Copyright Act 1976, s 107.

[13] See *Bowers v Baystate Technologies*, 320 F3d 1317 (Fed Cir 2003): '[A] state can permit parties to contract away a fair use defense or to agree not to engage in uses of copyrighted material that are permitted by copyright law if the contract is freely negotiated'. Note that a similar fact profile resulted in a different finding in *Vault Corp v Quaid Software*, 847 F2d 255, 7 USPQ 2d (BNA) 1281 (5th Cir 1988).

[14] See *Salinger v Colting*, 607 F3d 68 (2d Cir 2010).

[15] See *CUP v Patton*, 769 F3d 1232 (11th Cir 2014).

which are typically considered fair use – have been confirmed to be overridable by contract. Likewise, clauses which restrict the resale of works, an activity normally explicitly allowed in copyright law, have also been upheld as valid.[16] The key point here is that all of these uses which are allowed by law can nonetheless be modified by contract.

Elsewhere is a more scattered picture. In the UK, there is explicit legislative language for certain exceptions (including parody, text and data mining) which renders any terms that would restrict such exception unenforceable.[17] There are nonetheless lingering doubts about the scope of this particular limitation where a clause merely 'restricts' but does not outright prohibit an exception.[18] Likewise, in the EU, certain exceptions – particularly in the Computer Programme Directive – which allow for eg reverse engineering of software, cannot be overridden by contract.[19] However, the main regulatory mechanism for exceptions – the Information Society Directive – does not expressly address the relationship between these exceptions and contracts, leaving this to the discretion of Member States' implementation.[20] Judicial interpretations by the Court of Justice of the European Union have nonetheless given more weight to the role of exceptions in recent cases, suggesting an overarching principle of 'fair balance' between the interests of rightsholders and users. Indeed, in the *Pelham* case, the Advocate General's Opinion makes a specific reference to exceptions as 'user rights', suggesting a stronger and more affirmative entitlement to the user if a contract should try to override this.[21]

Importantly, the risk of contractual overridability is not a hypothetical problem – it is very real. Empirical research of audiovisual streaming platforms,[22] music,[23]

[16] See *Vernor v Autodesk*, US Dist LEXIS 90906 (WD Wash Sep 30 2009), and *MMDY Industries v Blizzard Entertainment*, 629 nF3d 928 (9th Cir 2010).

[17] See amendments to the Copyright, Designs and Patents Act 1988 via the Copyright and Rights in Performances (Research, Education, Libraries and Archives) Regulations 2014, SI 2014/1372.

[18] A Aronsson-Storrier, 'Copyright Exceptions and Contract in the UK: The Impact of Recent Amendments' (2016) 6(1) *Queen Mary Journal of Intellectual Property* 111.

[19] In the Computer Programmes Directive 2009, non-overridable exceptions include the right to make back-up copies of a computer program to decompile the program and to reverse engineer it for observation, study and testing.

[20] Directive 2001/29/EC of 22 May 2001 on the harmonisation of certain aspects of copyright and related rights in the information society [2001] OJ L 167/10 (the InfoSoc Directive), Art 5. Note that following Directive 2019/790 of 17 April 2019 on copyright and related rights in the Digital Single Market [2019] OJ L 130/92 (the CDSM Directive) in 2019 some exceptions – particularly for quotation and parody on online platforms – have since become mandatory.

[21] See Case C-201/13 *Deckmyn v Vandersteen* EU:C:2014:2132.

[22] P Mezei and I Harkai, 'End-User Flexibilities in Digital Copyright Law – An Empirical Analysis of End-user License Agreements' (2022) 5(1) *Interactive Entertainment Law Review* 2.

[23] U Gasser, 'iTunes: How Copyright, Contract, and Technology Shape the Business of Digital Media – A Case Study' (2004) Berkman Center for Internet and Society at Harvard Law School Research Publication No 2004–07 and L Grøndal, 'DRM and Contract Terms' (2006) 2(12) *Indicare*.

video games,[24] and the education sector[25] all confirm that override of copyright exceptions in user contracts is systematically used in practice. So not only is it legally tenable, but is enacted routinely in the 'real world'. Further empirical research confirms that these terms are doubly enforced through technical protection measures, or digital rights management systems, which may prevent the activity stipulated in the contract on a technological level.[26] As a result, users may be both legally and technically prevented from enacting an exception, if this is so chosen by the rightsholder.

The relationship between contract and copyright exceptions is significant for our examination of the player for two reasons. First, because it offers a more proximate lens through which we can view the player's relationship with the rightsholder and its work. Using contracts to say that a player is not allowed to do one of the activities permitted by law suggests that, regardless of the legislator's intent in the exception, the reality changes upon the receipt of a work because it is mediated through the 'legitimate interests' of the rightsholder. Second, it is significant that clauses which override exceptions exist even in those limited circumstances where an exception is mandatory and a contract term which prohibits it cannot be enforced. Even if it is not legally effective, it signals the rightsholder's intention, or a reliance on the user's unawareness or unwillingness to litigate.[27] In short, it tells us about the priorities of the person constructing the recipient of the work.

B. Copyright Overreach: User Licences and Non-Copyright Matters

While copyright protects many things, and for a long time, it does not protect everything forever. Nonetheless, contracts can bundle legally 'unprotectable' content and claim ownership of it through contract. For example, while copyright does not protect 'ideas', a contract can nonetheless claim this as a proprietary product and restrict how other people use that idea through those terms. Contracts can also set the conditions on which a user is given permission to access a work. These conditions may be related to copyright (eg the user can lawfully use a game so long

[24] E Reuveni, 'On Virtual Worlds: Copyright and Contract Law at the Dawn of the Virtual Age' (2007) 82 *Indiana Law Journal* 261; DC Miller, 'Determining Ownership in Virtual Worlds: Copyright and License Agreements' (2003) 22 *Review Litigation* 435; and C Roquilly, 'Control Over Virtual Worlds by Game Companies: Issues and Recommendations' (2011) 35(3) *MITS Quarterly* 653.

[25] R Xalabarder, 'Study on Copyright Limitations and Exceptions for Educational Activities in North America, Europe, Caucasus. Central Asia and Israel' (WIPO, 2009).

[26] K Erickson, and V Stobo, 'Survey on Technological Protection Measures: Impacts for Researchers, Libraries and Archives' (Knowledge Rights 21, 2024).

[27] CA Sullivan, 'The Puzzling Persistence of Unenforceable Contract Terms' (2009) 70 *Ohio State Law Journal* 1127.

as they do not copy it) but can also be unrelated (eg the user can lawfully use a game unless they harass another user). In the context of video games, breaches of player licences have been enforced against streamers when they have used a racial slur in (unrelated) game content,[28] where they have shared game 'spoilers',[29] and for resoundingly negative critiques of games.[30] Such examples have come to be known as the 'weaponisation' of copyright, per Smith, 'using copyright to vindicate noncopyright interests',[31] but the scope of contractual overreach is not limited to this.

Unlike exceptions where the occasional legislative language explicitly prohibits its contractual override, there is no general copyright policy on limitations to contractual overreach. In the US, in principle, copyright law – a federal matter – has superiority over contract law, which is regulated at state level. In determining whether the 'superior' copyright law should regulate the issue at hand (eg in saying that something cannot be copyrighted – like an idea) courts have asked whether the contractual clause is within the 'general subject matter' of copyright.[32] If so, this clause would be 'pre-empted' by the conflicting rule in copyright. However, in practice, pre-emption has not typically been applied to user contracts,[33] based on the (rather simple – and controversial)[34] logic that copyright and contract bind different parties, and so always operate differently. This means that contractual terms which overreach into non-copyright, on un-copyrighted, issues in the US are generally considered enforceable (absent any other contract-based irregularities). Or rather, the contract can shape and regulate an object of property, and the recipient's behaviour with it, regardless of the underlying copyright status of that object. Broadly, this parallels the similar attitude to copyright override, that contract can modify most default copyright rules in the US.

[28] M Ibrahim, 'Firewatch Creators Can Target PewDiePie with DMCA Takedowns, and It's Perfectly Legal' (*Polygon*, 12 September 2017) (*Polygon*, 12 September 2017) https://www.polygon.com/2017/9/12/16295412/pewdiepie-campo-santo-firewatch-dmca-legal-abuse.

[29] K Orland, 'Posting Persona 5 Spoilers Could Get You Hit With Account Suspension' (*Ars Technica*, 4 May 2017) https://arstechnica.com/gaming/2017/04/atlus-threatens-takedown-of-persona-5-spoiler-videos/.

[30] An issue which undoubtedly overlaps with the copyright exceptions doctrine outlined above: see J Alexander, 'Super Seducer Dev under Fire after DMCA Takedown Hits YouTuber, Twitter Fight' (*Polygon* 28 February 2018) https://www.polygon.com/2018/2/28/17058040/super-seducer-iampattyjack-dmca-takedown.

[31] C Smith, 'Weaponizing Copyright' (2021) 35(1) *Harvard Journal of Law & Technology* 193.

[32] *ProCD Inc v Zeidenberg*, 86 F3d 1447 (7th Cir 1996). This decision has largely been affirmed in subsequent decisions, as summarised by SY Chow, 'A Snapshot of Online Contracting Two Decades After *ProCD v Zeidenberg*' (2017) 73(1) *The Business Lawyer* 267.

[33] One notable exception is *Vault Corp v Quaid Software*, 847 F2d 255 (5th Cir 1988).

[34] Case notes on this are extensive, but for opposing views written at the time of the judgment – and somewhat in dialogue with each other – see first CL Pitet, 'The Problem with Money Now, Terms Later: *ProCD, Inc v Zeidenberg* and the Enforceability of Shrinkwrap Software Licences' (1997) 31(1) *Loyola of Los Angeles Law Review* 325 (from the perspective of the consumer), then JC Wang, '*ProCD, Inc v Zeidenberg* and Article 2B: Finally, the Validation of Shrink-Wrap Licenses' (1998) 16 *Journal of Computer and Information Law* 439 (from the perspective of the software developer).

No such balancing exercise exists for copyright overreach in either the UK or the EU, where national differences in contract law can be substantial.[35] Instead, the condition of 'lawful' access[36] is used as a proxy to determine whether the work is being used with the *consent* of the rightsholder.[37] This has an important interplay with contractual overreach because the conditions of the rightsholder's consent – the conditions on which lawful use or access is granted – can be dictated through contracts.[38] This has been used to prevent, for example, 'cheat' software in an online multiplayer game. In this case, it was irrelevant that 'cheating' is not defined (nor prohibited) in copyright law, only that the conditions of accessing the copyrighted work were that the player did not 'cheat'.[39] This leads Elkin-Koren to conclude that user contracts are not contracts at all, because the user's consent is irrelevant – rather, it is a unilateral action through which the rightsholder is exercising its property right and confirming the terms of the work's use.[40] And consent in itself can be generously construed because the legitimate interests of the copyright holder are *also* broadly construed – the interests, for example, in having an online multiplayer game where 'fair play' is ensured through the prevention of 'cheating'.[41]

Unlike research into copyright override, empirical evidence on contractual copyright overreach is scarce. There are some studies of copyright overreach in negative space literature, ie areas of creativity where the underlying copyright protection of that work is absent or uncertain.[42] Here, using contracts to 'package'

[35] Griffin (n 5) and JP Trialle et al, 'Study on the Application of Directive 2001/29/EC on Copyright and Related Rights in the Information Society (the "InfoSoc Directive")' (European Commission, 2013).

[36] On a side note, in the US, the requirement for 'lawfulness' is arguably subsumed within the fair use test, rather than as a standalone criterion to be achieved. The fair use test does not, by its nature, delineate between uses that are lawful or not – rather it is an interpretative mechanism for determining lawfulness as a defence to infringement. Contractual conditions are a determination of consent, and thus lawfulness. See JD Litman, 'Lawful Personal Use' (2007) 85(7) *Texas Law Review* 1871.

[37] Synodinou notes that the lawful condition is attached to different concepts across EU Directives, such as 'access' or 'use', which may have meaningful differences in interpretation. See TE Synodinou, 'Lawfulness for Users in European Copyright Law: Acquis and Perspectives' (2019) 10 *Journal of Intellectual Property, Information Technology and Electronic Commerce Law* 20.

[38] Readers may note the potential for conflict where copyright exceptions are concerned – if a work is accessed unlawfully for the purposes of enacting a lawful exception, which position should prevail? This is discussed in Guibault (n 4), and has subsequently been litigated in Case C-406/10 *SAS Institute v World Programming Ltd* EU:C:2011:787, and Case C-360/13 *Public Relations Consultants Associations Ltd v Newspaper Licensing Agency Ltd* EU:C:2014:1195. The answer appears to be that lawful use is still an important determinant of lawful access for the purposes of enacting an exception.

[39] See, for example, the UK case *TakeTwo v James* [2020] EWHC 179 (Pat), concerning *Grand Theft Auto* 'cheats' employed in multiplayer mode.

[40] Elkin-Koren (n 3).

[41] Deserving, per Recital 4 of the Preamble to the InfoSoc Directive 2001, a 'high level' of protection (as opposed to 'adequate' or 'fair', for example).

[42] Helpfully summarised in R Danna et al, 'Interim Report on Negative Space of EU Creative Industries' (ReCreating Europe, 2021).

the object of protection for trade may be more effective for commercial transactions than the underlying default legal protections. But otherwise, the existence of such provisions remains anecdotal for user contracts, if perhaps strongly suspected.

Again, in summarising this section, copyright *overreach* is also significant for shaping the player. Even where the behaviour being regulated appears distant from the concept of copyright, there is always the possibility that it is within the scope of the legitimate interests of the rightsholder – an interest construed broadly. This might be especially relevant in the context of games, because – as discussed in Chapter 1 and elaborated in Section II below – many of their elements have an uncertain or disputed copyright status. If a contract can be used to regulate both copyright and non-copyright elements of a game, this could be very strategically employed indeed.

II. The History and Development of Player Contracts

As illustrated, contracts are important legal tools which can control how a player interacts with a game. Copyright is essential in creating this relationship, because it is the law that gives the initial broad grant of rights that allows rightsholders – game companies – to mandate the specifics of ongoing, permission-based usage of a work via contract. The scope of what can potentially be regulated by contracts is enormous, and may bear little resemblance to the copyright system that it spawned from. As a preliminary conclusion, we might suggest that the player can potentially be 'anything and everything' under the terms of play.

In this section, 'anything and everything' is given a more concrete and temporal examination, analysing the real employment of player contracts in the games industry, and the history and development of these contracts in practice. In doing so, it shows that the inception and development of player contracts has always been in dialogue with copyright law, and that they have historically acted as a mechanism to realise rights via the player. As such, this section emphasises that contracts are not frozen, statutory law, but are responsive to the needs of the entity writing them, whether based on the fear of a real legal gap, or the desire for a commercial advantage. Table 2 presents an overview of the timeline presented in this chapter, substantively beginning from the early 1970s, and concluding with the state of the art today. Throughout, the key message is that the construct of the player in contracts is not stable, but rather highly strategic. Game companies have selectively shone a light on different facets of the player throughout history, drawing attention towards or from different facets depending on the broader social, cultural or legal context of the era.

Table 2 Timeline of user and player contract developments

Year	Key development
1969	First software licence
1978	First video game registered in the US Copyright Office
1980	Software officially recognised in (US) copyright law
1985	First (identified) player contract
1989	First open software licence
1996	First software licence litigation
2000	First open game licence
2007	First player contract litigation
2010	Phase out of game shrink-wrap

Side quest: some notes on methods

In the development of this chapter, I reflected on the adage that 'history is not a science – history involves the *use* of science'. This adage is intended to capture the inherent subjectivity of historical research, that we can never 'know' what we cannot experience firsthand. As such, a note on methods is appropriate, to understand the limitations of the possible corpus of historical material for player contracts, and ways of collecting this.

Perhaps unsurprisingly, the preservation of what equates to mass-produced terms and conditions is not particularly well served. There is no centralised resource for these contracts, nor a single point of collection for vintage games. Contracts may be issued in paper form with the work, digitally embedded within the work itself (eg as a readme file), or maintained on a third-party server. Access to these materials is of course theoretically possible – but practically (nearly) impossible. Likewise, verifying the existence of contracts in vintage games is dependent on access to working and compatible vintage hardware – a rarity, but also an increasingly expensive collectors' hobby which significantly curtails their availability on the open market. Indeed, the poor state of video game preservation has been presented as an imminent policy issue since I initially approached this research during my PhD.[43] As a result, access to older player contracts is dependent on access to limited institutional curation, personal collections, or company reporting. Many of these curatorial efforts are based in the US which, as the progenitor of many important game developments, is perhaps apt, but skews the geographical story – a lot of early game development was happening in, for example, Japan.

The risk to highlight here is that there may be survivorship bias in this research; that is, that I have not captured player contracts that actually existed but only measured those contracts that have been *preserved*. A key question in mitigating this risk is then whether those player contracts – particularly before the identified inception point of 1985 – did indeed exist. Certainly, it is *possible* – and that its absence forms part of larger problems with preservation of games. However, this possibility is unlikely. During this

[43] P Salvador, 'Survey of the Video Game Reissue Market in the United States' (*Zenodo*, 10 July 2023) https://zenodo.org/records/8161056.

research – which started in 2017 – and in conversation with a number of game archivists and historians, most indicated that the culture of early games development was framed as either/or: (i) hobbyist pursuits, combined with an open (or, in one book 'hippy-ish') culture;[44] or (ii) as 'toys' for children. Both aspects are discussed below, and in either situation we would not necessarily *expect* to see a contract, whether because the game was not 'propertised', or because this ostensibly formal relationship was inappropriate for the young target audience. In conclusion, before the identified inception point, there may be Schrodinger's contracts – a later event may yet prove their existence, but at the point of writing, I cannot evidence that fact.

I used multiple methods to build an impression of this historical timeline, primarily through reviewing materials in the Video Game History Foundation archive (archive.gamehistory.org), Internet Archive (archive.org), ReplacementDocs (replacementdocs.com), and with limited access to personal game collections (where I checked both the physical paper documentation, installation information, and/or readme files included with the game).[45] I use illustrative examples from surviving game materials throughout each era. The earliest point I considered for the possible existence of any *relevant* user contract is 1969, the inception date of software licensing more broadly.[46] From there, the second earliest point I considered for a player contract was 1971 (the date of the original development of *The Oregon Trail*, and first arcade game – *Computer Space*).

A. Pre-Contract: 1970s

The pre-contract era is characterised by the absence of a formal contractual relationship between the game company and the player.

Importantly, this is not because contracts were not a recognised legal tool – user contracts for software had been established since 1969 and had quickly become normalised throughout the 1970s in the computer industry. Predominantly, this was implemented through 'shrink-wrap' contracts, so called because by removing the cellophane (shrink) wrapping on the product, the user indicates their consent to be bound by its terms.[47] In the 1970s, these contracts performed an important commercial function because the contractual terms therein filled a real

[44] J Mailland, *The Game That Never Ends: How Lawyers Shape the Videogame Industry* (MIT Press, 2024) 20–21: 'Atari sounded like it was being run like a commune [where] "we were all a product of the Free Speech Movement at Berkeley"'.

[45] With thanks to Martin and Raymond. I did not attempt to reach out to individual game developers or companies to source this information, both the impossibility and undesirability of which are more articulately summarised in Mailland (n 44) 6–7.

[46] Detailed further in A Thomas, 'The First Software Licensing Agreement and its Relationship with Copyright Law' (*CREATe* 14 November 2018) https://www.create.ac.uk/blog/2018/11/14/the-first-software-licensing-agreement-and-its-relationship-with-copyright-law/, and A Thomas, 'The Copyright User: A Socio-legal Enquiry' (University of Glasgow, 26 May 2022) https://theses.gla.ac.uk/82902/.

[47] MA Lemley, 'Intellectual Property and Shrinkwrap Licenses' (1995) 68 *Southern California Law Review* 1239.

lacuna in the law – software was not yet unambiguously protected by copyright.[48] Previously, when software was 'bundled' together with hardware, and the intangible property was sold together with the physical chattel (ie the 'computer'), this would not necessarily have presented a problem – certain rights would have been protected by default property law rules. But for a distinct *software* market to be commercially viable, contract was the only mechanism that could alleviate that particular legal vulnerability – by regulating the user's behaviour with the work without relying on copyright.

Even though the first commercially viable games, outwith the hobbyist home-brew space, were published after the establishment of user contracts in the software industry, it does not appear that the practice of using shrink-wrapped contracts translated into the early days of the game industry. The reasons for this are twofold, and are reflected in examples of the primary game types of the era: arcade games, and early computer games. I deliberately use the term 'computer' here, rather than 'video' game, both to encompass the character of video *and* text-based games which were in development, and to acknowledge that the games discussed here were not available on purpose-built consoles, but rather multi-purpose home computers.

First, where arcade games are concerned, it is not clear that the game itself was actually conceived of as a standalone object to be protected. Instead, much like the earlier state of the software industry, the intangible aspects of the 'game' were sold within the physical chattel – namely, the arcade cabinet (the physical 'house' of the arcade game with, for example, the display and control panel). The game, such as it was, was not included in code, but rather custom-printed circuit boards. These circuit boards would have allowed for rudimentary game play mechanics – logic gates, for example – which were physically built into the physical wiring of the board itself. Any player input would physically send an electric signal to the board, which would then produce a corresponding output on the arcade screen. While patents were considered for these circuit boards, copyright did not evidently have a role in protecting physical technologies, being a property right more readily applicable to *soft*ware (not hardware).[49] In any case, at its inception, the game could not be meaningfully divorced from the hardware due to the limitations of the technologies employed at the time. And as a result, a separate contract to regulate the player of the game likewise would not have been perceived as necessary – neither appropriate to the technology, nor required where it could be regulated by default property laws. Indeed, in the earliest arcade game considered – *Computer Space* – produced in 1971, I found no evidence that this was sold on the basis of any contractual relationship with the player, nor that copyright was routinely invoked. Rather, the only documents accompanying the sale of the arcade cabinet are technical instructions, health and safety advisories, and

[48] M Kretschmer, 'Software as Text and Machine: The Legal Capture of Digital Innovation' (2003) 1 *Journal of Information, Law and Technology*.

[49] The Atari/Magnavox patent controversy regarding electronic circuitry is detailed in Mailland (n 44).

maintenance orders, issued from the manufacturer to the arcade owner.[50] This latter point also raises an important consideration that, where arcade games are concerned, the primary legal relationship would have been between the game company and the arcade owner, rather than a direct relationship with the player.

The second reason for the absence of player contracts in this era is more nebulous to capture, but largely pertains to the *laissez-faire* corporate culture of early *computer* game companies. The corporate culture of game development in the 1970s is at least suggestive of a more collaborative and open ethos, antithetical to a formal, legal contractual relationship. Computer game developers[51] of the 1970s are perhaps better understood as informal hobbyist groups, largely based in universities and research institutions – a culture which Mailland flatly describes as having 'commune-like' vibes.[52] Before the inception of the game *industry*, these developers would write 'homebrew' games – that is, titles compatible with proprietary systems, but without any intention of mass-marketing them.[53] *The Oregon Trail*, a game initially developed in 1971, was one such title developed under these circumstances, by a group of student teachers. Neither the readme file, nor the user manual published in 1977 contains a player contract, and no restrictions were specified when the code was publicly shared in 1978 via *Creative Computing* magazine.[54] An important aspect of the game code being shared in this way – other than its flagrant open ethos – is that the early computer player also had a quasi-programmer role. Before games had removable storage, if you wanted to play a game you would have to manually type in the program – to be a programmer first, then player second. For this reason, Swalwell notes that it would be erroneous to conceptualise early computers as a *consumer* good – rather, the player necessarily had to be a creator (or in their words, a 'maker') to operationalise it.[55] Again, here the player is not in a relationship with a *rightsholder* per se, but rather a relationship with a fellow programmer, or programmer in training where – as many early games were – they were employed in educational settings.

Importantly, even though there is no evidence of player contracts in this era, this does not mean that intellectual property was not considered a tool by game developers. In which case, we might conclude that the 'open' ethos described above

[50] Midway Manufacturing Company, 'Arcade Game Manual: Midway's Pac-Man Parts and Operating' (*Internet Archive*, 4 January 2011) https://archive.org/details/ArcadeGameManualMidwaysPac-manPartsAndOperating/mode/2up.

[51] The specific terminology of 'computer' games here as opposed to 'video' games is deliberate. The games developed at this time are specifically text-based games designed for general purpose personal computers; video games, by contrast, becomes the more specific term for video-based displays of games, typically via consoles rather than computers (though the delineation between the two is increasingly becoming less salient).

[52] Mailland (n 44) 20–21.

[53] B Keogh, 'From Aggressively Formalised to Intensely In/formalised: Accounting for a Wider Range of Videogame Development Practice' (2019) 12(1) *Creative Industries Journal* 838.

[54] 'Creative Computing Magazine (May 1978) Volume 04 Number 03' (*Internet Archive*, 18 January 2013) https://archive.org/details/creativecomputing-1978-05/page/n139/mode/2up, 140.

[55] M Swalwell, *Homebrew Gaming and the Beginnings of Vernacular Digitality* (MIT Press, 2021).

is more limited to computer game code and copyright, but not necessarily the hardware or skillset know-how that would be protected by patents or trade secrets, legal tools which were explored in earnest throughout the 1970s.[56] Despite its precarious legal status, copyright *notices* do occasionally appear on game documentation (see, for example, a copyright symbol © on the cover of the *Space Wars* Service and Owner's Manual, 1978). It is unclear, however, whether they are intended as a claim of copyright over the game itself or rather over the text of the accompanying documentation.[57]

Regardless, it is evident that the concept of the *copyright* player was both staggered and abstracted in the early days of video game development. The lack of uptake of using player contracts is not because these contracts did not exist as a concept, or because they had no function – arguably, at the date of its inception, the use of contract to 'patch' the law represented a very real industry concern for anyone in the software, or software adjacent industries. Instead, the absence of overt player contracting is influenced by both technology – the limitations of circuit board hardware – and cultural expectations of early game communities about how games *should* be shared.

B. Inception: 1980s

The culture of game development changed to a more proprietary mindset in the 1980s, where significant changes – legal, technological and cultural – made the commercial viability of a large-scale game industry possible. Three important developments happened at the outset of this era.

First, in 1980 the US Copyright Act explicitly recognised software as an object of copyright protection. Despite filling the previous lacuna in law, the Act – knowingly or unknowingly – left open the possibility for a dual role for both copyright *and* a contract for software-based works. While a rather technical point, the Act only gave software *owners* – that is, the software developers rather than the lawful possessors of a *copy* of the software – the right to permit the making of temporary reproductions necessary for running that software.[58] In doing so, the statutory language concretised the norm of using contracts as a means of granting rights of use to the user. Or rather, in order to lawfully use software for *any* purpose, a user would still need the permission of the rightsholder via contract.

[56] Detailed in Mailland (n 44).

[57] Note that when the first games and software were accepted for registration at the US Copyright Office they tended to be registered as 'literary works' – books or manuals of text with the accompanying code and specifications – rather than other hardware.

[58] Computer Software Copyright Act 1980, s 117. Note that this conflicts with the recommendation given by the recommending commission that the right to make temporary copies should remain with the lawful possessor of the software – ie the user: National Commission on New Technological Uses of Copyrighted Works, 'Final Report on the National Commission on New Technological Uses of Copyrighted Works' (1981) 3(53) *Computer Law Journal at* 62.

Second, as the accessibility and affordability of software and hardware improved, game consoles including the Sega SG-1000 and NES Family Computer (both in 1983) became more widely available, and were no longer the remit of very expensive and cumbersome hardware. New cartridge technologies also meant that games could be stored – and sold – in removable products which could be distributed separately from the game console. With new removable storage, games were also more evidently software rather than advanced circuit boards, as the cartridges were populated with pre-written code, and functionality in games now came from the execution of that stored code. Code, being closer to a typical 'literary' (written) work for the purposes of copyright had a more evident connection to the law. And in combination with the first development – that software was unambiguously now protected – this is a significant technological change with new legal dimensions.

The third (and final) variable of the 1980s pertains to the enablement of third-party games development. Prior to this point, the creator of a game console or arcade cabinet would also make the game itself, or would have to give someone else the tools or technologies to make a game that would be compatible with that hardware (through, for example, digital rights management systems).[59] The most notorious example is perhaps the 10NES chip employed on the Nintendo Entertainment System which had certain authentication features that meant only authenticated developers could access the hardware needed to make compatible games.[60] This requirement changed in the 1980s, in part because of the new technologies detailed above, but mostly due to a series of litigation concerning competition between new and old games companies. The settlement of a dispute between Atari and Activision – the defendants being defectors from the plaintiffs, dissatisfied with their working arrangements – was largely seen to condone third-party development of games without needing the consent of the hardware owner.[61] Subsequent court decisions which permitted reverse engineering for the purposes of making compatible products likewise influenced the development of the third-party market.[62]

The confluence of these issues means that at the outset of the 1980s, games started to be *thought of*, technologically, like software. At the same time, the law

[59] While the history of game digital rights management (DRM) is outwith the scope of this chapter, it undeniably has an important role in shaping usage rights to video games. See examples in PQ Rubin, 'A Brief History of DRM in Video Games' (*Prompting Culture*, 11 November 2024) https://promptingculture.substack.com/p/a-brief-history-of-drm-in-video-games.

[60] The rights to reverse engineer this were litigated between Atari and Nintendo in 1986–1992 (*Atari Games Corp v Nintendo of America Inc*, 975 F2d 832 (Fed Cir 1992)). Nintendo was also notable for introducing its 'control quantity/control quality' ethos by limiting access to the third-party development market, a vulnerability which it ascribed as contributing to the 1983 games market crash in Europe and the US.

[61] The settlement was reported in the June 1982 issue of *Electronic Games* https://www.ataricompendium.com/faq/faq_vcs_electronic_games_6-82_atari_activision_lawsuit_settled.jpg. While the terms of the settlement remain confidential, speculation includes a long-term licensing arrangement with royalty payments.

[62] See *Atari Games Corp v Nintendo of America Inc*, 975 F2d 832 (Fed Cir 1992) and *Sega v Accolade*, 977 F2d 1510 (9th Cir 1992).

confirms that software is definitely protected by copyright, but still relies on a contractual relationship to give rights to the player to use that product. And now third-party *software* companies can start making new products for games *en masse*.

These factors led to the beginning of player contracts. The earliest example known is from the user manual of the 1985 title *Pitfall II*, which is replicated in Appendix 1.[63] This game, developed by Activision, was distributed through Radio Shack, a subsidiary of Tandy Computers. In this iteration, the *software* licence is offered from Radio Shack, as a licensee of Activision, who had been commissioned to develop the game for compatible Tandy hardware. This relationship in itself suggests that the drive to offer the game via a contract is in part influenced by the presence of a software-hardware industry party, rather than a unilateral decision by the game developers.

The most notable feature of this primitive player contract is its brevity – a total of five clauses that barely exceed 100 words. These clauses are more apparently and directly limited to shaping the player's role in relation to the *copyright* of the game, clarifying that the contract takes precedence to the default law ('except as otherwise provided') and that title to the game is retained by the distributor. They are explicitly a 'CUSTOMER' – a lawful *purchaser* of the game – a title which becomes more significant in the context of widespread counterfeiting concerns detailed below. In any case, with the law now legitimating this contractual tool, and the clearer technological relation to *software*, game companies now begin to translate those established contract norms from the software industry. The placement of the contract in relation to the game documentation is also worthwhile noting – annexed to the warranty, itself appended to the user manual, which continues to take precedence in the text through its prominent placement. This suggests that the contract was developed *adjacent* to the initial, and well-established use of warranties and health and safety cautions to the player, rather than as a standalone agreement. It also suggests that it – like the warranty – acts as a legal caution and limitation of liability: it is a statement, rather than *agreement* per se (a fact that continues to be true today).

In another early example of player contracts, *Moria* (1985) is likewise notable for its brevity, and is better understood as a more detailed copyright *notice*, while sharing many functions of a primitive contract. This contract was distributed in a readme file included alongside the game's source code, which was widely shared by the game's developers:

> Moria may be copied and modified freely, but may not be sold or marketed IN ANY FORM without the permission and written consent of the authors Robert Alan Koeneke and James E. Wilson. We retain all copyrights to this program, in either the original or modified forms, and no violation, deletion, or change of the copyright notice is allowed.

[63] Tandy 'Pitfall II Programme Manual' [1985] (*Color Computer Archive*, date unknown) https://colorcomputerarchive.com/repo/Documents/Manuals/Games/Pitfall%20II%20(Tandy).pdf.

> Furthermore, we will have no liability or responsibility to any user with respect to loss or damage caused directly or indirectly by this program.[64]

From this example, we see echoes of the open culture of early computer game development in the 1970s remains – the contract permits copying and modification 'freely' while prohibiting the resale or marketing of it. Of note, the game was later re-released via an open licence in 2008.[65] It is nonetheless emblematic of a shifting perception of game *software* as an object of copyright protection, which is subject to ongoing permissions and regulation.

Importantly, while this is the earliest point that I find player contracts, there is no evidence these were *systematically* used, and the examples above are the exceptions rather than the rule for much of the 1980s. For example, the original *Rogue* (1984) was published without a contract (and was subsequently re-published under an open licence at a later date).[66] *Ultima III: Exodus*, despite famously including primitive digital rights management, also does not appear to have included a contract at first publication.[67] Instead, what is most prevalent and consistent is – as aforementioned – the warranty, which is prominently included in game documentation.[68] Many of these warranties – also typically accompanied by health and safety warnings – are more specifically directed towards limiting responsibility for adverse health reactions; note that the first publicly documented consideration that games may cause epileptic seizures occurred in 1981.[69]

While contracts remain absent for the most part of the 1980s, copyright notices continue to appear on game-related documentation and deserve some further consideration. In particular, the changes to new (copying and home-based) technologies meant that 'counterfeit' game products became a more viable concern for the developing game industry. Games were increasingly distributed on cassette tapes and floppy disks. Ordinary hi-fi and computer equipment could easily copy data from one removable object to another, enabling it to be re-sold or given away indefinitely. As a result, counterfeit warnings start appearing prominently on arcade games,[70] and evolve into lengthier anti-piracy calls in computer games. An example from the *Transylvania* game manual includes the Preston Penguin mascot (of Penguin Software, also appearing on badges and other merchandise),

[64] Free Moria, 'Moria Non-Free License' https://free-moria.sourceforge.net/moria-non-free-license.txt.

[65] B Asselestine, 'Freeing an Old Game' (*Free Software Magazine*, 12 March 2007) http://freesoftwaremagazine.com/articles/freeing_an_old_game_moria/.

[66] Djnym, 'RoguelikeRestorationProject: license.txt' (*Github*, 2011) https://github.com/RoguelikeRestorationProject/urogue/blob/master/LICENSE.TXT.

[67] Origin Systems, 'Ultima III: Exodus Manual' (*Internet Archive*, 11 October 2018) https://archive.org/details/c64man_ultima3/mode/1up.

[68] See eg Scott Adams, 'Adventureland' (Color Computer Archive, 1981) https://colorcomputerarchive.com/repo/Documents/Manuals/Games/Scott%20Adams%20Adventure%2001%20(Adventureland)(1981)(Adventure%20International).pdf.

[69] Video games were also at the centre of many 'fad-induced' injuries in the 1980s, including so-called 'Pac-Man elbow' (a kind of ulnar nerve compression).

[70] Mailland (n 44) 105.

a penguin in a workman-like pose, wearing a hat and holding a shovel, who says 'only you [the player] can prevent software piracy'.[71] This is a soft, preliminary movement towards what would ultimately become stronger anti-piracy messaging in subsequent eras – for now, it is caged in the friendly face of a cartoon penguin.[72] But unambiguously, the suggestion that only '*you*' can prevent piracy indicates an inherent suspicion of a player's behaviour with the *protected* game product.

Another notable example of the copyright-counterfeit notices is in the 1981 full-page *Compute!* magazine spread forwarded by Atari, headlining 'PIRACY: THIS GAME IS OVER'.[73] The spread includes a thin implication that not only players, but new (legitimate) third-party developers (read: Activision) are associated with a criminal enterprise. Making duplicate copies of games at home, or buying third-party developed game products not authorised by the computer or console developer, are treated as the same 'harm'. The prominence of this document suggests that the rise of the third-party development market led larger game companies to consider that *anyone* – private players and commercial enterprises – could make a copy of a game, or make a similar *competing* game. And the player, as the recipient of the game, is no longer in the quasi-programmer role of the 1970s where there is somewhat a relationship of parity, but rather is part of the mass, home-based, and slightly suspect audience – anyone from a naïve child (who is both vulnerable – annexed to the warranty – but complicit in the fight for/against piracy) to a bad-faith defector, corporate competitor. While contracts are not yet a central feature of regulating the player, it is an important part of the larger picture of the player-as-pirate ethos, and shifting proprietary mindset towards games. As the perceived copyright application – and risk – increases, so do the rights that are claimed vis-à-vis the player.

C. Acceleration: 1990s and 2000s

The 1990s and 2000s[74] are marked by rapid technological development for games, which changes the way that copyright and player contracts are approached. This era is characterised by an acceleration in the uptake of player contracts, if not quite reaching systematic use. Plentiful examples of contracts appear towards the end of the 1990s, an acceleration which is likely fuelled by the 1996 decision in *ProCD*

[71] Strangely, there is no literature on the symbology of Preston Penguin, but I suspect the connotations of manual labour in the hard hat and shovel represents the 'hard work' of Penguin Software.

[72] The use of cartoons and mascots to convey anti-piracy messages continued throughout the 1980s and 1990s. See Quinn, 'The Eerie Art of Anti-piracy Screens' (*Medium* 15 May 2024) https://medium.com/counterarts/the-eerie-art-of-anti-piracy-screens-d92efc433b1f.

[73] M Reed, 'The Atari Anti-Piracy Advertisement' (*Matthew Reed's TRS-80.org*, 2007) http://www.trs-80.org/atari-anti-piracy-advertisement/.

[74] As will become evident later in this sub-section, these decades are merged together because of the blurriness of dating the inception of *online* gaming, which has been in practice since the early 1990s, but only reached the zeitgeist in the mid 2000s.

v Zeidenberg in the US, which confirmed both the enforceability of shrink-wrap contracts, and the legality of using contracts to change default copyright rules.[75] This decision may have been read as a legitimation of the form which allowed it to be normalised in the industry.

Player contracts of the 1990s are typically annexed to a user manual within the game packaging and are now presented *separately* from any warranties, suggesting their importance is increasing. While still comparatively brief by today's standards, they steadily acquire more proprietary characteristics than those in the 1980s, including the use of dense legalese and more restrictive use policies:

> You agree not to adapt or otherwise modify, create any derivative work, or decompile, disassemble, reverse engineer, or otherwise attempt to derive any source code from the Program (or any portion thereof) except and only to the extent that, notwithstanding such restrictions, such activity is expressly permitted by applicable law.[76]

These restrictions are a concretisation of the developments in the 1980s which legally and technically sought to curtail the development of third-party and 'homebrew' game development. Per Keogh, the 1990s became marked by the absence of any alternative, commercially successful modes of game development outside of a dedicated corporate space.[77] Through the professionalisation of game development, the game industry homogenises the view of games as a consumer *product*, and the player becomes concretised as a *consumer*. In turn, a contract which gives more restrictive *usage* rights both affirms that the player should be a passive recipient of that product, and that the professional corporation holds the right and the power to regulate it. Note the stark difference in the view of the player as a consumer in the 1990s, versus the player in the 1970s as a co-creator, receiving free code in a magazine (just two decades previously).

While the inclusion of a player contract is becoming normalised in shrink-wrap format, the more obvious cause of changes to contracting behaviour in this era is the inception of PC games with online, multi-player capabilities. Early online multiplayer game *Neverwinter Nights*, launched in 1991, was accompanied by a lengthy player contract in a readme file.[78] Valve, launched in 2003, exclusively relied on contracts for game distribution, with accounts-based agreements for distribution of digital games downloadable via the Internet. *Second Life*'s 2003 click-wrap contract was famously subject to a lawsuit about the ownership of virtual goods in 2007.[79] Despite settling this lawsuit – which was largely

[75] *ProCD Inc v Zeidenberg*, 86 F3d 1447 (7th Cir 1996).

[76] 3D0, 'Army Men 3D' (*Internet Archive*, 28 May 2013) https://archive.org/details/Army_Men_3D_1999_3D0_US_SLUS-00491/page/n9/mode/2up.

[77] Keogh (n 53).

[78] Neverwinter Nights Wiki, 'End-User License Agreement' https://nwn.fandom.com/wiki/End-User_License_Agreement.

[79] *Bragg v Linden Research Inc*, 487 FSupp 2d 593 (ED Pa 2007). The original terms are replicated in 'SL Modifies Terms of Service and EULA (Sort of)' (*The Alphaville Herald* 6 October 2004) http://alphavilleherald.com/2004/10/sl_modifies_ter.html.

understood as affirmation that certain provisions of the contract were unenforceable – the use of contracts for online games persisted, with *World of Warcraft* employing a lengthy contract even after the settlement.[80]

A curio of these early online games is that many – including all of the aforementioned – still required a piece of physical hardware for the initial installation of the game, typically an installation disk (or several). This is a limitation of the technology of the 1990s, where slow broadband speeds combined with large game sizes made it unfeasible to download all game data from a remote source in a reasonable time. Installation disks instead did a lot of the initial 'heavy lifting', paving the way for the player to access the online aspects of a game via a personal account. In this respect, it is important to recognise the nuance that games of the 1990s are not entirely 'online' because of the tie to the physical, local component. In other words, in this era, there is still a meaningful delineation between the game *product* and the online *service*, even if neither could *usefully* be divorced from the other.

The systematic use of contracts at the inception of online gaming suggests that it is not the product *itself* that determines whether a contract will be used – this was still being patchily employed in shrink-wrap format for 'offline' games – but rather whether the player would be accessing a *service* through the use of the product. Here, qualifying the player as the recipient of condition-based *usage* permissions could have an important function by allowing the rightsholder to withhold access to that service if its product was being used in a way that breaches those terms – for example, if the player was harassing another player in a game. The connection to copyright here becomes increasingly abstracted because, on the face of it, it is being used to regulate behaviour that seems to have little to do with the law. But the initial grant of a copyright is essential in enabling this contractual relationship in the first instance. Instead, if a player is closer to being a consumer, they may also benefit from many consumer rights which – throughout the 90s and 00s – are becoming firmer and more inflexible.[81] A consumer cannot be bound by unfair terms, or a term that unfairly burdens them, for example. Instead, by framing the player as a condition-based *user of proprietary software* – a licensee – game companies could avoid being limited by the implications of the player as a *consumer of a game product*. The game, as is often iterated at the outset of player contracts of this era, is 'licensed, not sold'.

The duality of the player – as both consumer *and* user – becomes widespread when game consoles and mobiles also develop embedded online capabilities. An

[80] Blizzard Entertainment, 'World of Warcraft End User License Agreement' (on file with the author).

[81] For example, in the EU, the Maastricht Treaty 1992 includes a specific title dedicated to consumer protection. The Unfair Terms in Consumer Contracts Directive was subsequently introduced in 1993. Changes in the US are much more incremental, but include litigation surrounding the labelling of toys and children's products, which acted as a model for subsequent legislation (see *Toy Mfrs or America Inc v Blumenthal*, 806 F Supp 336 (D Conn 1992)). A series of United States Senate Committees held between 1993 and 1994 concerned the effects of violence in video games on children: see SL Kent, *The Ultimate History of Video Games: The Story Behind the Craze that Touched our Lives and Changed the World* (Prima Publishing, 2001).

early example is the Nintendo DS, launched in 2004, which while being the first Nintendo console with (very limited) online capacities, is also the first Nintendo console that systematically includes a contract for its games in paper and via the console interface.[82] Towards the end of the noughties, hybrid shrink-wrap and click-wrap contracts became widely employed across the entire game industry, with terms presented in both the game packaging and on screen.[83] The clear delineation between games as a product (player as consumer) and games as a service (player as a user) starts to erode as the hardware itself becomes service-based and, as we will see in the following section, the player becomes more firmly a 'user' as we leave this era.

D. Critical Mass: 2010–Today

Having given an overview of the development of player contracts and its relationship with copyright, we are now in a good space to explore how contracts construct the player today. Illustrating today's 'terms of play' is a task largely left for the following chapters, but for the purposes of completing the timeline here, a brief overview of some key characteristics of modern player contracts is necessary.

First, click-wrap and browse-wrap formats are now the default mode of contracting in the games industry today. Shrink-wrap has been all but phased out, and while it is difficult to offer a concrete date for when this occurred, Ubisoft – an influential games developer – stopped including paper documents in its physical games in 2010.[84] Most players will be prompted with the contract when they initially access the game, typically a virtual box that embeds or links to the contract, with the option to click 'I agree' (or equivalent) to proceed. Alternatively, the player can close the box, rejecting the terms, and in doing so will no longer be able to access the game.

The key characteristic of the modern player contract is that – unlike in previous eras – it is now embedded *within* the game itself. It is another virtual device for the player to interact and 'play' with. And indeed, this 'hidden' quality, only available post-purchase and post-installation of a game, has raised many of the same questions on its enforceability as with previous litigation surrounding shrink-wrap, with no universal consensus yet being reached.[85]

[82] See Humongous Inc, 'Backyard Football 09' https://dn790007.ca.archive.org/0/items/NintendoDSManuals/BackyardFootball09usab.pdf.

[83] See, for example, Midway Games 'Mortal Kombat: Armageddon – manual' https://www.gamesdatabase.org/Media/SYSTEM/Sony_Playstation_2/Manual/formated/Mortal_Kombat-_Armageddon_-_2007_-_Midway_Games.pdf.

[84] M Fahey, 'Ubisoft Does Away With Tree-Killing Instruction Manuals' (*Kotaku*, 19 April 2010) [*archived*] https://web.archive.org/web/20210729215057/https://kotaku.com/ubisoft-does-away-with-tree-killing-instruction-manuals-5520261.

[85] See F Marotta-Wurgler, 'What's in a Standard Form Contract? An Empirical Analysis of Software License Agreements' (2007) 4(4) *Journal of Empirical Legal Studies* 677; J Grossklags and N Good, 'Empirical Studies on Software Notices to Inform Policy Makers and Usability Designers' (2007)

While player contracts have become more available to the player – viewable in a single click – they have simultaneously become less accessible. They are long,[86] and full of increasingly dense legalese or, as a participant to a 2005 study on privacy notices expressed it, full of 'legal mumbo jumbo'.[87] Indeed, the most well-known characteristic of player contracts is that hardly anyone will read them,[88] and the declaration that 'I agree to the terms and conditions' has been dubbed the 'biggest lie on the Internet'.[89] More informal experiments using hidden clauses within contracts (eg that the recipient agrees to sell their soul, or wins a prize upon finding the hidden clause) similarly confirm an overall low rate of reading.[90] Studies on reading habits of privacy policies, which are similarly distributed, find that the click-wrap format is deliberately designed to induce a low read rate with 'skippable' characteristics:

> (clickwraps) maintain flow to monetized sections of services, while diverting attention from policies that might encourage dissent. Clickwraps accomplish this through an agenda-setting function whereby prompts encouraging circumvention are made more prominent than policy links. Results emphasize that clickwraps discourage engagement with privacy and reputation protections by suggesting that consent materials are unimportant, contributing to the normalization of this circumvention.[91]

When reflecting on the state of player contracts today compared with the origins of the game/copyright relationship in the 1970s, we see the player is far from their original position of equivalence – the quasi-programmer and mutual games enthusiast. Instead, the assumptions entrenched in the 1980s – that the player is part of a mass, and impliedly naïve, audience – situates them as a layperson, for

International Conference on Financial Cryptography and Data Security; and N Good, 'Noticing Notice: A Large-Scale Experiment on the Timing of Software License agreements' (2007) CHI'07: Proceedings of the SIGCHI Conference on Human Factors in Computing Systems.

[86] Quite famously, as early as 2012, the iTunes agreement at 56 pages long was longer than Shakespeare's *Macbeth*. See U Pidaparthy, 'What You Should Know about iTunes' 56-page Legal Rerms' (*CNN*, 6 May 2011) [*archived*] https://web.archive.org/web/20110509075256/http://edition.cnn.com/2011/TECH/web/05/06/itunes.terms/.

[87] N Good et al, 'Stopping Spyware at the Gate: A User Study of Privacy, Notice and Spyware' (2005) SOUPS '05: Proceedings of the 2005 Symposium on Usable privacy and security 50.

[88] See Y Bakos et al, 'Does Anyone Read the Fine Print? Testing a Law and Economics Approach to Standard Form Contracts' (2009) Working Papers 09–04, NET Institute, where it was discovered in an experiment on nearly 50,000 households that only 1 or 2 of every thousand will access terms, and even those who do purport to read them do not spend nearly long enough to comprehend them.

[89] JA Obar and A Oeldorf-Hirsch, 'The Biggest Lie on the Internet: Ignoring the Privacy Policies and Terms of Service Policies of Social Networking Services' (2008) 23(1) *Information, Communication and Society* 128.

[90] See experiments by PC Pitstop (PC Matic Cybersecurity, '4 Years Later – PC Pitstop EULA Experiment Still the Buzz' (*Tech Talk*, 14 December 2009) https://techtalk.pcpitstop.com/2009/12/14/4-years-later-pc-pitstop-eula-experiment-still-the-buzz/) and Gamestation ('7,500 Online Shoppers Accidentally Sold Their Souls To Gamestation' (*Huffpost*, 25 May 2011) https://www.huffingtonpost.co.uk/entry/gamestation-grabs-soulso_n_541549).

[91] JA Obar and A Oeldorf-Hirsch, 'The Clickwrap: A Political Economic Mechanism for Manufacturing Consent on Social Media' (2018) 4(3) *Social Media and Society*, quotation from the article's abstract.

whom the contract is at best a nuisance to be clicked *through*, rather than held within the product, and owned on the shelf. And, if the player has attributes of the 'pirate', then any form of legal agreement ensures some form of risk management in the event they behave in a contrary way. In sum, this suggests that some concepts about who the player is are 'stickier' than others, and easier normalised.

Finally, low readership means that many are surprised by the reality of what is contained in the terms of the contract, as their expectations tend to be more generous than what is permitted in reality.[92] When discovered, some may attempt to resist them while continuing to participate in their use of the copyrighted work. For example, users on social media have posted 'warding charms' on their profile that attempt to 'opt out' of disagreeable automated updates to terms of service.[93] However legally ineffective these 'charms' may be, they do evidence the final and perhaps most important characteristic of the player contract today: that they remain non-negotiable and stubbornly unilateral. They are a one-way dialogue initiated and maintained by the rightsholder. It is for this reason that the remainder of the book will evidence how the player is constructed through the contract in a *non-dialogic* process. While we may be the intended *recipients* of these contracts, we are evidently not intended to be their *readers*. We cannot penetrate the discourse (it is hidden behind click-wrap, and largely unreadable) or change it. Instead, the intended reader is more likely to be a lawyer, charged with interpreting the 'legal mumbo jumbo' of the text. For the player, the baseline readability is – candidly – hostile. Rather than a direct communication to the player themselves, the main function of the modern contract is to influence the *legal* interpretation of the player, by situating them in a way that anticipates litigation – the type of litigation that has waxed and waned since its inception.[94] In doing so, this helps explain the puzzling ongoing existence of a legal mechanism which has facially become redundant – software, and games are now unambiguously protected by copyright such that there is no 'gap' left in the law that demands an alternative form of contractual protection to fill.[95] Instead, the persistence of player contracts, which cherry-picks different characteristics accrued across the timeline of its development, can be understood as an exercise in strategic legal *power* to help

[92] C Fiesler et al, 'Reality and Perception of Copyright Terms of Service for Online Content Creation' (2016) CSCW '16 Proceedings of the 19th ACM Conference on Computer-Supported Cooperative Work and Social Computing.

[93] Z Friedman, 'Stop Falling For This Facebook Scam' (*Forbes*, 19 August 2019) https://www.forbes.com/sites/zackfriedman/2019/08/19/facebook-scam/?sh=5efafd01a4cf.

[94] There is only limited evidence that licences are being made more 'user' friendly. See MA Campos-Pardillos, 'End-User Agreements in Videogames: Plain English at Work in an Ideal Setting' in A Ensslin and I Balteiro (eds), *Approaches to Videogame Discourse: Lexis, Interaction, Textuality* (Bloomsbury, 2019) and crowdsourced efforts to help understand implications of terms agreed to (see ToS;DR, 'Terms of Service; Didn't Read' https://tosdr.org/ and tl;drLegal, 'Software Licenses in Plain English' https://tldrlegal.com/).

[95] eg Digital Millenium Copyright Act 1998 in the US and the Computer Programs Directive 2009 in the EU. Formal recognition of copyright protection of software was included in international instruments, both in Trade-Related Aspects of Intellectual Property Rights, Art 10(1) and WIPO Copyright Treaty, Art 5.

realise a myriad of different rights, adjacent to, and sometimes including, copyright. Copyright is the legal mandate that lets a game company *tell* the player who they are (or rather, who they would *like them* to be) – whatever that may mean – without inviting a conversation about it. Who then, is the player today?

III. Save Point: Chapter Summary

This chapter sets the scene for illustrating the present day 'terms of play', which is the task of the following chapters. It does so by first illustrating the system that makes the legal mandate of player contracts possible. Copyright law gives the initial grant of a right to a game company which allows it to specify the rules on which lawful access to its work is granted. In doing so, this may override lawful exceptions – carve-outs in the law which permit socially, culturally, or economically beneficial uses – or overreach into regulation of non-copyright (or non-copyright*able*) matters. While the law is increasingly abstracted from some of the functions that contracts now occupy – regulating 'fair play', for example – it is nonetheless essential in creating this system. As such, player contracts can be understood as an exercise in legal power, because they are fundamentally grounded in a law which grants property rights.

The legal aspects of the player contract then develops into a narrative about the history and development of contracting in practice. The second section of the chapter shows that contracts have been used as a legal tool that can give, or hide, characteristics to the player depending on the strategic priorities of the rights-holder in the time and space it occupies. In other words, the needs of the industry bleed into the text of the contract. This can re-affirm copyright law, or attempt to correct its perceived defects. In the 1970s, the absence of a contractual relationship was reflective of the cultural, legal and technological expectations and constraints of the era. Here, the player is a welcome enthusiast in the early game development space, interacting with an object that does not clearly have the qualities of a copyright 'work'. At this time, the player is neither conceptually – nor legally – weak, nor in an exceptionally unbalanced contractual relationship. In the 1980s, legal and technological developments concretise the propertisation mindset towards game *software*, in turn leading to the earliest examples of player contracts. While both sporadic and brief, these early contracts evidence industry concerns surrounding counterfeiting, performing a dual role of thanking the lawful customer (the player) and condemning unauthorised players and competing developers. The player is more specifically a potential pirate – an omnipresent threat where power is being negotiated between them and the game company. The 1990s and 2000s continue to be marked by rapid technological change, where eras become merged because of the significance of the Internet in creating the expectation that players are recipients of use-based, transient services. Normalising this expectation through the embeddedness of online capabilities in game hardware and software concretises the player as a *user of a proprietary work*, whose access to that work is conditional on ongoing permissions granted by the rightsholder. In the current era, this ethos has been firmly accepted, and the ability to shape the conditions of this access – as to who the player *is* – can be understood as an exercise in legally mandated power.

Two key points are worth synthesising from these findings before proceeding further. First, copyright law and player contracts run in parallel with each other. The law is responsible for granting the initial right that allows game companies to specify the exact terms of player behaviour in a contract. So, the text of the contract has a function in allowing the realisation of rights via the shaping of a player in a way that anticipates legal challenge or litigation. Second, the player being described in this contract *does not exist*. As evidenced throughout the historical timeline, players are highly malleable and adaptable entities in the contract. They are, more accurately, an *idealised* version of what the game company needs – a mutual game enthusiast, a welcome customer but wary pirate, or a new inhabitant of an online space that demands expectations in behaviour. The shaping of the player is not an inevitable result of technological determinism or cause-and-effect when games become copyrightable software; rather, it is an object of industry construction. How to measure that construction, and what that says about the player today, is the task of the following chapters.

Level 2

3

Research Design

This chapter outlines the research design showing *how* contracts construct the player in parallel to copyright law. Section I concerns methodology which, broadly put, details the theoretical assumptions of 'why' the contract is being studied. More so, this section shows how contracts have a function beyond a legal list of permissions and prohibitions, to a window into the broader social, cultural and economic concerns of the time in which they are written. As such, this section provides an overview of Critical Discourse Analysis (CDA), a qualitative, interpretative methodology which offers a critical theory of *language*, a language of which contracts clearly form part. The section shows how this methodology is an apt means to study the player as a subject of law and quasi-legal texts, with frameworks understanding identity, power, and construction. Section II concerns the methods, or the 'how' of the research itself. This section details how contracts were identified and collected, alongside summary statistics evidencing key characteristics of the dataset, and limitations of the selection process. The section also outlines the procedure for coding the contractual discourse across textual, discursive, and sociocultural dimensions of analysis.

I. Methodology: Critical Discourse Analysis

As illustrated in Chapter 2, contracts are legal tools that are deeply intertwined with the subjective needs of the games industry. Contracts are certainly in dialogue with copyright, because it is copyright that gives a games company the initial authority to claim those rights through contract in the first instance. But the story being told in the contract is quite separate from the law; it is a narrative about the player in its *own* words. Fundamentally then, this becomes a question about the subjective nature of language, and how language can be employed to construct certain concepts both in relation to law, and outwith it.

The language-orientation of this question resulted in the identification of CDA as an appropriate methodology through which to understand the construction of the player in contracts. CDA is a flexible, multi-disciplinary methodology, with multiple and distinct theoretical and methodical approaches, to the study of discourse. Despite this plurality, there is an agreed understanding that CDA is a critical theory of language, and that language is itself a social practice.[1] In essence, CDA proposes that language can be used to shape reality, and in turn is shaped by it; and that this reality can comprise certain identities and concepts (eg 'player'). Within this methodology, there are both theoretical assumptions (Section A) and established frameworks for their implementation (Section B) which are outlined in turn.

A. Theoretical Assumptions

The main characteristic that distinguishes CDA from competing methodologies which study language is its 'critical' component, which forms a key aspect of its theoretical assumptions. CDA draws from a group of loosely connected 'critical' theorists in both sociolinguistics and social theory, including Althusser, Bourdieu, Foucault, Gramsci, Habermas, and Halliday, and their studies of linguistics, semiotics, and communication.[2] While there are many important distinctions between these theorists in terms of the concepts they employ and their respective disciplines,[3] we might summarise them as all sharing a healthy scepticism about power, and how power can be wielded through language to achieve potentially harmful outcomes that we may not be aware of. We might observe, for example, that the manner in which player contracts are presented to us – a bland wall of black-and-white 'legalese' – can purposefully disguise some disagreeable clauses being presented in it, on a mandatory, non-negotiable basis.

The following sub-sections outline three core theoretical concepts in CDA that help frame this research: power (section i); ideology (section ii), and; common sense (section iii). While these are presented as exclusive categories, readers may rightly find that they have a dialectical relationship that often feeds into the others.

[1] TA van Dijk, *Elite Discourse and Racism* (Sage, 1993) 131: CDA is 'at most a shared perspective of doing linguistic, semiotic or discourse analysis'.

[2] Namely, Althusser's ideological state apparatus and interpellation (L Althusser, *Lenin and Philosophy and Other Essays* (New Left Books, 1971)); Bourdieu's habitus (P Bourdieu, *Language and Symbolic Power* (Harvard University Press, 1991)); Foucault's order of discourse and power knowledge (M Foucault, The Order of Discourse' in M Shapiro (ed), *Language and Politics* (New York University Press, 1984)); Gramsci's hegemony (A Gramsci, translated by Q Hoare and G Nowell-Smith, *Selections from Prison Notebooks* (Lawrence and Wishart, 1971)); Habermas's theory of communicative rationality (J Habermas, translated by T McCarthy, *The Theory of Communicative Action: Reason and the Rationalization of Society* (Heinemann, 1984)); and Halliday's functional linguistics (MAK Halliday, *Language as a Social Semiotic: The Social Interpretation of Language and Meaning* (Edward Arnold Ltd, 1978)).

[3] Which formed part of the series of critiques leveraged against CDA as a methodology in HG Widdowson, 'Discourse Analysis: A Critical View' (1995) 4(3) *Language and Literature* 157 and HG Widdowson, 'Reply to Fairclough: Discourse and Interpretation: Conjectures and Refutations' (1996) 5(1) *Language and Literature* 57.

i. Power

Most CDA scholars adopt the classic Weberian definition of power: that it is the ability to exercise one's will over others.[4] Power can be held for myriad reasons – economic, political, cultural, or social. And understanding *who* holds this power is important because it affects the control of how texts and discourses are produced, distributed and consumed.[5] For example, the unilateral offering of a contract would be an example of how a game company can control the distribution and content of that text. And we might assume that the game company has more power than the player because they hold an exclusive economic right to permit or deny access to that game – a legal right that can generate income for them.

Power can be achieved and sustained through two chief mechanisms: coercion and consent.[6] Of the two, coercion is often the more obvious to measure, because it may be evidenced by overt threats or pressures (eg 'stop making this thing or I will sue you in a court'). Consent, by contrast, is more opaque, because it is a more subtle influence that frames things in a way that makes us think it would be a *good idea* to agree to the exertion of power (eg 'we think it's really cool when you do this thing, so it would be cool if you would keep doing it'). Again, we see parallels of this in the nature of the contract, which has elements of both coercion and consent. Being based in law, contracts can have coercive functions – they designate what is lawful or unlawful, with the real threat of state-sanctioned enforcement measures behind it. But as a tool of consent, it also has the subtle qualities of naturalising assent to (generally unfavourable) terms to permit access to games, as a socially desirable product. They are, in short, systematically encountered, and systematically ignored, even where it may not be in our best interests. Our identity as players is not something we construct ourselves or choose, but rather is one that has been constructed for us by the powerful 'other' – one offered, accepted, but not negotiated. And this identity has been established and reproduced institutionally within the games industry.

Because contracts have both elements of power, they might evidence power either *behind* discourse or *through* discourse (or both).[7] The former – power *behind* discourse – is where power is 'real' outside of the text itself, in that it is bolstered by, for example, the sovereign and inherently powerful character of law. Where the licence claims ownership to a work protected by copyright, this is a reference to the real rights granted to the game company in law. The latter – power *through* discourse – is more subtle, and shows how power may be manifested in the language use itself. For example, if a licence were to suggest that

[4] M Weber, *Wirtschaft und Gessellschaft* (JCB Mohr, 1925).

[5] N Fairclough, *Critical Discourse Analysis* (Longman, 1995) 1.

[6] N Fairclough, *Language and Power*, 2nd edn (Longman, 2001) 33 – this is developed from Foucault's distinction between sovereign and disciplinary power (M Foucault, *Discipline and Punish* (Penguin, 1979)).

[7] ibid.

a certain activity is more or less socially desirable (eg 'we think it would be cool if you …'), this may be a way of manufacturing consent to its terms by presenting it as a 'good idea', regardless of its anchoring in 'real' power behind the text.

ii. Ideology

Ideology refers to a worldview, a collective set of beliefs about how one understands the world and oneself in relation to it.[8] Importantly, this is not a reference to the way the world *is*, but rather how it is idealised or *ought* to be; again, with reference to the 'critical' bite of CDA, ideologies are not a neutral view of reality, but rather the perspective of a dominant interest group as to what might best forward their interests. For example, for most orthodox CDA scholars, the specific ideology being scrutinised is capitalism, an ideology that perpetuates a system of private property, free markets, and the pursuit of profits, manufactured by an identifiable 'ruling class'.[9]

While class is not absent from this analysis, the object under study here is narrower: it is a group of *legal* subjects (ie rightsholders, game companies) who have been given constitutive and generative power through law to construct the player, another legal subject. Those relationships are more specifically stratified along the lines of property and law: one with property, the other without; one with *power*, and one without. Indeed, as discussed throughout Chapters 1 and 2, the presentation of games as property has not always been unequivocal or broadly accepted, but has clearly been *desirable* for certain facets of the games industry – it forms part of the industry's dream of the world, its ideology. As a preliminary view then, we might conclude that games-as-software or games-as-property – a *proprietary* view of games – is the ideology which would be perpetuated through a contract, by packaging and 'selling' games on this assumption.

CDA scholars stress that language cannot be removed from the influence of ideology. As such, consciously or unconsciously, we must assume that the text of the contract will always present a particular worldview. This may or may not be harmful, depending on the intentions of the entity 'wielding' that language, and whether that language is being used to legitimise ideologies that are potentially harmful – eg that a player's legitimate interest could be overruled by the (more powerful) games company. As such, an omnipresent question throughout this research is about *who* benefits from the use of the language in a contract, and *why* is this benefit sought?

[8] N Fairclough, *Discourse and Social Change* (Polity Press 1992) 87.

[9] An orthodox Marxist dichotomy of class – between bourgeoise (owners of the means of production) and proletariat (the wage-working class) – is often forwarded in the work of key CDA scholars, including Fairclough, van Dijk and Wodak, referenced throughout this chapter.

iii. Common Sense

Common sense, sometimes known as naturalisation,[10] refers to the process of how discourse becomes dominant and universal. This concept is closely tied to power, because power is only successful where it is re-enacted in routine activities that go unquestioned and are seen as normal; if it forms part of the 'subtle, routine, everyday forms of text and talk that appear "natural" and quite "acceptable"'.[11] Being sceptical of the 'common sense' aspects of the world is important for CDA scholars because things that are presented as natural, inevitable, or commonsensical, may in fact be artificial constructs that only benefit a particular dominant interest group. In sum, we may be unaware of our pre-constructed identities as players, because we are taught to ignore the text that tells us about this. For this reason, CDA is inherently interpretative and subjective, to look behind the neutral presentation of a word or a text to understand the intention behind it.

Again, this theoretical proposition is important for understanding the nature of the contract as a 'common sense' tool to manufacture consent in a relationship of power. The contract is both ends and means for the player: one must agree to proceed, therefore there is no alternative but to agree to its construction – its terms of play. As such, players will ultimately acquiesce to the terms of the contract, even if they balk at them when read, because consent to them has become naturalised in the digital environment. In doing so, the ideological claim to games-as-property becomes self-sustaining.

With reference to this disguised ideology, CDA has an inherently progressivist or 'biased and proud of it'[12] stance: these commonsense presentations – hidden ideas, assumptions, values, positions or perspectives – *should* be de-mystified, de-naturalised and ultimately changed where they perpetuate inequality or injustice. For the purposes of this research then, we might understand the player as a marginalised subject in copyright discourse, whose constructed identity, given by a powerful actor, is disguised by the commonsensical acquiescence to harmful contractual terms. The very effort to disguise this is, for the CDA scholar, suspicion enough to warrant further enquiry.

B. Frameworks

The theoretical concepts illustrated above are important, but largely abstract. To methodise this, we must consider the pragmatics: *how* would we measure power, ideology, or common sense? How would this be routinely structured or

[10] Fairclough (n 6) 76.

[11] TA van Dijk, 'Principles of Critical Discourse Analysis' in M Wetherell et al (eds), *Discourse Theory and Practice: A Reader* (Sage, 2001) 300.

[12] TA van Dijk, 'Multidisciplinary CDA: A Plea for Diversity' in R Wodak and M Meyer (eds), *Methods of Critical Discourse Analysis* (Sage, 2001) 96.

institutionalised in practice? There are several established frameworks for implementing these considerations in CDA research.[13] However, not all are appropriate to the study of fixed legal text, which is, admittedly, an oddity for discourse studies. It may be, for example, more obvious that power relations are at play in a heated meeting between a manager and their employee ('oral-conversational' discourse), than in the silent, flickering light of the 'click to agree' box that temporarily interrupts our screens.

I adopt the CDA framework proposed by Fairclough (the 'dialectical-relational' or 'three-dimensional' model), a holistic means of evidencing how *sociocultural practices* – a more pragmatic distillation of the theoretical concepts illustrated above – can influence, and are influenced by, language.[14] Fairclough's approach to CDA is illustrated into a model of three, interconnected dimensions or levels of discourse, shown in Figure 2. Broadly conceived, the framework evidences how textual, micro levels of discourse reproduce, challenge, or perpetuate the sociocultural practice in macro discourse. The macro level embodies the theoretical concepts such as power and ideology, whereas the micro level deals with more granular linguistic concepts such as grammar, style, and rhetoric in the text itself. The model also factors in a mediating meso level which examines the discursive practice through which the text is produced and distributed.

Figure 2 Representation of Fairclough's Three-Dimensional Model of CDA

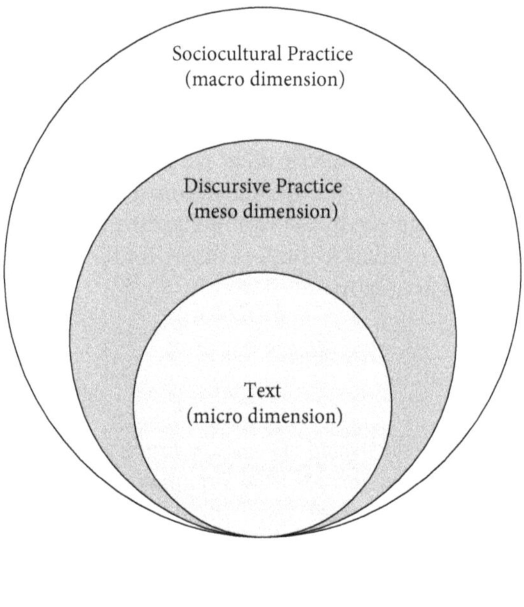

[13] Key alternative approaches, not suitable for this research, include Wodak's discourse-historical approach (R Wodak and M Reisigi 'The Discourse-Historical Approach (DHA)') and van Dijk;s socio-cognitive approach (TA van Dijk, 'Socio-Cognitive Discourse Studies'), both in J Flowerdew and JE Richardson (eds), *The Routledge Handbook of Critical Discourse Studies* (Routledge, 2017).

[14] Fairclough (n 6).

For Fairclough, each of these levels is interrelated, with language being capable of influencing our sociocultural practices, and vice versa. For example, contracts may refer to the game as the 'property' because this is part of the legal precedent that says this term is most effective, but likewise the repeated claim to the game as 'property' might perpetuate the (inaccurate) impression that *all* aspects of the game are equally owned. In this respect, the term 'dimension' may be more accurate than 'level', because 'level' implies an ascending or descending process, whereas, and as the embedded circular structure of Figure 2 illustrates, each of these is interdependent, and tends to overlap, with no prescriptive or linear process.

i. Textual Dimension

The textual dimension of Fairclough's framework involves a micro-level analysis of the specific linguistic and semiotic features of a text – the language of the contract itself. This is otherwise known as an analysis of the 'descriptive' characteristics of the text, in the sense that this involves looking at the vocabulary (eg word choice, meaning, metaphor – formality), grammar (eg transitivity, modality – imperatives) and text structure (eg sentence length, complexity – emphasis, narrative). This may also include analysis of more granular features such as the choice of voice (active or passive), speech (direct or indirect) and emphasis (eg capitalisation, italicisation, underlining). The aim of the textual dimension is to look for particular linguistic patterns that assist in identifying shared, underlying conceptualisations or constructions of – in this case – the player. For this reason, some elements of content analysis are appropriate in the textual dimension – eg a quantitative metric of how often a term appears – in part because this can indicate the prevalence of a particular textual feature where appropriate (eg how often do UGC policies refer to UGC as 'fan' content?). However, any such content analysis should only be understood as complementary to the main, qualitative, and interpretative CDA methodology.

At the textual dimension, where the textual meaning of a word may have a quite separate meaning in law, I offer doctrinal analysis where appropriate to highlight a difference between the concept in the text and the legal meaning. For example, Chapter 6 illustrates the differences between the contract's definition of 'commercial' activities, which permits passive revenue-making through monetisation on online platforms, versus the meaning given in copyright law, which would not permit such monetisation. Illustrating the differences between the legal meaning and alternative meaning as constructed in the licence is required as it impacts how word choice is interpreted in the text. The contract may deliberately engage with, or subvert, the meaning enshrined in law and thus differ in the power it claims *behind* or *through* discourse. In this dimension, the parallels between the methods adopted in this research and 'rules lawyering' should become more clear – that words have particular meanings, and when employed in particular contexts, have very specific conclusions.

ii. Discursive Dimension

The discursive dimension of Fairclough's framework occurs at the meso level and is mainly concerned with the methods and circumstances by which the text is produced, circulated, and distributed. Importantly, in this dimension the typical CDA scholar would also examine how a text is *consumed* by the recipient of the discourse. However, it is outwith the scope of this book to examine the player's interpretation of the contract – instead, the core focus is on how the player is constructed, and idealised *by* particular legal actors with particular ideologies, and how this identity is constructed in the contract, rather than received.

In this research, the discursive dimension examines the circumstances in which the contract was produced, circulated, and distributed. For the most part, this is a static and linear relationship in that there is only one 'speaker' – the game company – and one recipient – the player. However, distribution of the contract may change in terms of whether it is distributed physically or digitally, whether there is a singular agreement or multiple agreements, and where those agreements can be found (eg as a static version on an institutional webpage).

iii. Sociocultural Dimension

The sociocultural dimension of Fairclough's model has the explanatory function of tying the micro and meso textual and discursive dimensions together by situating them within the broader social, cultural and/or historical context in which the contract was written. In doing so, this dimension questions the extent to which a text changes or copies existing *social practices* within the context in which they are made. These social practices can be understood as a way of framing the influence of power, ideology and common sense so that they can be measured.

In the context of this research, for example, we might ask 'what type of ideology does this contract perpetuate?'. And in doing so, we need to take account of the particular context in which that contract was written and distributed – was it written by (or more likely on behalf of) a large company with an established publishing profile, or a small, independent game developer? What interests might such a company have in perpetuating this idea – and what does it stand to benefit? Do other companies behave similarly? In doing so, the sociocultural dimension mechanises ways of evidencing relations of power, the worldview adopted by particular companies, and the veneer of neutrality in which they are often dressed.

Side quest: legal texts as discourse

CDA is not unheard of in legal studies, and does occasionally appear as an analysis method for conversational speech acts such as unscripted discourse in courtrooms and policy debates where, as suggested above, power relations may be more evidentially 'visible'.[15] However, the choice to study legal language in the form of a written and

[15] Of most relevance to this research, see M Favale et al, 'Who is Steering the Jurisprudence of the European Court of Justice? The Influence of Member State Submissions on Copyright Law' (2020)

fixed text – a contract – as discourse is quite unorthodox.[16] As such, this side quest is included for those who may need further convincing on this treatment, and to show how the methodology proposed here may extend beyond its application to the contract, to any fixed, written legal text.

In part, hesitancy to engage with CDA to analyse legal texts is because law is a language for a specific purpose – it is functional. And the need for clarity, neutrality, and consistency over time all inform the ways in which the rules of law are written. The strange, often archaic, formulation of legal language is not accidental, but rather has purposeful conservative characteristics which results in a frozen written style.[17] Written legal text is typically characterised by its formality, impersonal nature, textual complexity, lengthy sentences, formulaic expressions (eg binomials 'represent and warrant', 'disburden and dispone') and legal jargon (eg 'heretofore').[18] Frequent intertextual references to pre-existing cases (eg legislation or statutes) are another typical textual feature of discourse which have a functional purpose of establishing precedent and authority.[19] This frozen style may lead to the belief that there is nothing meaningful to be gained from approaching a written legal contract as a discourse, as the reason it 'speaks' in a particular way is purely functional. Lawyers write the way they do because that is the way things have always been done to achieve a specific purpose: securing legal ground, and enforcing rights, by 'casting a legal spell' with all the correct rhymes and incantations.[20]

Yet, written law is also conceptual. Indeed, if CDA supposes that reality is created through language, and law is in its essence language, then we also have to assume that law *cannot* be objective. As well as having a function which manifests in a specific textual style, it is also a tool of *social* construction; law criminalises the undesirable, and legitimates the approved, if only tacitly by omission. As an institution of power, the law delegates the superordinate and subordinate – who has rights, who doesn't – and manifests asymmetrical power relations between them.[21] From a CDA perspective then, the very fact that legal language is often presented as objective, neutral, and purposeful

83(4) *Modern Law Review* 831; K Erickson, 'User Illusion: Ideological Construction of "User-generated Content" in the EC Consultation on Copyright' (2014) 3(4) *Internet Policy Review*; L Edwards et al, 'Discourse, Justification and Critique: Towards a Legitimate Digital Copyright Regime?' (2015) 21(1) *International Journal of Cultural Policy* 60; H Kalimo, T Meyer and T Mylly, 'Of Values and Legitimacy – Discourse Analytical Insights on the Copyright Case Law of the Court of Justice of the European Union' (2018) 81(2) *Modern Law Review* 282.

[16] But not unheard of. Of contracts see M Nartey and H Huang, 'Situated Identities in the Discourse of Insurance: A Comparative Critical Discourse Analysis of Chinese and British Contracts' (2018) 6(2) *Language, Discourse and Society* 119. Of legislation, see V Hollis, 'A Critical Discourse Analysis of the Intellectual property Chapter of the TPP: Confirming What the Critics Fear' (2017) 6(1) *Communication.*

[17] See R Hultunen, 'The Grammar and Structure of Legal Texts' in LM Solan and PM Tiersma (eds), *The Oxford Handbook of Language and Law* (Oxford University Press, 2012); E Finegan, 'Discourses in the Language of the Law' in M Handford and JP Gee (eds), *The Routledge Handbook for Discourse Analysis* (Routledge, 2012); JP Kaplan, *Linguistics and Law* (Routledge, 2019).

[18] Kaplan (ibid).

[19] ibid.

[20] E Martinez et al, 'Even Laypeople use Legalese' (2024) 121(35) *Proceedings of the National Academy of Sciences.*

[21] See J Niemi-Kiesilainen et al 'Legal Texts as Discourses' in A Gunnarsson, E Svensson and M Davies (eds), *Exploiting the Limits of Law* (Ashgate, 2007).

because of its function, makes it *in itself* a worthwhile object of study, precisely because it can disguise the conceptual, constitutive element underlying it.

By extension, this logic applies to the contract. Contracts are a form of quasi-legal text which are both sanctioned by the law, and that repurpose the law. Much like the law, the contract is also partly functional; it is a technical, if not necessarily legal, document that follows certain conventions to grant access to a particular copyrighted work. However, and like the law, we must assume it can also be conceptual.[22] The contract continues to exist long after its initial legal justification has expired (as discussed in Chapter 2), and now forms a hidden part of a player's everyday interactions – an interaction that has become so naturalised that the player completely ignores it. Likewise, the same logic can by extension be granted to the player as a *legal* subject in copyright. The player, despite its abstract construction in law, is not merely a functional label that is objective, but is instead a subject situated within a particular historical, social and cultural condition. Much like the language of law or the contract, the label of 'player' may in part be functional (simply describing the quality of interaction with a work), but its conceptual construction is never neutral or natural under the CDA paradigm. This is precisely why the player should be understood from the specific context of where and by whom they are being constructed, an aspect given form in the methods section below.

II. Methods

Having outlined 'why' contracts can be studied as a form of language through CDA, this section now shows how the 'terms of play' were collected and analysed.

A. Dataset

In the process of this research, I have shied away from (over)stating the size and growth of the game industry – because, whilst undoubtedly eye-catching, I do not think evidencing their economic scope is necessary to justify their importance as an object of study. But this factor is indeed a relevant consideration when *designing* the research. In this context, it is worth noting that games are, globally, the largest entertainment industry in both volume and revenue – larger than music, or film and TV.[23] The game industry is composed of multiple actors – some of them, the largest 'Big Tech' companies in the world – spread across different platforms, all of whom may have vested interests at different levels of the supply chain.[24] The

[22] ibid.

[23] Statista, 'Games – Worldwide' (*Statista*, 2025) https://www.statista.com/outlook/amo/media/games/worldwide.

[24] A Thomas et al, 'Competition in the Cloud Gaming Market: Proposing the Innovation-Creativity Dichotomy' (2025) 9(1) *Interactive Entertainment Law Review* 1.

audience of potential players to be constructed is, likewise, enormous. Given this scale, the sub-sections that follow explain how the dominant contractual discourse(s) in the games industry were identified, the characteristics of this dataset, and the challenges of the selection.

B. Selection Criteria

The dataset of contracts used in this research is derived from a sample of 30 popular game titles, each of which is published by a separate game company. Importantly, these contracts do not tend to be purpose-written for only those individual titles, but rather are blanket policies for the entire catalogue of titles owned by that company. As a result, while the selection process was driven by reference to a small sample of game titles, the contracts under study apply to approximately 1,500 individual games.[25]

At the outset of selection, the definition of 'contract' was broad and holistic, emphasising the *purpose* of the text in regulating the usage of the game, rather than the specific label applied to the document. For example, games that are played wholly online (eg *Dota 2*) or are free-to-play (eg *Fortnite*) are typically regulated under 'terms of use' or 'terms of service'. While such terms are not strictly a contract in a copyright sense (they are not a 'licence' per se), they still constitute the only permission to the player to play the game. In other cases, particularly where the game company is also the owner of the game platform, titles may be made available under the platform's general terms and conditions, rather than as a standalone regulation (as is the case with Sony, Microsoft and Valve). Again, these documents are functionally equivalent to a contract because they constitute the only permission to the player which regulates their usage of a game. So where functionally there is a primary document concerned with giving the player permission to use the game, this is embraced as the main unit of analysis, regardless of its branding.

Contracts usually do not exist in a vacuum, and instead incorporate many supporting documents, such as UGC policies and codes of conduct, or additional terms of service that are complementary to the 'main' contract or may

[25] To be more precise, I estimate 1,538 individual game titles are covered by the contracts in this sample. For various reasons, it can be difficult to give an exact figure for the number of individual game titles published by a given games company. For example, a 'title' may be published multiple times across multiple platforms (eg each instance of *Minecraft*), be re-published or included in game bundles (eg Mass *Effect Legendary Edition*), or be published multiple times for regional variations or localisations (eg the *Resident Evil* franchise vs *Biohazard* in Japan). As such, this figure is based on an aggregate sum of the average number of all game titles listed on each game company page on Wikipedia, after removing simple ports, re-releases or remasters, or obvious compilation bundles (see Appendix 2). For companies with over 100 titles (eg Nintendo), I rounded up the average number of titles (~100–120) to 120. This aggregate figure also includes discontinued games which in principle would also be bound by the same terms even if no longer being actively published by the game company.

be contingent on its acceptance. This is both a consideration for methodology – because it concerns the process of production and distribution of the text(s) – and method, because it is a pragmatic consideration for data collection. As such, where further documents are incorporated by reference to the main contract, or accompanying it, those documents were also gathered and treated as an extension of the main contract. Documents for more specific purposes, such as privacy policies and warranties, were excluded from the scope, instead focusing only on documents which regulate the player in their experience of the creative content in a game (ie the 'copyright' player). As a result, while there are 30 game companies represented in this dataset, in total there are 70 individual documents, making for an average of two documents per title.

In conducting keyword searches for these documents, it became apparent that some game companies were communicating, particularly UGC policies, more informally through other means of communication, such as social media and contact forms. While it is not possible to take an exhaustive account of such communications, given the multiplicity of people involved in game development, examples of these types of communication are used where relevant to illustrate alternative approaches of communication (a factor for the 'discursive' dimension of CDA). These examples are supplementary to the primary dataset of contracts and are only used for illustrative effect.

As a final consideration of dataset collection, throughout the process of gathering this data, it became evident that the contract is very much a 'live' document which is frequently updated and modified. When gathering the initial dataset between late 2019 and mid-2020, eight of the primary contracts were updated at least within the last year (and most within the last six months),[26] with only 11 failing to state their date of last update.[27] Further changes were noted during the revision process for later work in 2023, and again in late 2024, particularly as a result of merger and acquisition activity.[28] This is in itself an interesting finding – that the contract is not a static document that is created to accompany the initial release of a game which is subsequently left untouched. Instead, this frequency of update suggests that the contracts are responsive to any subsequent developments in their respective markets.[29] Unfortunately, the lack of version control offered via publishers' websites means that a full historical appreciation of these changes is

[26] Electronic Arts (18 July 2019), Magic Online (25 September 2019), Microsoft (September 2019), Psyonix (8 July 2019), PUBG (28 June 2019), Valve (30 April 2019), Rockstar (11 July 2019), Warner Bros (September 2019) (Appendix 2).

[27] Being Epic Games, Ubisoft, Bandai Namco, Bethesda, Studio MDHR, Nintendo, Red Barrell, Sony, Superhot Team, Take 2, and Toby Fox (Appendix 2). Note that most of the games which omit this are indie titles, and may be a byproduct of less financial investment in re-drafting.

[28] Namely the Microsoft/Activision Blizzard merger, which was considered in the UK, EU and US (for further details, see Thomas et al (n 24).

[29] Virality can also be a factor in changing policies. See, for example, a substantive change in Capcom's video-sharing policy in 2021, released in response to the virality of *Resident Evil: Village*: Capcom, 'Capcom Video Policy' (*Capcom*, 15 March 2021) https://www.capcom.com/video-policy/.

not possible, with similar limitations to game preservation having previously been noted in Chapter 2. As contracts are subject to multiple updates during their lifespan, each agreement was retained as a static copy from the particular date it was gathered. As a result, the selection on file is reflective of the discourse occurring between late 2019 to mid-2024.

C. Sample Selection

Given the multiplicity of games available, I considered that the most *popular* types of discourse would be the most *prevalent*, and so used popularity as a metric to select game titles and their respective contracts. I therefore treated popularity and prevalence as a proxy for the most dominant discourse in the industry and, by extension, the most dominant vision of the player.

However, the diversity of game titles makes the metrics of assessing popularity difficult, particularly as games are distributed in many ways, across multiple platforms. Choosing popular titles based on the number of players online at any given time tends to be skewed towards particular genres, such as MMOs (eg *World of Warcraft*) and would not capture offline titles (eg *Undertale*). Best-*selling* lists will not capture free-to-play titles (eg *Fortnite*), and depending on their configuration may selectively include either physical or digital sales, but not both.[30] In short, most ways of determining the popularity of a game title based on volume or revenue are not representative of the full and diverse market.

An alternative metric for assessing video game popularity is to use a hybrid of community and critic-sourced ranking systems. For many years, Metacritic has been the 'go-to' source for determining game popularity, being an aggregation website that can be used to determine popularity based on weighted average reviews from users and critics alike.[31] Earlier versions of my research design used Metacritic scores as a metric to determine popularity, but this was subsequently dropped towards the end of the initial data-gathering period, as the reliability of the site was called into doubt. In particular, a spate of 'review bombing', where large numbers of negative reviews are deliberately posted in an effort to reduce sales, appeared to be artificially skewing aggregated scores.[32] Instead, the most popular video game titles were determined with reference to Ranker, a community-sourced

[30] See eg J Sirani, 'Top 10 Best-Selling Video Games of All Time' (*IGN*, 9 February 2021) https://www.ign.com/articles/2019/04/19/top-10-best-selling-video-games-of-all-time, which notes that 'free mobile downloads don't count toward sales'.

[31] Metacritic, 'Games' https://www.metacritic.com/game.

[32] Most notably in response to *Last of Us: Part II* (see P Tassi, 'After "The Last of Us Part 2" Insanity, Metacritic Has Changed User Score Submissions' (*Forbes*, 18 July 2020) https://www.forbes.com/sites/paultassi/2020/07/18/after-the-last-of-us-part-2-insanity-metacritic-has-changed-user-score-submissions/?sh=57f869617e6f).

polling site which is more resilient to review bombing than Metacritic.[33] One key difference is that Ranker does not incorporate critic reviews into its determination of popularity, and instead is purely user sourced (perhaps more fitting given the overall theme of this book, a selection of popular titles as determined by their players). Resultingly, the first half of the dataset was constructed with reference to Ranker's 'Best games of 2010s' vote to establish the 15 most popular video game titles, as determined by a community vote on their quality.[34]

I then expanded the dataset with additional material from games which would address more creative or engaged players, particularly the kind that may seek to monetise game content through, for example, streaming or UGC (see Chapter 1 for more detail on different player types in copyright law). To do so, I gathered a further sample from eSports games, which have an explicit commercial element as they are played professionally, and often have a money-making purpose through eg sponsorships, tournaments, and prize-setting.

As with video games, in respect of the eSports sample there is no definitive metric of defining popularity. The same considerations which limit the capacity to measure video games' popularity also apply with eSports in terms of genre, business models, and self-reporting. In looking for an authoritative source from which to reference for this sample, the British eSports Association estimate approximately 30 recognised eSports titles, though these are, unhelpfully, unlisted.[35] Given the inability to cross-check between them and verify the identity of these titles, it is not possible to infer popularity in this way. Instead, similarly to the initial sample, the eSports sample draws from a crowdsourced website in order to determine an appropriate selection of eSports titles and corresponding contracts. The sample was drawn from eSports Earnings, which is described as a 'a community-driven competitive gaming resource based on freely available public information',[36] dependent on user submissions for its accuracy. The 'Game Rankings' list details the top 100 eSports titles based on overall prize money, from which popularity, and hence prevalence, is inferred within the community.[37] From this list, 15 further titles were selected.[38]

[33] Ranker, 'How Do Rankings Work?' (*Ranker*, date unknown) [*archived*] https://web.archive.org/web/20211122141043/https://blog.ranker.com/faqs.

[34] K Townsend, 'The Best Video Games of the 2010s, Ranked' (*Ranker*, 22 October 2020) https://www.ranker.com/list/best-video-games-2010s/kyle-townsend.

[35] British eSports Association, https://britishesports.org.

[36] eSports Earnings, 'eSports Earnings' https://www.esportsearnings.com/.

[37] eSports Earnings, 'Game Rankings' https://www.esportsearnings.com/games.

[38] One important observation in this selection process relates to how condensed the market for eSports is. Unlike video games, where a diversity of rightsholders is noted, it appears that only a small number of large games publishers specialise in eSports titles, resulting in many titles being owned by the same company, and therefore often regulated by the same contract. In order to obtain 15 different contracts from the sample, it was necessary to uncover the ownership of the first 25 titles listed within the 'Game Rankings' list; or to put this another way, the top 25 eSports games are owned by only 11 games publishers. Only one of the titles examined here can be categorised as indie (*Rocket League*). eSports titles therefore appear to be the exclusive remit of those with the budget and capacity to maintain the more demanding technical upkeep of larger, multiplayer games.

As a note of caution for the eSports sample, while eSports titles are used in this research as a proxy for the professional (commercial) player, because these are titles that are known to be played professionally, it is not a *guarantee* that every player of an eSports title is a professional eSports player: it is just more likely. For titles such as *Fortnite*, it is entirely possible to engage with this game casually and for personal enjoyment rather than in a professional capacity. However, in any case, as the contract is a frequently updated 'live' document, one could anticipate that both types of players are accounted for within the text.

After aggregating both samples – from video games more broadly and eSports titles – the dataset constitutes 30 game titles, equally split between video games and eSports, comprising 70 total individual documents. A complete list of game titles examined and constituent documents, including dates of retrieval, is included in Appendix 2.

Side quest: the platform effect

In illustrating how this dataset was constructed, it is important to acknowledge that games do not exist in a vacuum. The game will always require a facilitatory medium to make it playable via, often third-party, hardware and system software. Facilitation is typically via a mobile device (via eg Apple App Store), game consoles (eg Sony's PlayStation, Microsoft's Xbox), or PC (either via a disk, or downloaded from a virtual marketplace)[39] – a platform on which the game can be played. This has characteristics of a two-sided market,[40] with players who have a consumerist demand for the platform itself, and the third-party game publishers and developers who seek to make their wares available via the platform. As a result, that platform – by mediating this relationship – may also have a role in constructing the player, both technically and contractually. For example, at the technical level many platforms have integrated sharing features that exist outwith the game itself: the PlayStation 4 and 5 have integrated 'share' buttons (in the PlayStation 5, now a 'create' button) in the game controllers, which allows the player to share screenshots and videos of gameplay, and stream directly onto authorised platforms, such as Twitch and YouTube. This invites the possibility that even if a game company's contract prohibits sharing of certain content in the text, this is made technically possible by merit of the platform on which the game is played (or vice versa).

As the hardware-software divide in this market means that game platforms can also have a role in constructing the player, I conducted a brief pilot study of the terms of four of the main gaming platforms (Sony, Microsoft, Valve and Apple) to determine whether this could have a significant effect. Both Sony (in respect of its PlayStation 4) and Valve

[39] Titles that are exclusive to certain platforms from the dataset include: *Dota 2* (Valve/Steam), *Halo 5* (Microsoft/Xbox), *The Last of Us* (Sony/PlayStation), *The Legend of Zelda: Breath of the Wild* (Nintendo/Switch).

[40] V Landsman and S Stremersch, 'Multihoming in Two-Sided Markets: An Empirical Inquiry in the Video Game Console Industry' (2011) 75(6) *Journal of Marketing* 1024.

(in respect of Steam) take the position that any terms imposed by a third-party game company apply in *addition* to the terms of their own platform:

> 'If another company is the publisher of the Software, they license you to use it on terms which include, but may not be limited to, these Terms. That company may tell you about other terms it imposes on your use of its Software, in which case those terms apply in addition to these Terms, not instead of them. In the case of any conflict between the additional terms and these Terms, these Terms apply.[41]
>
> Some Subscriptions may impose additional terms specific to that Subscription ("Subscription Terms") (for example, an end user license agreement specific to a particular game, or terms of use specific to a particular product or feature of Steam).'[42]

The Sony example makes for a particularly interesting reading, because in the event of any conflict between its own terms and the terms of a third-party game company, Sony's will prevail. If, for example, Sony prohibited an act of sharing, but the third-party game company permits this, then Sony's rule would prevail. As such, the construction of the player is ultimately the ambit of the platform, rather than the game company itself. By contrast, Microsoft and Apple hold that third-party contracts, where provided, shall take precedence over any platform terms:

> 'Your use of the Software is governed by the terms of the end user licence agreement, if any, which accompanies or is included with the Software ("Licence Agreement").[43]
>
> Any App that you acquire is governed by the Licensed Application End User Licence Agreement ("Standard EULA") set forth below, unless Apple or the App Provider provides an overriding custom licence agreement ("Custom EULA").'[44]

These groupings and differences in approach are difficult to explain with reference to any industry-specific factor. If Sony and Microsoft had similar terms, it may be explained by their positioning together in the console market as necessitating a particular approach; instead, the two companies have different approaches. Similarly, Valve and Apple operate more accessible digital marketplaces where third-party publishers can more easily and accessibly make games available, yet again their approaches are different.

While this curious differentiation and 'layering' effect of contracts is worthy of further study, it is ultimately outwith the ambit of this research to conduct a full assessment of each contract's compatibility with the relevant terms of the platforms that facilitate

[41] Sony, 'Software Usage Terms' (*Sony*, October 2020) https://www.playstation.com/en-gb/legal/software-usage-terms/.

[42] Valve, 'Steam Subscriber Agreement' (*Steam*, date unknown) https://store.steampowered.com/subscriber_agreement/.

[43] Microsoft, 'Microsoft Services Agreement' (*Microsoft*, 1 April 2021) https://www.xbox.com/en-GB/legal/XboxComTOU.

[44] Apple, 'Apple Media Services Terms and Conditions' (*Apple*, 16 September 2020) https://www.apple.com/uk/legal/internet-services/itunes/uk/terms.html.

them. Instead, the contracts examined here offer a window into the vision of an *idealised* player from the perspective of a *game company* and how that player is conceptualised by this particular actor, rather than the platform itself. It measures intention and idealisation rather than legal effect, as the reality of what is technically or contractually permitted to the player may be very different depending on the medium through which a player accesses a game.

D. Dataset Characteristics

Some initial, brief observations are worth measuring to give an appreciation of the sociocultural context for this research. In CDA, an awareness of the characteristics of game companies can help us understand the context in which the contract is being written, and where the player is being constructed. In particular, competing cultural specific considerations, both from the company's country and date of origin, and its corporate structure, are noted in this section.

At the outset, there are indications of a potential US hegemony in both the video game and eSports industries. Of the 30 game titles examined, over half were published in the US (16), followed by Japan (five), as illustrated in Figure 3. Predominantly then, this dataset offers a construction of the player from a US perspective, with its associated legal, cultural, and social assumptions.

Figure 3 Pie chart showing country of origin of game rightsholder across all titles

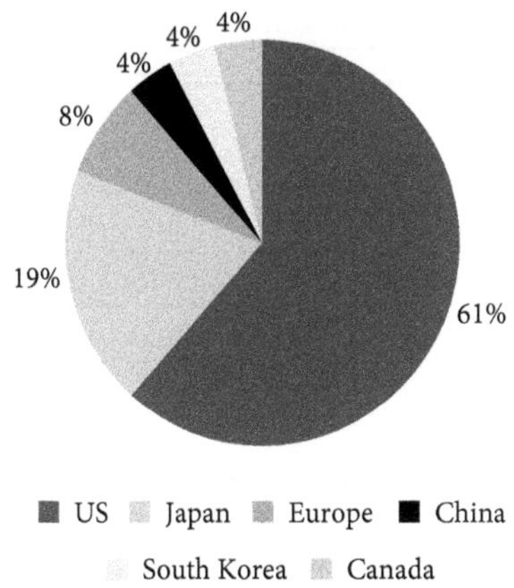

As illustrated in Table 3, most game companies in the dataset were established between 1990 and 2006, meaning that most companies have been operational for around 20 years at the time of this research. Nonetheless there is a sizeable difference in the earliest date of establishment – 1889 (Nintendo) – and the most recent observation – 2018 (PUBG) – where we may anticipate differences in constructions of the player and their embeddedness or 'stickiness' within that company.

Table 3 Game companies by date of establishment

Date of establishment[45]	Game company
1889	Nintendo
1955	Namco (part of Bandai Namco)
1960	Bandai (part of Bandai Namco)
1969	Konami
1979	Activision, Capcom
1982	EA Games
1986	Ubisoft, Bethesda
1990	Wizards of the Coast
1991	Epic Games, Blizzard
1993	Sony Interactive Entertainment, Take-Two Interactive
1994	CD Projekt Red
1996	Valve
1998	Wargaming, Rockstar Games
2000	Psyonix, Microsoft Game Studios
2003	Proxima Beta (Tencent)
2004	Warner Bros. Interactive Entertainment
2005	Hi-Rez Studios
2006	Riot Games, Bandai Namco (merger of Bandai & Namco)
2009	Mojang
2011	Cygames, Red Barrels
2018	PUBG Corporation

It is also worth noting differences in corporate structures of games companies represented in this dataset. For the purposes of this research, I delineate between triple A (or AAA) titles and 'indie' titles, a common dichotomy in game-related research and reporting. The former (triple A) is analogous to the Hollywood blockbuster, and is characterised by large budgets and development teams. Such games tend to be the sole remit of major developers and publishers. The latter (indie) refers to the 'independence' of a game company from larger financial structures and major publication houses, ranging from a single person to a small or

[45] Note that for three companies there is no given 'establishment' date, but rather 'active from'. They are: Toby Fox, Superhot Team, and Studio MDHR.

mid-sized team. In this dataset, there are only seven indie titles.[46] The relatively small number of indie titles is in line with expectations, given the more limited reach of titles with less financial backing (limiting advertisement and promotion, for example). Indeed, this would seem to be supported by the fact that only one title (*Rocket League*) falls within the eSports sample, as larger, multiplayer titles tend to be the remit of those with the substantial financial backing to support it.

While these company characteristics are illustrated here as standalone categories, there is the capacity for interplay between them. For example, many of the oldest game companies originated in Japan, due to the development of arcade and early home console gaming in this market pre-1980. For the purposes of CDA, this may be indicative of more established economic, cultural or social power given the longevity and importance of these companies in influencing the industry. We might also observe that indie game development heightens around 2009, and is the purview of relatively newly established 'all digital' companies. This may be useful for the purposes of CDA, because different ideologies may have developed in game companies that work outwith established, traditional publishing models. In a dataset that is mainly composed of established (older), US-based, triple A game companies, we can therefore make some preliminary assumptions about the level of power held by the companies under scrutiny, and the particular ideologies they may be interested in perpetuating.

E. Research Design Challenges

While efforts have been made to optimise the selection of video game and eSports titles, there are challenges in constructing a dataset worth noting.

First, titles were excluded from consideration where contracts were not available via the company's website. However, there is a lack of transparency as to which contract is actually presented to, and agreed by, the player upon installation of the game itself. It is entirely possible that this is different (and in the case of one game in this dataset – *Superhot* – entirely purposeful). The contracts in this dataset are static versions captured from the institutional webpage of the relevant game company. While there is a strong presumption that this is the same document, which can be accessed by the player any time post-installation via a hyperlink in a game, this version may nonetheless not correspond to the version the player accepts upon installation of a game. It is impossible to verify this without technical access to each title and each corresponding game platform in the dataset. Where possible, the version presented to the player upon installation was verified using keyword searches on search engines (including image searches) and with reference

[46] Being *Rocket League* (Psyonix), *Smite* (Hi-Rez), *Minecraft* (Mojang: note that this may be understood as 'indie originating' following a subsequent acquisition by Microsoft), *Superhot* (Superhot Team), *Undertale* (Toby Fox), *Cuphead* (Studio MDHR) and *Outlast* (Red Barrels).

to private collections of games.[47] However, and in any case, I cannot claim to have conducted an exhaustive verification of the contracts actually presented to the player during installation of a game, due to lack of full technical access to all titles across the dataset.

Second, the dataset is limited in that it does not attempt to differentiate between titles available on particular platforms, and the hierarchy between the platform's contract and the game company's. As noted in the side quest 'the platform effect', above, the layered aspect of the hardware-software market leads to a huge amount of variety in terms of which contract will legally and *technically* prevail in the event of a conflict between a publisher and a platform. And indeed, depending on which contract prevails may influence what we view as the 'dominant' vision of a player (in a 'top trumps' sense), if not the most prevalent view of them. However, given that this research focuses more narrowly on the construction of the *idealised* player by a game company – the contract as a statement of what they wish the player to be, regardless of its technical effect – the exclusion of the platform intermediary is perhaps a reasonable limitation of the research design.

Third, treating crowdsourced websites, including Ranker.com and eSports Earnings, as a proxy for popularity is not without problems. While I explicitly outline the problem of meaningfully understanding popularity in video games and eSports, there nonetheless remains no way of testing the veracity of the voting system or crowdsourced information for either website. This lack of transparency presented a bias problem for the initial design to use Metacritic, justifying its exclusion. To account for any such bias, where possible, other sources (a sort of triangulation, including other ranking websites[48] and best-selling/highest-grossing[49] lists) were used to verify that the selection was representative of genuine popularity, and not a result of trolling.

And indeed, relying on crowdsourced sites has potentially led to certain skews in the dataset. Despite no deliberate attempt to exclude mobile games from the ambit of the sample, none appeared in either of the samples presented. In respect of the eSports sample, this exclusion is perhaps understandable, given that the market tends to be the exclusive remit of PC and console-based games. However, the exclusion from the video games sample is a notable omission, as mobile gaming is undeniably an important market in itself. Nonetheless, it is the result of the 'crowd-wisdom'

[47] Where possible, I confirmed which contract was presented upon installation through my own game collection, which only has limited cross-referencing with the research dataset (being *The Witcher 3: Wild Hunt*, *The Elder Scrolls V: Skyrim*, *Red Dead Redemption II*, *The Last of Us*, *Batman: Arkham City*, *The Legend of Zelda: Breath of the Wild*, *Minecraft*, *Dark Souls III*, *Resident Evil 2* and *Metal Gear Solid V: The Phantom Pain*). Screenshots of in-game contracts were checked via keyword searches on Google Images for those titles which could not be technically accessed in-person.

[48] Bearing in mind the caution to using Metacritic noted above, see J Dietz, 'Highest-Scoring Games of the 2010s' (*Metacritic*, 4 January 2020) [*archived*] https://web.archive.org/web/20191211033941/https://www.metacritic.com/feature/best-videogames-of-the-decade-2010s.

[49] See eg A Willings, 'Best Selling Games List of 2010s is Surprising for its Lack of Surprises' (*Pocket Lint*, 20 January 2020) https://www.pocket-lint.com/games/news/150785-best-selling-games-of-the-last-decade, which includes five cross-over titles.

of Ranker.com. In this case, the omission of mobile games may in fact give parity between the eSports and video games samples, by removing this capacity for variance between different gaming platforms.

Finally, the contracts were gathered only in the English language, and accessed using a UK network. As a result, there is a risk that the contracts examined here are specific to players in the UK and may not be reflective, for example, of what a player in Japan would receive. To confirm whether this was the case, each institutional webpage per title was checked to confirm if the game company offered alternative versions of contracts which were tailored for other countries that could be verified against the UK versions retained on file. Checks were conducted for Japanese and US versions of the contracts as the two most common jurisdictions from the dataset. Only one publisher's webpage offers such a service that is not simply a translation of the English contract, but is in fact customised per country: Bethesda.[50] However, when comparing the UK, US and Japanese versions against each other, they are almost verbatim copies with no substantive differences between them (even when accounting for slight differences in translation of the Japanese version). The UK version has slightly more content in terms of refunds, returns, unfair terms and privacy than the US or Japanese versions (possibly to account for the influence of EU privacy legislation),[51] but otherwise the language itself is highly homogenous.

After this initial assessment, a VPN was used to check a selection of titles[52] using both US and Japanese IP addresses to access the game company's institutional webpages and reroute to the appropriate country-specific contract. However, again it seems that the contract is a verbatim copy (or close, accounting for post-translation differences for the Japanese version) of the UK version in both countries, with the exception of the same provisions on eg privacy, refunds, and returns. As such, there is relative universal stability in terms of the contracts across different countries. And while it is outwith the scope of this research to investigate this further, one possibility for this highly homogeneous language is due to the inclusion of clauses on choice of law or jurisdiction,[53] which would seemingly usurp the need for a tailormade version particular to different countries.

[50] Bethesda, 'Fallout 76 EULA' (*Bethesda*, date unknown) https://bethesda.net/en/eulas/fallout-76. This contract includes versions for: US/Latin America, UK, Germany, France, Spain, Italy, Australia/New Zealand, Japan, Poland, Russia, and Brazil.

[51] eg Regulation 2016/679 of 27 April 2016 on the protection of natural persons with regard to the processing of personal data and on the free movement of such data [2016] OJ L 119/1 (the General Data Processing Regulation or GDPR).

[52] Being the first three titles listed in each dataset. From eSports: *Dota 2* (Valve), *Fortnite* (Epic Games), *League of Legends* (Riot Games). From video games: *The Witcher 3: Wild Hunt* (CD Projekt Red), *Red Dead Redemption II* (Rockstar Games), *The Last of Us* (Sony).

[53] Note that in each case the choice of law is US-based, with the exception of CD Projekt Red, which designates Polish law as the choice of jurisdiction for European users (see Appendix 2).

F. Coding and Analysis

No text analysis software was used when coding the contracts, and instead a plain reading of the text was conducted in order to capture the types of granular nuance required at multiple levels of the CDA analysis. Working 'bottom-up', the coding process began at the micro dimension of the text, identifying particular linguistic patterns (eg grammar and vocabulary that implies a degree of formality or informality). Whilst a holistic approach was applied to evaluating the entirety of the contract, given the research focus on the *copyright* player, concern was focused more specifically on clauses that regulate the *creative content* of the game. To this end, clauses concerning eg indemnification, warranties and privacy, are largely excluded from the ambit of analysis as being more specifically orientated around consumer protection, litigation and data protection, rather than copyright.[54] Thereafter, the meso discursive dimension was analysed to understand how the text was distributed to the player, eg physically or digitally, in-game or outwith. Finally, in the sociocultural dimension of analysis, the prevalent themes of the text and discursive levels were tied together, seeking an explanation as to why these particular features were present, with reference to the theoretical concepts identified above. At this final level, the textual and discursive features are demystified to uncover the concept of player constructed within the contract, and the strategic significance behind this designation with reference to sociocultural practices in the games industry. Table 4 illustrates the types of questions considered at each level of analysis.

Table 4 Example questions across CDA dimensions of analysis

Textual	Discursive	Sociocultural
How does the contract describe the characteristics of the player? (eg as consumer, customer) How do vocabulary, grammar and structure of the text create the impression of a particular concept? (eg if formal, a distanced relationship – if informal, a more proximate one) Does the contract use specific terminology that is indicative of a particular underlying or hidden opinion (eg 'user-generated content' or 'fan-made content')?	How is the contract distributed? (eg physically or digitally, in-game or outwith the game) Are there any alternative means of communicating to the player outwith the set space of the contract? (eg in a contact form or on social media) How is the contract presented to the player? (eg in a check box, or within an in-game menu)	Does the contract construct, maintain or challenge existing power relations? (eg between the game company and player) Is the construct of the player reflective of a particular ideology? (eg a strong, proprietary vision of software) Does the contract contribute to normalising a particular view of the player? (eg as a consumer, or non-owner of a game)

[54] Note that, as established in Chapter 2, there is good reason to believe that the modern day player contract/copyright licence developed from initial warranties and indemnification notices.

Following the coding process, three themes were iteratively derived given their salience and delineation in the dataset: *Authority*; *Access*, and; *Artifice* (literally, 'triple A', the salience of which will become evident in the following chapters). These themes were derived from the textual dimension of analysis, where clusters of keywords indicated the forming of a broader concept. For example, the *Authority* theme was inferred by clusters of keywords including: copyright, intellectual property, property, ownership, title, (exclusive) rights, law, legal or the reference to a specific legislative act. The prevalence of entire clauses could also be captured within this keyword coding approach. 'Ownership' and 'intellectual property' clauses, for example, appear early, prominently, and repeatedly in the text of the contract, stressing their importance in constructing the player. The use of these terms in combination suggested that the concept of player was tied to law, and the power claimed through the invocation of law, hence the designation of the *Authority* theme.

III. Save Point: Chapter Summary

This chapter outlines the 'how' of this research, offering a methodological approach for constructing the player via a discourse analysis of contracts. The chapter presented an overview of CDA, a qualitative, constructivist methodology which can be used to uncover naturalised identities and concepts that have been artificially constructed by powerful 'others'. CDA is well-suited to the aims of the research, which necessarily must take an interpretative approach to uncovering the identity of the player, who is obscured in both legal discourse and the discourse of the contract. And further, the critical component of CDA not only obliges us to *expose* the player's artificial construct, but also to *challenge* its presentation and suggest how this can be changed or improved (eg in copyright policy).

In illustrating the merits of CDA, the chapter engages with three key, interrelated concepts which are omnipresent throughout the analysis in the following chapters: power, ideology, and common sense. To systematise the measurement of these concepts more pragmatically, Fairclough's three-dimensional CDA model offers a method that interlinks the micro-linguistic textual details of the contract with the broader sociocultural context in which it takes place. In short, the method adopted allows us to see how the way the contract is written is a reflection of the needs of the industry in which it was made, and how these needs can be realised via the player.

In respect of data collection, this research builds upon a primary dataset of 30 individual game titles, equally split between video games and eSports titles (15/15), with a total of 70 individual documents. These titles were selected based on their popularity, measured with reference to secondary datasets curated on crowd-sourced, ranking websites, Ranker and eSports Earnings. Popularity is treated in this research as a proxy for prevalence of discourse, and hence the dominant construction of the player in these industries. Importantly, that construction is in itself not neutral – it is, more specifically – a construction mainly from US-based, well-established, triple A game companies.

In respect of data analysis, the research was conducted in line with Fairclough's approach to CDA, with coding across three dimensions of discourse: textual, discursive, and sociocultural practice. Working from the micro (text) to the macro (sociocultural practice), the data analysis derives three themes iteratively from the coding process, given their delineation and importance to the construction of the player: *Authority*; *Access*; and *Artifice*. The following chapters outline the findings across each of these themes in turn.

Level 3

4

Authority

Every player contract is a claim to authority. Through copyright, games companies are enabled to speak as lawmakers, presenting their rules as natural and unavoidable. However, not every company uses its (copyright) authority to the same ends. This chapter shows how different material relations of game companies influence the extent to which they engage with copyright law, and the authority it conveys, in their contracts. To the triple A company – the equivalent of the Hollywood blockbuster game – the player is a legal object, bound and commanded. However, to the indie company, the player is recognised somewhat closer to a playful subject – a kind of countercultural signifier to the mainstream. These differences in engagement with legal authority reveal wider ideological tensions between profit-driven creativity and artistic freedom in the games industry.

I. Textual Dimension

Triple A discourse frames the player as the recipient of a copyrighted *work*, in a close relationship with copyright law. Engagement with the law, and particularly the formality and authority conveyed by the law, manifests prominently within the text in two interrelated ways: first, through the adoption of the legal genre in language, terminology, and format (Section A); and second, through direct, intertextual references to copyright law (Sections B and C). Collectively, these give the impression that the player is a weak party to the contract, and also perhaps one whose intentions are slightly suspect.

A. Legal Genre

Triple A discourse presents the contract as a distinctly *legal* agreement. The seriousness of its legal character is often emphasised explicitly at the outset of the text by reminding the player that '[this] is a legal document …'[1] or 'this Agreement is enforceable like any written contract signed by you':[2] it is emphatically an

[1] Epic Games, 'Fortnite End User License Agreement' (Appendix 2).
[2] Riot Games, 'League of Legends Terms of Use' (Appendix 2).

'IMPORTANT LEGAL NOTICE'.[3] The intention to engage in a *legal* relationship with the player is also mirrored in the contract throughout the text by the adoption of particular styles, characteristics and formatting that are typical of the legal genre.[4] The most common manifestation of this is the tendency towards a high-degree of formality, complexity, and lexical denseness. The following example from Activision is emblematic of many of these characteristics:

> To the fullest extent permitted by applicable law, by submitting any UGC (including without limitation, images, videos, customer service submissions, idea submissions, suggestions and message postings) you automatically grant (or represent and warrant that the owner of such rights has expressly granted) Activision a perpetual, worldwide, royalty-free, irrevocable, non-exclusive right and license to use, reproduce, modify, adapt, publish, translate, sub-license, create derivative works from and distribute such UGC or incorporate such UGC content into any form, medium, or technology now known or later developed throughout the universe, and agree that Activision shall be entitled to unrestricted use of the UGC for any purpose whatsoever, commercial or otherwise, without compensation, notice or attribution.[5]

The complexity and length of this *single sentence* is not typical of oral-conversational discourse – it is not how anyone 'speaks'. As a result, it is difficult for the reader to engage with. The sentence contains 112 words – which should be compared against the average of 20 in non-legal genres of discourse.[6] The language is dense and technical ('irrevocable', 'sub-licensable'),[7] favouring the legalese version of a term rather than more colloquial appropriations (eg 'attribution' rather than 'credit' or 'acknowledgement').[8] The text also borrows specific legal tropes, such as the use of binomials ('represent and warrant'),[9] passive referral in the third person ('you automatically grant … Activision')[10] and catch-all conditions to anticipate all potential scenarios ('technology now known or later developed throughout the universe').[11] Much like the law, the contract also mimics the infringement-consequence ('if-then') process.[12] The contract emphasises the seriousness of its terms by detailing consequences for non-conformity, ensuring obedience is enforced (or rather, has the impression that it *could* be enforced). Penalties for non-conformance include termination of the agreement and temporary or

[3] Hi-Rez, 'End User License Agreement' (Appendix 2). Note that the use of all caps to denote emphasis is often utilised in contract writing to draw attention to a particular clause, or the use of defined terms to refer to contract subjects.

[4] JP Kaplan, *Linguistics and Law* (Routledge, 2019).

[5] Activision, 'Terms of Use' (Appendix 2).

[6] The Acropolitan, 'Sentence Length Has Declined 75% in the Past 500 Years' (*Medium*, 29 August 2017) https://medium.com/@theacropolitan/sentence-length-has-declined-75-in-the-past-500-years-2e40f80f589f.

[7] Rockstar Games, 'Limited Software Warranty and License Agreement' (Appendix 2).

[8] ibid.

[9] Bandai Namco, 'Terms of Use' (Appendix 2).

[10] Activision, 'Terms of use' (Appendix 2).

[11] ibid.

[12] Kaplan (n 4).

permanent bans from online servers (though more often this is in relation to breaches of codes of conduct/player behaviours).[13]

By utilising characteristics of the legal genre, the cumulative impression is that of a formal legal text written by a powerful legal actor – they know the special, magic words, and we do not. They know the pre-set rules, and how to ensure conservatism through precedent and technical specificity. As a result, the (non-lawyer) player is excluded both from participating and comprehending the contract.[14] This textual construction significantly weakens the position of the player in the face of the more powerful, legal character of the game company.

Here, the player is clearly constructed as a *recipient* of a one-way discourse. They are unilaterally obliged and commanded to act by the authority of the text ('you automatically grant').[15] Indeed, the objectification of the player continues throughout the contract, where they are obliged through the prevalence of modal verbs, such as 'shall'[16] and 'must,'[17] denoting necessity, obligation, and a particular force behind the text, which contribute to its perceived power. By comparison, the company behind the contract is framed by conditionals and hypotheticals – it 'may'[18] act, 'if'[19] something happens, unless in its 'sole discretion'[20] it decides otherwise (and in the example above, 'for any purpose whatsoever').[21] These are examples of a linguistic technique known as 'hedging'[22] which, by avoiding precision, also avoids commitment, and tends to be indicative of a more powerful speaker – a speaker who will not be obliged. The contrast in this language (modality vs hedging) suggests that the game company's position is *optional*, whereas the player's position is *mandatory*; the player is a passive object, rather than an active subject, within the discourse. The result is a distanced relationship between the game company, which presents itself as a powerful legal actor, and the player who, if not equipped with the appropriate resources, is excluded from even comprehending the conversation.

The legal genre of discourse is dominant across the majority of triple A contracts surveyed – however, it is not the *exclusive* discourse. Instead, the dominant 'triple A' discourse is subverted, if not outright rejected, by the smaller, indie companies

[13] e.g. Riot Games, 'League of Legends Terms of Use' (Appendix 2) permits termination or suspension of an account for the breach of any terms or if 'doing so would be in the best interests of our community or the Riot Services'.

[14] J Niemi-Kiesilainen et al, 'Legal Texts as Discourses' in A Gunnarsson et al (eds), *Exploiting the Limits of Law* (Ashgate, 2007).

[15] Activision, 'Terms of Use' (Appendix 2). Note that the use of 'you' to address the player, as opposed to formalistic passive third person, is a departure from the legal style. Only on two occasions is the player addressed as 'user' (interchangeable with 'you') (Capcom and Ubisoft) and once as 'customer' (Cygames).

[16] Konami, 'Terms of Use: Metal Gear Solid V: The Phantom Pain' (Appendix 2).

[17] ibid.

[18] ibid.

[19] ibid.

[20] ibid.

[21] Activision, 'Terms of Use' (Appendix 2).

[22] P Baker and S Ellege, *Key Terms in Discourse Analysis* (Continuum, 2011).

in the dataset – those without any affiliation within a larger corporate entity. In contrast to the highly formal, legal relationship implied by the triple A discourse, indies adopt an informal and friendlier approach to the contract text by altering their register and style, 'inviting' the player to converse and understand. As a side-by-side comparison, Table 5 illustrates differences in the textual approaches between Capcom (triple A) and the Superhot Team (indie).

Table 5 Comparison of triple A and indie discourse styles: Capcom and Superhot

Capcom	Superhot Team
Capcom shall grant a non-exclusive license to users who install the Program to their own personal computer only for the purpose of playing the game for its personal use under the condition that the users shall abide by and comply with the provisions hereunder.[23]	This Agreement entitles you to install and personally use as many copies of the Software Product as you in your heart of hearts desire.[24]

This essential clause – the most necessary part of the 'copyright' contract, forming the licence – permits the use of a game through an express grant. The legal effects of the two clauses are the same. But in these examples, the indie expression is couched in a more friendly, playful way than the more traditional, formal approach of the triple A company. While some legal tropes are still apparent for the indie title, such as the capitalisation of defined terms ('Software Product'), many of the more formalistic and technical terms typical of the genre are not present ('non-exclusive' or 'hereunder' as in the Capcom example). Instead, there is permission to use 'as many copies' as 'you in your heart of hearts desire'. The use of this idiom and informal expression is evident of a less *serious* stance by the indie company. As a natural extension of the adoption of this oral-conversational discourse, the relationship between the player and game company is more proximate than the formal legal relationship in the triple A discourse: the player is instead being 'spoken' to in a language like their own. Even if the player ultimately still cannot change the discourse in the indie contract, they are not automatically excluded from a conversation through the technical invocation of the (powerful) legal genre.

Mojang, creator of *Minecraft*, makes for an interesting case study of this 'indie effect' and subversion of the legalistic triple A discourse.[25] While Mojang was subsequently acquired by Microsoft (a triple A company), its indie roots or 'spirit' are still preserved in its contract.[26] We might contrast the way in which the triple A company usually makes clear at the outset its intention to form a formal, legal

[23] Capcom, 'End User License Agreement' (Appendix 2).

[24] Superhot Team, 'End User License Agreement' (Appendix 2).

[25] More extensively discussed in MA Campos-Pardillos, 'End-User Agreements in Videogames: Plain English at Work in an Ideal Setting' in A Ensslin and I Balteiro (eds), *Approaches to Videogame Discourse: Lexis, Interaction, Textuality* (Bloomsbury, 2019).

[26] Note that the Microsoft, 'Game Usage Rules' (Appendix 2) specifically exclude *Minecraft* from their ambit of regulation.

relationship with the player, where Mojang instead express an explicit hesitancy to engage with the contract itself:

> In order to protect Minecraft (our 'Game') and the members of our community, we need these end user license terms to set out some rules for downloading and using our Game … We don't like reading license documents any more than you do, so we have tried to keep this as short as possible.[27]

While Mojang acknowledges that the contract is necessary ('we need these …'), it also actively describes itself as an unpleasant reading experience ('[w]e don't like reading license documents any more than you do'). Immediately, this expression of solidarity and complicity lessens the social distance between the player and game company, creating a shared commonality between them – it is suggested here that they play the same games, accessing them in the same way – rather than opposition. Even if Mojang is participating in the format of the dominant, triple A discourse (in the sense that it is indeed nonetheless using a contract), it does not necessarily agree with the formalistic, legal relationship it typically implies.

The creation of a common space by the indie company also manifests in other textual elements of the Mojang contract which mimics the language of the player. Mojang differentiates itself from the dominant discourse by avoiding technical, legalese terms, instead substituting them for specific colloquialisms, for example 'griefing' and 'trolling' (respectively meaning 'annoy/frustrate' and 'insult/provoke', rather than 'offensive or harmful behaviour'),[28] 'general stuff' (rather than miscellaneous),[29] or describing something as 'no fun' (rather than 'prohibited')[30] or 'okay' (rather than 'permitted').[31] Where the use of a technical term is unavoidable, its meaning is explained ('… unless done so in good faith (eg to develop mods').[32] Many other legal tropes are subverted in the Mojang contract, with the use of oral-conversational discourse (such as 'Oh'),[33] metaphor ('put a lid on it' rather than 'enforce'),[34] and idioms. Legal threat, while present, is toned down where, if necessary, the company '… might even have to ask our lawyers to help out'.[35] The hesitancy expressed in this condition suggests an unwillingness to engage in the same enforcement procedures ('if-then') endorsed in the dominant, triple A discourse. This friendlier and conversational approach, being much more personable, was noted even in early versions of the Mojang contract, which were signed by 'Marcus Persson and friends'.[36]

[27] Mojang, 'Minecraft End User License Agreement' (Appendix 2).
[28] ibid.
[29] ibid.
[30] ibid.
[31] ibid.
[32] ibid.
[33] ibid.
[34] ibid.
[35] ibid.
[36] Noted by Campos-Pardillos (n 23) 120. Including this signature resembles the *politique des auteurs*, whereby the hallmark of an independent production is to recognise the author's name in paratexts around indie games (a personal stamp of the auteur).

In sum, in the textual dimension, we see that indie companies differentiate themselves from the 'mainstream' dominant discourse of triple A by lightening their engagement with the legal genre of writing: it sounds less like a magical, legal spell, and more like a conversation with the player. In doing so, they present the player – and indeed, themselves – as more of a countercultural signifier to the dominant, triple A discourse, which instead situates the player as a conceptually weak – and distinctly serious – legal object. Importantly, authority is still present in both types of contract; they are indeed, both ultimately an exercise of a legal right and permissions granted. But the way in which the specific authority of law is presented to the player *in* the text suggests a different ideological stance as to what the player should be: a legal object to be constrained, or a fellow gaming compatriot.

B. Intertextuality: Copyright Ownership

In the triple A discourse, the contract's perceived power is bolstered by its repeated, intertextual claims to *ownership* of the underlying (intellectual) property rights comprising the game. Much emphasis is put on the power of ownership to legitimise the company's entitlement to construct the player (note that in Section C, we will see that this is nonetheless a *selective* engagement with ownership where copyright exceptions and limitations are concerned). References to rights ownership appear early and prominently in the text, usually within the introductory or first clause of the contract:

> All title, ownership rights and intellectual property rights in and to the Content and Services and any and all copies thereof, are owned by Valve and/or its or its affiliates' licensors. All rights are reserved, except as expressly stated herein. The Content and Services are protected by copyright laws, international copyright treaties and conventions and other laws. The Content and Services contain certain licensed materials and Valve's and its affiliates' licensors may protect their rights in the event of any violation of this Agreement.[37]

In the above example, there are multiple repetitions and variants of claims to ownership ('title', 'ownership rights', 'intellectual property rights', 'owned by Valve', 'all rights reserved') which are substantiated with a more vague and general reference to protection by 'copyright laws, international copyright treaties and conventions and other laws'. Other contracts make more specific reference to named legal acts, such as the Japanese Copyright Act[38] or the 'copyright laws of New Zealand, the United States …',[39] which, while perhaps having a more limiting legal effect, more specifically frame the discourse around the issue of *copyright* within a named jurisdiction. By stating this ownership as factual, the introductory clause claims,

[37] Valve, 'Steam Subscriber Agreement' (Appendix 2).
[38] Capcom, 'End User License Agreement' (Appendix 2).
[39] WB Games Inc, 'End User License Agreement' (Appendix 2).

without dispute, the authority to mandate the rest of the agreement through an intertextual reference to the law – an entity that at least implies something close to state-sanctioned truth. The contract may also employ a complementary reversal of this mechanic, and oblige the player to recognise this authority, rather than claiming it per se:

> As between you and Hi-Rez, you acknowledge Hi-Rez's exclusive rights in and to the Software Product and that the Software Product is unique and original to Hi-Rez and that Hi-Rez is the exclusive owner thereof.[40]

In this example, the obligation of the player to recognise the company's authority is stated in the active voice ('you acknowledge' that the game is 'unique and original'): it is a direct command to the player. Whether claiming ownership or obliging it, these are manifestations of power *behind* discourse, as the contract is making an intertextual reference to an authoritative text through which its power has been derived: the law. In this respect, the contract is more specifically constructing the player as a *user of proprietary software* – an entity subject to copyright regulation – rather than a player of a game, who lives outwith this space. The significance of this framing resonates with many of the delineations explored in doctrinal analyses in Chapter 1.

Similar intellectual property clauses which appear later in the text reiterate and repackage this initial claim through repetition. CD Projekt Red offers a particularly interesting example of this repetition. CD Projekt Red's contract is split into two columns: the 'Full Text' and the 'Quick Summary', accompanied with a cautionary note that only the Full Text is legally binding, whereas the summary is only intended to 'help you understand what it means'.[41] Differences in textual approaches between the Full Text and Quick Summary at clause 7 ('Ownership and Intellectual Property Rights') are included for illustration in Table 6.

Table 6 Comparison of intellectual property clauses: CD Projekt Red 'Full Text' vs 'Quick Summary'

Full Text	**Quick Summary**
CD PROJEKT RED games and services, including (but not limited to) their graphics, computer code, user interface, look and feel, audio, video, text, layout, databases, data and all other content and all legal and exploitation rights regarding them, are either owned by us or we license them from third parties. All rights are reserved except as we have explained in this Agreement. You may not use or exploit any part of CD PROJEKT RED games or services except as explained in this Agreement.	We spent years building CD PROJEKT RED and our games/services. Enjoy it all, but please behave and do not cause trouble.

[40] Hi-Rez, 'End User License Agreement' (Appendix 2).
[41] CD Projekt Red, 'User Agreement' (Appendix 2).

The Full Text version of this clause is typical of many other contracts which intertextually claim similarly 'all legal and exploitation rights'[42] to a lengthy list of game components, some or most of which are copyrightable (eg graphics, computer code, audio etc). By contrast, CD Projekt Red's Quick Summary column reveals that this clause is also intended to have a *deterrent* effect ('please behave and do not cause trouble'). This is a hidden value that is not otherwise expressed, except implicitly, in the Full Text.[43] The Quick Summary reveals a more explicit view that claims to ownership through the invocation of law are not just factual statements, but *warnings* to the player.

These repeated claims, obligations to recognise, and warnings concerning legally sanctioned ownership are all examples of textual claims to power. Consequently, and despite most often classifying itself as an 'agreement' *between* the player and game company (suggesting reciprocity), most of the contract is dedicated to listing the responsibilities, rules and conditions placed solely upon the player. So, while the player is omnipresent throughout the contract and constantly foregrounded as the subject through an active voice, this is always conditioned by the authority of the game company (see eg 'You agree to only use the Software, or any part of it, in a manner that is consistent with this Agreement …').[44] The player is again an object of construction, and the power to do that construction is justified through the invocation of legal ownership.

However, while the law is treated with great importance in establishing this initial ownership, contracts do not treat copyright, or indeed any other law, as a *superior* or conflicting legal regime external to the contract (ie important ≠ superior). Instead, the game company frames the law as a conditional application that is paralleled with the authority of the contract itself:

> Except as otherwise permitted under this Agreement (including any Subscription Terms or Rules of Use), or under applicable law[45]

While each contract in this dataset caveats itself as only applying to the fullest extent of applicable law (or variants thereof), in this example the key use of 'or' suggests that the law is not the dominant text to which the contract defers to, but rather a parallel regime which is complementary to the agreement. In doing so, the contract situates itself as not only having power *behind* discourse (the intertextual reference to the law) but also claims power *through* discourse, by framing itself as being paralleled with an authoritative institution. It deflects responsibility for determining compliance with the law by omission and imprecision: exactly what

[42] ibid.

[43] Of interest, the Steam version of *The Witcher 3: Wild Hunt* contract is even more informal than the version accompanying console and PC games (CD Projekt Red, 'The Witcher 3: Wild Hunt' (*Steam*, 18 May 2015) https://store.steampowered.com/app/292030/The_Witcher_3_Wild_Hunt/).

[44] Psyonix, 'End User License Agreement' (Appendix 2).

[45] Valve, 'Steam Subscriber Agreement' (Appendix 2).

is the relevant 'applicable law' is never defined in the contract; instead, it is often the responsibility of the player to seek out this understanding:

> Any other use of Nintendo's intellectual property and creation of content outside of this scope is subject to the relevant laws of the applicable jurisdiction. Nintendo cannot provide legal advice to you, so we encourage you to seek your own legal counsel if you have any questions about whether your particular proposed use is permitted.[46]

This imprecision is a linguistic technique known as 'obscurification'[47] for which two potential explanations may apply: first, it may be that the information is omitted because it is too obvious to include. This would suggest that the reader's knowledge of applicable law, and the extent to which the contract is compliant with this, is obvious. Given that this is unlikely, the alternative is that this information is suppressed (obscured) because it conflicts with the dominant discourse that may be idealising something that the law would not permit (such as eg the subversion of copyright exceptions discussed in Section I.C below). This suggests that if the law likely conflicts with the contract, the game company will seek to obscure this fact in order to maintain its authority.

Indeed, copyright law is more deliberately obscured throughout the contract by the *adaptation* of specific legal terminology. The contract frequently uses specialised copyright terms which, initially, demonstrate both an awareness and willingness to invoke its technical specificities in line with the legal genre of discourse. This includes claims to work being 'original',[48] and deserving of 'moral rights'[49] and 'authorship',[50] with corresponding prohibitions of 'reproduction',[51] 'modification',[52] 'distribution'[53] and the creation of 'derivative works'.[54] Each of these terms has a fixed, technical, meaning in copyright which, we would assume, is what is being invoked alongside the legal genre of discourse. However, the contract instead applies a degree of flexibility and adapts these concepts to obscure both the limits of the company's exclusive ownership, and the beginnings of player entitlements. For example, Mojang places great emphasis on prohibiting 'distribution' of its game, which the contract defines as giving copies of the game to anyone, making commercial use of the game, trying to make money from the game, or letting other people access any aspect of the game in a way that is unfair or unreasonable.[55] A

[46] Nintendo, 'Game Content Guidelines' (Appendix 2) and recalling Lessig's quip about a 'user' being someone who can afford a lawyer (L Lessig, *Remix: Making Art and Commerce Thrive in the Hybrid Economy* (Penguin Press, 2008)).

[47] Baker and Ellege (n 22).

[48] Hi-Rez, 'End User License Agreement' (Appendix 2).

[49] Nintendo, 'End User License Agreement' (Appendix 2).

[50] Blizzard, 'End User License Agreement' (Appendix 2).

[51] Wizards of the Coast, 'Magic Online End User License Agreement and Software License' (Appendix 2).

[52] ibid.

[53] ibid.

[54] EA, 'Electronic Arts User Agreement' (Appendix 2).

[55] Mojang, 'Minecraft End User License Agreement' (Appendix 2).

strict reading of 'distribution' under a pure copyright context does not ascribe the same meaning,[56] and instead this invocation of a technical copyright term is given a much broader interpretation in the text of the contract. This should be read as a cautionary note that, even where the discourse in the contract appears to be *mimicking* copyright, there is rarely a shared commonality on the interpretation of what it technically means.

In sum, we can see that the invocation of rights *ownership* holds a prominent place within the textual dimension of the contract. Through intertextual reference to the law, whether implicitly (eg 'ownership rights') or explicitly (eg 'copyright laws') the game company claims a particular type of authority derived from previous, institutionally and societally-backed power that legitimates and justifies the content of the contract. This is both a claim to power, and a warning to the player; rights are claimed, and by extension penalties for non-compliance. This extension into enforcement is presented as a natural consequence of rights ownership, rather than a deliberate choice of the game company. And while the law is relied upon to establish this power, it is not treated within the text as a superior regime that may place limitations upon the contract itself. Rather, it is a complementary system that applies in *tandem* with the contract. The co-existence between contract and copyright is not necessarily unusual but, in this instance, it is highly selective. It is clearly important for establishing the initial title awarded by copyright, but willingness to engage with its ongoing principles and limitations, are rejected. Copyright concepts are only clear in the contract when they apply in favour of the company to establish ownership of a defined *property*, but are otherwise obscured in their application to the player. This obscurification is perhaps more obvious in the interplay between the contract and copyright limitations and exceptions discussed below.

C. Intertextuality: Copyright Limitations and Exceptions

The contract parallels the (desired) structure of copyright law by claiming an exclusive right (the intertextual claims to copyright ownership discussed above) to which conditional exceptions and limitations may apply. The contract first mandates itself with an encompassing exclusivity to 'ALL RIGHTS'[57] over the game. Then, it creates a conditional that this shall be the case unless certain permissions are '… EXPRESSLY GRANTED TO YOU IN THIS AGREEMENT'.[58] Crucially, the

[56] For example, in Case C-516/13 *Dimensione Direct Sales Srl and Another v Knoll International SpA* EC:C:2014:2415, Art 4(1) of the Directive 2001/29/EC of 22 May 2001 on the harmonisation of certain aspects of copyright and related rights in the information society [2001] OJ L 167/10 was interpreted to mean 'that it allows a holder of an exclusive right to distribute a protected work to prevent an offer for sale or an advertisement of the original or a copy of that work' (para 20) but does not extend to eg access of a work by another.

[57] Psyonix, 'End User License Agreement' (Appendix 2).

[58] ibid.

contract *itself* ('*THIS* AGREEMENT') claims to determine the existence and scope of any such rights (conditional on being 'GRANTED'): anything not expressly *excused* by the contract is therefore forbidden. By contrast, in copyright law, exceptions and limitations are normally characterised by the *absence* of infringement (being 'excepted'). The contract, in arrogating itself the mandate to determine the ambit of use of the game, instead changes these exceptions into *excused* infringement. Resultingly, both infringing and non-infringing activities of the player – acts that invoke the game property and those that do not – are constructed *within* the text of the contract, not the law.

Indeed, for the most part, the bulk of the contract is not overly concerned with copyright-specific behaviour as such (eg copying aspects of the game or distributing it), but rather on player behaviour more generally (eg banning unfair play practices or offensive, harassing behaviour).[59] References to copyright exceptions, such as parody or quotation, are particularly rare, and when they do manifest this is presented as an excused activity by the game company, rather than a positive entitlement granted to the player by the law. For example, the Hi-Rez contract includes a broad restriction on general copying but includes the caveat that the player may 'make one (1) copy of the Game Software … for archival purposes': essentially a back-up copy exception.[60] No other equivalent copyright exceptions, such as using the game for the purposes of education, are included within the contract. Instead, by only including this specific, named exception explicitly within the text of the contract, all other exceptions are – by its own definition – omitted.

Only two contracts prove an exception to this general no-exceptions rule: *Minecraft* and *Outlast*, both indie titles. Mojang reminds the player (twice) in its UGC policy that they may '[d]o things that are specifically covered by "fair dealing" or "fair use" exceptions to copyright and trademark laws'[61] notwithstanding the rest of the restrictions in the agreement. Red Barrels, creator of *Outlast*, has no specific policy for making content other than video recordings and streams of gameplay, but reminds the player that in any case they have rights to make 'certain kinds of user-generated content' under Canadian copyright law.[62] Again then, this is some limited evidence of an 'indie effect' in the construction of the player; the player's entitlements are less obscured for indie companies than for triple A.

Contracts similarly obscure the limits of copyright by, for example, claiming indefinite ownership of content (copyright duration)[63] or claiming ownership of uncopyrightable content. The latter is particularly notable for its broad,

[59] See, for example, the Konami, 'Terms of Use: Metal Gear Solid V: The Phantom Pain' (Appendix 2) code of conduct, which contains 26 provisions, of which only four concern copyright-related activities.

[60] Hi-Rez, 'End User License Agreement' (Appendix 2), largely paralleling the private copying exception.

[61] Mojang, 'Minecraft End User License Agreement' (Appendix 2) and Mojang, 'Brand and Asset Usage Guidelines' (Appendix 2).

[62] Red Barrels, 'Message to YouTubers' (Appendix 2).

[63] Per the Berne Convention, Art 7, most countries will be limited to a minimum of copyright protection for the life of the author plus at least 50 years after their death.

indiscriminate, and all-encompassing claims to ownership of lengthy lists of game content which includes both protectable and unprotectable content:

> … any titles, trademarks, service marks, and trade names, computer code, themes, objects, characters, character names, stories, dialog, catch phrases, locations, concepts, artwork, animations, sounds, musical compositions, audio-visual effects, methods of operation, moral rights, and any related documentation.[64]

Other examples of the types of content the contract claims to own includes colour schemes, concepts, ideas,[65] locations, functionalities, and re-enactments,[66] and 'catch-all' claims to 'all other original works of authorship contained [herein]'.[67] This textual framing, muddying the protected with the unprotected, gives the impression that everything within the list of the contract is part and parcel of the legitimate ownership derived through copyright. As such, much as with how the contract deals with copyright exceptions, there is only willingness to engage with copyright insofar as it establishes the initial ownership claim, with the corresponding limitations of the system being disguised.

Concluding, we see that the dominant discourse of the contract cherry-picks aspects of copyright which support the power of the game company – the claim to an all-encompassing propertisation of the game – while suppressing or misrepresenting the aspects which do not support this. It disguises what is otherwise permitted by law (copyright exceptions) or unregulated by it (copyright limitations eg on non-copyright-related activities or content). The construction of the player in this respect is very strategic indeed. Lawful uses are presented as being mediated by the contract, which selects only the aspects of law that best suit the business strategy of the game company – to permit, or to constrain. Curiously, in the case of the indie company, the best business strategy appears to be, conversely, to be more transparent about the entitlements of the player in law.

II. Discursive Dimension

In the textual dimension, the contract is often presented – at least in the dominant, triple A discourse – as a formal, legal document. However, this formalistic legal tradition is less obvious in the discursive dimension when we consider *how* the contract is presented to the player. The fact that games can be distributed physically, digitally, or via account membership, does not change how the contract itself is distributed, as a static, digital document. And often, these 'serious legal

[64] Activision, 'Terms of Use' (Appendix 2).
[65] Psyonix, 'End User License Agreement' (Appendix 2).
[66] Blizzard, 'End User License Agreement' (Appendix 2).
[67] ibid.

documents' are also presented to the player within the interface of the game itself, effectively absorbing into a broader aspect of play (Section A). Some indie titles appear to take this absorption a step further, in turning the contract into a kind of performance art rather than the presentation of a formal, legal contract (Section B).

A. Integration within the Game Interface

The shifting character of the distribution of games and contracts is important in the context of this theme. Historically, contracts were included within the shrink-wrap of a game, denoting assent to its terms when the player broke a seal on the game packaging. As illustrated in Chapter 2, paper documentation has been steadily phased out of game production since 2010, with click-wrap instead becoming the favoured method of distribution.[68] This means that the contract is presented to the player post-purchase, post-installation, indicating assent by clicking a digital checkbox (or equivalent) before proceeding. While all of the games observed in this dataset have a static version of their contract available via their institutional webpage (a necessary limitation of the method for data collection detailed in Chapter 3), the contract is also now built *into* the game interface itself, accessible upon first installation of a game, and usually subsequently through an in-game menu, for example. The effect of this is that the contract becomes transformed into another tool that the player may interact with within the game space, in much a similar way as a player may access a game character's inventory. For example, in *Fortnite*, all 'Legal' information (including the contract) can be accessed in the game 'lobby' – a gathering space for players pre-match, where they can also customise their character and communicate with other players. In *Metal Gear Solid V: The Phantom Pain*, the contract can be accessed – alongside other in-game tools – against the visual backdrop of the protagonist resting in a helicopter between game missions.

Turning briefly to contrast this new transformation with the origins of the player contract, there is a notable evolution. The digital interface removes any performative, formalistic context typically associated with a legal document. The material act of breaking a seal or (in even earlier examples of user contracts) signing a document creates, I would argue, a different relationship with a work than simply clicking a button or skimming text to click 'I agree'. Particularly, by integrating the contract within the game interface, and changing this into another virtual device for the player to interact with, the contract simply becomes another aspect

[68] M Fahey, 'Ubisoft Does Away With Tree-Killing Instruction Manuals' (*Kotaku*, 19 April 2010) [*archived*] https://web.archive.org/web/20210729215057/https://kotaku.com/ubisoft-does-away-with-tree-killing-instruction-manuals-5520261.

of *play*. It becomes no more significant that an interaction with a character inventory or in-game map, simply sharing the game space, rather than as a standalone legal document. For the triple A company, adopting a legal and formalistic textual discourse, this informal interaction through a game-space does not match the seriousness of the text it contains.

Surprisingly, these discursive features do not change even for more 'professionalised' eSports titles. Here, the player is not necessarily a casual enjoyer of the product, who may be relatively uninvested in occupying a more powerful or 'serious' position, but instead a professional who may be reliant on access to the game for their career. As such, we might anticipate that the distribution of contracts to eSports players would mimic this formality and professionalism – perhaps a separately negotiated, or custom agreement. However, of the limited number of titles[69] which include standardised eSports permissions, players are nonetheless ultimately subservient to the primary (user) contracts included with *all* versions of the game:

> '[We may] make changes to this Code of Conduct from time to time … ESPORTS PROFESSIONALS WHO DO NOT AGREE TO ANY OF THE PROPOSED CHANGES, MAY WITHDRAW FROM RIOT ESPORTS COMPETITIONS AND THE PROPOSED CHANGES WILL HAVE NO EFFECT ON ESPORTS PROFESSIONALS WHO WITHDRAW.'

Evidentially then, this method of distribution of the contract is a complete norm in the industry, regardless of the characteristics of the player. It does not change in response to a professionalised context. In this sense, we might conclude that even if the construct of the player in the textual dimension is not stable (eg changing depending on whether the game company is triple A or indie), the methods of communicating to the player are.

The cumulative effect at the discursive dimension minimises the role of the player, by giving them no input on the contractual relationship with the game company; the company's authority alone is presented as being sufficient to unilaterally offer and change the terms.[70] This is, of course, further legitimated at the textual dimension by reference to the institutional backing of law. The production, distribution and consumption of the text is entirely unilateral, with no room for agency by the player. Discursively then, the transformation to click-wrap and particularly the inclusion of the contract as part of the game interface, which obscures its existence within play, situates the player as the weaker object of the relationship, with no agency as an active subject. By design, the player is invited to agree to the terms therein, or walk away.

[69] Of interest, at the original time of writing my thesis (2021), only one company (Blizzard) had an eSports policy. Upon revisiting for this monograph in 2025, this has increased to 7: Activision-Blizzard, EA, Hi-Rez, Nintendo, Ubisoft, Valve and Wizards of the Coast.

[70] See eg Bandai Namco, 'Terms of Use' (Appendix 2): 'At its sole discretion, BNEE reserves the right to change, modify, add or remove parts of these Terms of Use.'

B. Parallel Indie Discourses

Indie games, in keeping with a less formal textual approach also differentiate themselves at the discursive dimension by creating two separate, parallel discourses: one which is presented to the player through the static, institutional webpage, and a separate agreement which is more ephemerally presented to the player upon installation of the game through the in-game interface. While it is not possible to survey each game title to check whether the online version of the contract corresponds with the in-game version presented to upon installation (a challenge explored in Chapter 3), at least one of the indie game titles, and one indie game sequel[71] display an alternative contract to the player upon installation through the game interface, which is different in form and content from the static online version on their institutional webpages.

The first example, *Superhot*, displays an alternative, parody version of its contract upon installation. The contract automatically scrolls at great speed during installation, making it impossible for the player to read in real time. This appears to be both a reference to the most common approach the player takes when interacting with a contract (scrolling as fast as possible to agree before proceeding with the game, while indeed not actually reading its contents) and an inversion of the actual game mechanics. In *Superhot*, time only moves when the player moves – it is like playing a game in slow motion. The contract, in scrolling incredibly fast, is therefore also an acknowledgement of this mechanic: the malleability of time and space:

> Your viewing of game spoilers constitutes your acceptance of the following agreement between yourself (heretofore referred to as 'player') and SUPERHOT (heretofore referred to as 'system') and constitutes a contract that shall be considered binding in all municipalities, counties, states, countries, territories, continents, protectorates, dominions, planets, systems, galaxies and temporary autonomous zones, both physical and digital from today's date and extending 67,867,967 years or until the heat death of the universe, whichever shall occur first. For events occurring after the heat death of the universe, see relevant section below.[72]

The *Superhot* parody contract is deliberately contradictory in satirising its own existence. It uses hyperbole and humour, exaggerating the overreach of the typical triple A contract, purporting to last '... until the heat death of the universe' (note that previous examples of contracts examined here also claim, in all sincerity, to reach to the extent of the universe)[73] and exaggerating formalism ('heretofore'). It

[71] Boolean search strings were used to search for screenshots of in-game contracts on Google – eg 'Superhot' AND 'EULA' OR 'contract' OR 'licence' OR 'license' OR 'terms of use' OR 'terms of service' AND 'install' OR 'menu'.

[72] Superhot Fandom, 'End User License Agreement' (*Superhot Fandom*, date unknown) https://superhot.fandom.com/wiki/End_User_License_Agreement.

[73] 'Heat death of the Universe' is indeed defined by the parody contract: 'In the event that all energy has been exhausted from the universe and all matter has reverted to cold lifeless husks, this contract shall remain in effect and all rights, properties or consciousnesses abrogated to the system shall remain part of the system': Superhot Fandom, ibid.

deflates the seriousness of the dominant, triple A discourse that emphasises the formalistic and legal nature of the contracts by analogising the company to an authoritarian superintelligence (the 'system' – also, the ostensible antagonist in *Superhot's* metanarrative).

However, this ironic and humorous in-game contract does not exist in isolation, and in fact is accompanied by a different, static version available via the *Superhot* institutional homepage. While the in-game contract subverts the dominant discourse by mocking it and exaggerating its reach, the official contract largely feeds into the very system it purports to mock: namely, the authority of copyright. Table 7 shows a comparison of clauses from both the official and parody contract which have approximately the same function of introducing the purpose of the document.

Table 7 Comparison of *Superhot* contracts: official vs in-game version

Superhot: official contract	Superhot: in-game contract
This copy of SUPERHOT ('the Software Product') and accompanying documentation is licensed and not sold. This Software Product is protected by copyright laws and treaties, as well as laws and treaties related to other forms of intellectual property. SUPERHOT Sp. Z o.o. or its subsidiaries, affiliates, and suppliers (collectively 'SUPERHOT Team') own intellectual property rights in the Software Product. The Licensee's ('you' or 'your') license to download, use, copy, or change the Software Product is subject to these rights and to all the terms and conditions of this End User License Agreement ('Agreement').[74]	System stipulates that while it does not relish needing to create this document (heretofore referred to as 'the EULA') it feels it must in order to protect its rights against those who seek to harm or destroy system. System sincerely hopes you are not part of this regrettable, misguided group of dissidents and apologizes for any future actions it might take against you, provided such apology does not infringe upon its legal and/or physical ability to destroy you, your livelihood and those who love you.[75]

This evidences two simultaneous discourses for the indie player, separated in the discursive dimension. The first, being the official, static contract uses many of the legalistic tropes examined in the textual dimension (eg defined terms, intertextual reference to copyright, immediate claims to ownership of the game), more typical of the dominant triple A discourse. This version is in some ways less accessible to the player because it must be actively sought out via the institutional homepage. The second discourse, the parody contract, is a satire of the first, exaggerating the formalism, seriousness, and all-encompassing nature of triple A contracts. The parody version is more outwardly presented and accessible to the player through the game interface upon installation, giving us an immediate impression of an

[74] Superhot Team, 'End User License Agreement' (Appendix 2).
[75] ibid.

entity who ostensibly *rejects* the dominant discourse – yet we know it is also being perpetuated by it in parallel.

The choice to create this differentiation in the discursive dimension is curious. The safeguard of the 'true' binding contract on the institutional webpage creates the same legal effect. But the existence of the parody contract may look to media scholars like hypermediacy, being a way of reminding the player of the medium that they are using.[76] In this case, the game is a ludic medium, with a ludic, playful introduction that matches the theme of the game itself. The game's antagonist (the authoritarian superintelligent 'System') is presenting a contract (with threatening, but ostensibly civilly expressed terms) in an unreadable format and impossible speed (a core mechanic of the game). Presenting the contract as a parody of itself within the game interface may be a deliberate strategy of matching the contract to the ludic tone and atmosphere of the game – a metanarrative within a metanarrative. However, while the outward presentation of the contract has clear ludic intent, the existence of a separate, static, and formal document on the institutional webpage suggests there is ultimately still an underlying and cautious legal approach. To the indie company, it is apparently not acceptable for power relations to be played out within the game interface that the player 'inhabits', but authority can legitimately be present elsewhere. And while the player, outwardly, appears to be engaging with a less powerful actor, who creates a shared space where the dominant discourse is mocked, authority is still omnipresent: it is simply disguised by a layer of humour.

As a second example, much like *Superhot*, the in-game contract presented to the player upon installation of *Deltarune* (sequel to *Undertale*) has ludic features.[77] The original version of this contract simply reads 'YOU ACCEPT EVERYTHING THAT WILL HAPPEN FROM NOW ON', to which the player can click 'I agree' or 'Cancel'. As with *Superhot*, the intent here seems to be to use hyperbole to satirise the severity and overreach of mainstream discourse. The in-game contract for *Deltarune* imitates the legal genre features of using all caps, direct designations ('YOU') and an all-encompassing claim for every eventuality that happens post-acceptance. Ultimately, this is indeed what many triple A contracts seem to imply.

However, unlike *Superhot*, *Deltarune* has no alternative, static contract to compare with. Instead, the true intent in this case is more apparently hypermediacy of the kind described above. Indeed, the principle of *Deltarune* itself is that any choices you make within the game (eg the interactions with different characters or story choices) ultimately do not matter, as the ending will always be the same. The contract therefore again becomes absorbed both within the game

[76] M Hancock, 'Playing It By the Book: Instructing and Constructing the Player in the Videogame Manual Paratext' in A Ensslin and I Balteiro (eds), *Approaches to Videogame Discourse* (Bloomsbury, 2019).

[77] While *Deltarune* does not strictly appear in the primary dataset, it is incorporated as supplementary data given its billing as the 'parallel story' of *Undertale* (analogous to a subsequent chapter in a book, and indeed, an anagram) (see Steam, 'Deltarune' (*Steam*, 2021) https://store.steampowered.com/app/1671210/DELTARUNE/).

interface, and as a paratext of the game itself. The player's only interaction with the contract is as a further element of play, and thus they are more analogous to a true *player of a game*, rather than a *user of proprietary software*, per the dominant triple A discourse. This construction is quite deliberate in rejecting the dominant discourse, which engages with the power of law to turn play into proprietary space; instead, the indie company seems to reject the notion that law should have a role in regulating the play of a game at all.

In both examples, *Superhot* and *Deltarune*, the in-game contract rejects the dominant discourse of player-as-legal-subject, lessening the social distance between them by using humour and camaraderie. Indie companies lean into the changing medium of the contract, from physical to digital, and embrace it as simply another feature within the game that a player may interact and play with. By mocking the dominant discourse, the indie company simultaneously creates a shared space in which both it and the player are vaguely oppositional to that discourse – that is, they are oppositional to a discourse that primarily relies on a heavy-handed use of copyright. Again, this does not mean authority is absent – the player still cannot shape or engage with the indie discourse (it is still 'agree or walk away'). But the differentiation at the discursive level suggests that the player is invited to enjoy the contract as a paratext of the game itself, situating them as a *play*ful subject in the relationship, rather than a legal object.

III. Sociocultural Dimension

Unlike the early days of player licensing illustrated in Chapter 2, copyright law is no longer an afterthought in the contract. Copyright instead plays an important symbolic and legitimating function in establishing relationships of power, mainly – but not exclusively – adopted by triple A companies. Evidentially, copyright has not *replaced* the need for the contract, but rather its generative role – the authority it entails – has allowed the contract to evolve into a parallel system of player regulation. For the triple A company, it is crucial to transform the act of 'playing a game' into the 'use of proprietary software' – that is, into an activity that can be regulated by copyright. This in part explains the omnipresence of law and legal concepts throughout the text of the typical triple A contract. Through intertextual references to the law and adoption of tropes from the legal genre, the power of the company to define the player is rooted in a claim to ownership of the underlying game software, which is legitimated by reference to the legal regime of intellectual property, and particularly copyright. This is an example of power *behind* discourse, as copyright is used as a badge of authority, which is both real because it is generated from the institutionally and socially-backed power of copyright law, but also *constructed* through a re-packaging of this in the contract. The utilisation of the law is both functional and conceptual, because it achieves the desired outcome of establishing a legal relationship, while at the same time more conceptually framing the player as a weaker object – the recipient of the proprietary game software.

Power dynamics have also shifted as the discursive form of the contract has evolved. The sociocultural significance of this evolution is more important when framed within the historical context outlined in Chapter 2. Where the game company was once in a weakened, vulnerable position before software was unambiguously recognised as an object of copyright protection, there was a more explicit need for performative consent to the contract. Achieving that consent by constructing the recipient as a rational legal party, deliberately choosing to assent through breaking a seal (or, in the very early days, signing and returning) was important. Now, as companies have become bolstered by the generative power of the law, the player is by default in a weaker position – they simply do not have the same rights. As a result, the construction of the player as a consenting legal party is less important to the game company. Changing contracts to ephemeral click-wraps, embedded within the game interface itself, is standard. The strange result is that the formal legality implied in the text has outgrown the discursive form it has evolved into – there is a very serious legal story embedded within, for example, a multiplayer games lobby. Returning to the theoretical underpinnings of Critical Discourse Analysis (for more detail see Chapter 3), common sense is useful as an explanatory factor here, having overtones of coercion, consent, and hegemony; players may balk at the terms of the contract (if and when they read them), but ultimately agree to them in order to play the game. This routine acceptance has become normalised, and ultimately disguised in the discursive dimension.

In combination, the textual and discursive features of the contract suggest that the position of the player is *mandatory*, compelled as it is by the authority of the game company, whose position is entirely *conditional* and can be occasioned by a range of factors. This is a mirror of the structure of copyright; the rightsholder's position is conditional in the sense that it is initially divested with exclusive rights to which it may, or may not, choose to use or forsake. Similarly in the contract, the game company 'may', 'might' and 'could', linking itself explicitly with the discretionary execution of rights. The player's ambit is limited to a pre-set range of situational conditions, they 'will', 'shall' and 'must', much like the situational conditions of the copyright exception system. And the contract, by positioning itself as speaking from a place of legitimate, legal power, situates itself as having the mandate to determine the construct of the player. By contrast, the player's baseline access to this discourse is discouraged both textually and in the discursive dimension, by transforming the contract into a unilateral, non-negotiable offering within the game interface, and through the adoption of the legal genre with (often impenetrable) specialist language. Given the elitist nature of the law, to invoke this specialist language is to create a social distancing effect between the game company and the player; unless the player can engage with this language, the former is utilising specialised knowledge to exercise power over the other. Indeed, the ongoing use of elements specific to the legal genre, particularly the choice to use dense, technical language, is striking considering the mounting evidence that this is indecipherable to the 'average' layperson.[78] The player is, by design, excluded from being a *reader* of this discourse, and is instead a *recipient* of it.

At the sociocultural level, we might surmise that for the triple A company, the dominant discourse ideologically feeds into, and feeds from, an exclusive rights-based system to which all subsequent use is conditioned upon and subject to the authority granted to the games company as a rightsholder. The rightsholder is authoritative because of the legitimacy it claims through the law, an institution with significant power and societal backing; the player, by contrast, both textually and discursively, is a comparatively far weaker object. These unbalanced power relations and structural inequities are present even in an industry where this would not be anticipated: eSports. In eSports, with the potential for a professional player, this still does not seemingly change their relatively weak position; they are still compelled or constrained to act by the authority of the game company.

However, the ideology of games-as-proprietary-software is not omnipresent throughout all contracts examined here. Instead, the 'indie effect' offers an interesting window of critique to the dominant, triple A discourse. Whereas the triple A contract is a very literal exertion of power that relies heavily on the symbolic backing of copyright, indie games demonstrate more of an ideological struggle in their invocation of law. In the textual dimension, they are differentiated through their colloquial and conversational approach. In the discursive dimension, the use of in-game hypermediacy recognises the ludic nature of games; the player is here to *play*, rather than act as a legal subject. The contract is a paratext of the game itself.

Importantly, there is a possible Occam's razor argument in explaining the indie effect: one might argue that, as indie companies do not have the same financial support systems as triple A companies, there is simply not enough money to invest in the legal advice to create a 'proper' contract like the triple A companies, who tend to have larger budgets for legal support. However, I have found this argument to be unconvincing, not least because myriad copy-and-paste boilerplate contract templates are freely available online.[79] In fact, there is no suggestion that indie companies that use more informal ways of writing invest less in their contract at all; *Superhot*, for example, arguably invests *more* by creating two parallel versions. Some might also suggest that indie companies, having less financial support for advertisements and promotions, rely more on the value of being seen as socially responsible, rather than as having a draconian approach to propertising their game. *Minecraft* is both a good and bad example of this, given its many variables. *Minecraft*'s target demographic skews towards a younger audience and is also

[78] C Fiesler et al, 'Reality and Perception of Copyright Terms of Service for Online Content Creation' (2016) CSCW '16 Proceedings of the 19th ACM Conference on Computer-Supported Cooperative Work and Social Computing.

[79] TermsFeed, 'EULA Generator' https://www.termsfeed.com/eula-generator/.

increasingly used in educational settings.[80] As such, it could be that it is simply not appropriate to engage with a high level of legal formality with, for example, a nine-year-old in a school setting. Yet, it seems implausible that Mojang, in being socially responsible, would anticipate that a nine-year-old, or their teacher, would read the contract regardless. Improved reader-friendliness of the contract is therefore not necessarily responsive to the likely audience, nor explanatory of the informal approach adopted in indie contracts.

Instead, the indie rejection of the dominant triple A discourse is more likely explained by the sociocultural context in which indie games have been formed. Historically, the rise of indie game development was in *opposition* to a perceived lack of innovation in the mainstream games industry, and particularly the corporate culture of triple A companies, which tended to re-invest only in limited, repetitive 'crowd-pleasing' genres.[81] Such genres have historically been commodified under branded, intellectual property-intensive series, such as *Call of Duty* (Activision), *Resident Evil* (Capcom), or *Assassin's Creed* (Ubisoft) which, whilst certainly valuable, have been criticised for causing market stagnation in the industry and a lack of creativity.[82] These profit-driven incentives to re-invest only in well-known, branded series, is oppositional to the indie mentality of original creativity and experimentation. Indeed, many of the games surveyed in this dataset share little to no ludic similarities to the triple A titles – they look and feel very different. Whereas triple A titles mainly comprise the 'first person shooter' genre or large open world exploration games, mainly differentiated on different graphical styles, indie titles are much more varied, ranging from the time-based mechanics of *Superhot*, to the hand-drawn, stylised arcade format of *Cuphead*.

For the indie company, the repetition of genres in triple A titles is therefore in part due to the commodification of the branded *series*, which, far from copyright's intended purpose to stimulate creativity, ironically results in stagnation. Opposition to commodification in the corporate culture of triple A therefore also bleeds through to oppositional indie opinions on copyright more generally. For example, Markus 'Notch' Persson, creator of *Minecraft*, has previously claimed that 'piracy isn't theft' and 'if you steal a car, the original is lost. If you steal a game, there are simply more of them in the world'.[83] Toby Fox, creator of *Deltarune*,

[80] See Mojang, 'Minecraft: Education Edition' (*Mojang*, date unknown) https://education.minecraft.net/en-us/homepage.

[81] F Dutton, 'What is Indie?' (*Eurogamer*, 18 April 2012) https://www.eurogamer.net/what-is-indie.

[82] GameCentral, 'Triple-A Games Are Killing Gaming' (*Metro*, 5 April 2020) https://metro.co.uk/2020/04/05/triple-games-killing-gaming-readers-feature-12506993/. See also A Thomas et al, 'Competition in the Cloud Gaming Market: Proposing the Innovation-Creativity Dichotomy' (2025) 9(1) *Interactive Entertainment Law Review* 1.

[83] R Purchese, 'Minecraft Man: "Piracy Is Not a Theft"' (*Eurogamer*, 3 March 2011) https://www.eurogamer.net/articles/2011-03-03-minecraft-man-piracy-is-not-a-theft. Note: the inclusion of this quotation should not be construed as condoning any of the other personal beliefs held or expressed by Persson, who has been critiqued for a number of controversial comments on, among other issues, feminism and LGBTQ+ representation.

has distributed his game for free.[84] Others, such as the Superhot Team, relied on crowd-funding to develop their game, supported by the same people who would go on to play it.[85] The indie origins of a game thus indicate an oppositional stance to the triple A corporate culture; for the indie company, engagement with copyright is more analogous to this profit-driven creativity, and greed at the expense of artistic freedom. This ideological position has a direct effect on the textual and discursive features of the indie contract that rejects the dominant discourse of triple A. Indie companies align themselves as sharing the same ideological space as the player, who is likewise conceptualised as being oppositional to this dominant discourse (recall: 'We don't like reading license documents any more than you do'). Ironically, triple A companies must ultimately also support this construction – that the player is vaguely oppositional to copyright – but the manner of treatment results in copyright *maximalism* rather than *minimalism*. But for the triple A company, the player is framed more as an opponent, with a resultantly stronger and more punitive source of power: an exact iteration of what is owned, what can and cannot be done, and with corresponding penalties for noncompliance. For this reason, where the triple A company must insist that the recipient of the contract is a *user of proprietary software*, bound by legal responsibilities, for the indie company, the player is instead a *player of a game*. To the triple A company, invoking copyright and law is necessary to communicate a proprietary ideology. But for the latter, copyright may be oppositional to the aims of artistic freedom, and anti-commodification, at least on the surface. We must remain mindful that in both cases, authority is nonetheless omnipresent: both triple A and indie companies are ultimately relying on their authority as rightsholders to justify a contract that regulates the player in the first instance. However, the interpretations of the ideologies *behind* this authority are meaningfully different.

IV. Save Point: Chapter Summary

The *Authority* theme is about how power is claimed through engagement with copyright law and legal principles to construct the player as either conceptually weak or strong. The theme shows how the textual and discursive features of player contracts reflect different material relations of game companies at industry level. Differing levels of engagement with the law can be explained by the corporate culture in which they are written. For the triple A company, the ideology of games-as-property emphasises copyright ownership, making the (propertyless) player conceptually weak. However, for the indie company, an industry sub-set born out of opposition to the creative stagnation in 'mainstream' triple A gaming, the ideology

[84] T Fox, Deltarune (*Deltarune*, date unknown) https://www.deltarune.com.
[85] Superhot Team, 'Superhot' (*Kickstarter*, 2015) https://www.kickstarter.com/projects/375798653/superhot.

of artistic freedom results in the construction of the player as a more ludic – playful – subject. They are invited to 'play with' and mock triple A contracts while – somewhat ironically – also often relying on the same legal system. Resultingly, while it may be too bold to say the player is stronger to the indie company, they are at least not actively weakened through heavy-handed engagement with the authority of law.

Importantly, while ultimately arriving at different conclusions about *how* to regulate the player, both the triple A and indie companies share an underlying assumption that the player must be someone who is *vaguely oppositional to copyright*: either as a threat to be constrained, because they are trespassing upon the game property; or as someone who has no intent to engage with the law at all, and who is welcomed to share in the mockery of those who do.

5

Access

Even those on the periphery of gaming and the games industry will be aware of the claim that 'you don't own the games you buy', even if they are not convinced by the truth of it. And those on that periphery will also be aware that this claim is nothing new – it is said loudly, and often, by various industry stakeholders.[1] For the uninitiated, however, this claim may either seem perplexing, given that many people do seem to indeed have copies of a game in their possession that they seem to *own*. Or perhaps, it is otherwise self-evident, if we consider other norms around ownership of content we access through subscription-based services. Regardless of the reader's familiarity with this claim, it is fair to say that the status of player-game ownership is at least *presented* by game companies as an industry imperative – something that *must* be regulated in the interests of its survival. And indeed, in this theme, I show how the player is constructed by the contract strongly, and consistently as a *non-owner* in furtherance of that aim. Rather, the player is positioned as having temporary and conditional *access* to the game. This chapter shows that the player undeniably has qualities of a consumer: in principle, they earn this title when they pay for, and access, a game for their personal use. They are indeed the transactional end-point in the sale of a game from the game company. However, the contract attempts to deny them consumer status. It instead constructs an *ongoing* relationship between the player and game company after that transaction is complete; an access-based relationship subject to ongoing restrictions where the player adopts the more ephemeral mantle of 'user'.

Unlike the other themes, which have significant inter-theme variability, *Access* is highly homogeneous. The construction of the player as a non-owner of a game is so strongly and consistently expressed across all contracts that there is little room for debate about the intention behind the discourse. Section I illustrates the presence of a strong, textual construction of the player as a non-consumer and its mirror image as non-reseller: in combination, and emphatically, the player is a non-owner. These textual characteristics are so strong and consistent that variations in the discursive dimension, illustrated in Section II, do not change this construction. The consistency of this discourse across textual and discursive dimensions is explained by persistent industry concerns surrounding the recoupment of game investment by companies in the sociocultural dimension

[1] At the time of writing the most vocal advocate is Ubisoft, which has confirmed same in response to a lawsuit filed by two players who have lost access to the game *The Crew* following planned server shutdowns (*Cassell and Liu v Ubisoft* (2024) 2:24-cv-03058).

(Section III). In concluding, while framing the non-consumerist qualities of the player is important in the contract, it is *resale* which is more specifically forwarded as the 'imaginary dragon' of the games industry – something that must be slayed to ensure its ongoing survival. In this respect, the player may more accurately be conceptualised in this theme as a non-reseller.

I. Textual Dimension

The construction of the player in the textual dimension of this theme is strongly expressed through two related and complementary constructions: first, that the player is a non-owner, in the sense that nothing is transferred to them (Section A); and second, that the player is a non-reseller, in the sense that nothing can subsequently be transferred *by* them (Section B). This construction is then ensured by the addition of a moral deterrent in the text, which likens the act of reselling to piracy (Section C).

A. Player as Non-Owner

The player is explicitly and repeatedly framed as a non-owner of their game within the contract. Importantly, this transcends the interpretation that they are not the *copyright* owner of the game – a matter which is perhaps a statement of fact rather than a legal obligation. Instead, the text more broadly claims that the player is not even the owner of the individual *copy* of a game which they are currently using. In the true spirit of the player being granted a *licence*, this condition of non-ownership is often explicit, and set out early in the contract, taking precedence within the text. Notably, in the case of both Nintendo[2] and Psyonix,[3] it is in fact the very first sentence. Often, this statement of non-ownership is capitalised and/or emboldened to denote emphasis: the player has 'NO OWNERSHIP OR OTHER PROPERTY INTEREST'[4] in the game, and in any case '**THIS SOFTWARE IS LICENSED, NOT SOLD**'.[5] These techniques of ensuring prominence of the designation in the text (primacy, capitalisation, emboldening) suggests that non-ownership is an important construction of the player. Note how the contract also presents the retention of ownership and refusal of transfer as a statement of *fact* ('no', 'is'), precluding competing constructions of the player as, eg the owner of a copy, without further consideration. From the outset, the player is therefore constructed as being allocated a series of permissions to access a copy of the game, rather than having any property interests or ownership over it.

Claims and statements of non-ownership are made repeatedly within the contract, in different iterations but having the same functional purpose. Often,

[2] Nintendo, 'End User License Agreement' (Appendix 2).
[3] Psyonix, 'End User License Agreement' (Appendix 2).
[4] Activision, 'Terms of Use' (Appendix 2).
[5] Psyonix, 'End User License Agreement' (Appendix 2).

this extends into other aspects of game content, creating a tiered effect: the game itself is not sold, and therefore neither is anything within it. For example, the Riot Games contract provides a simple, plain-English explanation of the non-ownership status of virtual goods: **'[d]o I "own" the Virtual Goods I unlock? (No. What you "unlock" is not the virtual good itself, but rather, a qualified right to access it in the Game)'.**[6] This is then immediately re-iterated in an expanded format:

> Once again: I don't *own* these Virtual Goods? ('No!' shouted all the lawyers.) **NOTWITHSTANDING ANYTHING TO THE CONTRARY HEREIN, YOU ACKNOWLEDGE AND AGREE THAT YOU SHALL HAVE NO OWNERSHIP OR OTHER PROPERTY INTEREST IN YOUR ACCOUNT, AND THAT ALL RIGHTS IN AND TO YOUR ACCOUNT ARE AND SHALL FOREVER BE OWNED BY AND INURE TO THE BENEFIT OF RIOT GAMES. YOU FURTHER ACKNOWLEDGE AND AGREE THAT YOU HAVE NO CLAIM, RIGHT, TITLE, OWNERSHIP, OR OTHER PROPRIETARY INTEREST IN THE GAME CONTENT THAT YOU UNLOCK OR ACCUMULATE, REGARDLESS OF ANY CONSIDERATION OFFERED OR PAID IN EXCHANGE FOR RIOT POINTS OR VIRTUAL GOODS.**[7]

The importance of non-ownership is doubly emphasised here through capitalisation and emboldening of the statement. The repetition of this string of words immediately after a plain-English explanation suggests that this particular iteration has a functional, quasi-magical quality, that gives them a special, legal effect. As part of the legal genre of discourse (detailed in Chapter 4), the nature of the player contract is partially functional – to achieve a specific purpose – and to be so it must be expressed in a particular way such that plain language alone is seemingly not satisfactory. Instead, it must be conveyed with authority, which seemingly has particular (convoluted) qualities in textual discourse.[8]

This string of magical words may also be functional in that it is a response to what is, fundamentally, a confusing situation. The game, alongside any virtual goods a player might purchase within that game, such as in-game loot crates or skins, is typically advertised as being 'sold' to the player. These virtual goods may also have a monetary value separate from the currency of the game; they have been purchased, and are possessed by the player, in exchange for 'real' money. Yet, they are not in fact 'owned' per the terms of the contract. The contract seems to recognise that separating these ideas is conceptually challenging, and so the matter is repeated:

> Notwithstanding any use of the terms 'purchase', 'buy', 'sell', 'order' or the like, Virtual Currency and Virtual Goods you obtain using Virtual Currency are licensed, not sold, and you do not obtain title to or any ownership interest in any Virtual Currency or Virtual Goods.[9]

[6] Riot Games, 'League of Legends Terms of Use' (Appendix 2).
[7] ibid.
[8] See for example an experiment which confirms that the convoluted – less legible – structures of legal writing may be perceived to signal authority to others: E Martinez, D Mollica and E Gibson, 'Even laypeople use legalese' [2024] *PNAS* 121(35).
[9] Rockstar Games, 'Limited Software Warranty and License Agreement' (Appendix 2).

The conceptual vocabulary to describe the differences between ownership and *licensee*ship become strained as the contract explicitly outlines contradictory definitions, and tells us that they don't really matter. Apparently, these words do not mean what the player *thinks* they mean; but there is a lingering doubt that the severability between buying and owning has not yet been firmly established in their mind. As such the difference between them is stressed explicitly, and often, in the text of the contract. This suggests the status of the player is difficult to pinpoint on the spectrum between licenseeship and ownership, but rather it is defined by what it is not: a buyer, a purchaser, or a consumer.

The only suggestion of a more affirmative and explicit construction of the player's status is tied to the distinctly *personal* right to the *use* of the game. Complementary to this, the player is often limited to non-commercial uses of a game for their 'enjoyment'[10] and 'entertainment purposes'.[11] The contract makes assumptions that the player is a natural person, making use of a game for *play* in the true sense of the word. 'Play' is in fact a common condition of the contract. The contract is given 'for the sole purpose of *playing* the game',[12] or granting a 'personal right to play'.[13] Others conceptualise these as two different permissions altogether; the player may 'play *and* use [the game]' (emphasis added).[14] In another curious example from CD Projekt Red's contract, the contrast between the informal 'Quick Summary' and adjacent legally binding text, illustrated in Table 8, reveals a hidden quality about the connection between ownership of a game and 'fun'.

Table 8 Comparison of textual approaches: CD Projekt Red 'Full text' vs 'Quick Summary'

Full text	**Quick summary**
We (meaning CD PROJEKT RED) give you the personal right (called a 'licence' legally) to download, install and play *The Witcher 3: Wild Hunt* on your personal computer as long as you follow these rules. This licence is for your personal use only (so you can't give a sublicense to someone else) and doesn't give you ownership rights. At all times we continue to own all of *The Witcher 3: Wild Hunt*, all in-game content, any updates or additional content for them, manuals or other materials about them and the intellectual property rights in them, including all copyright, trademarks, patents and legal things like that …[15]	We grant you the right to play *The Witcher 3: Wild Hunt* and we sincerely hope you will enjoy it. We spent over 3 long years working on it, so let us add that it is our creation and remains our ownership. This will not limit you in having fun with it, will it?;)[16]

[10] CD Projekt Red, 'User Agreement' (Appendix 2).
[11] Cygames, 'Terms of Service Agreement' (Appendix 2).
[12] Bethesda, 'End User License Agreement' (Appendix 2) and Wizards of the Coast, 'Magic Online End User License Agreement' (Appendix 2).
[13] CD Projekt Red, 'User Agreement' (Appendix 2).
[14] Mojang, 'Minecraft End User License Agreement' (Appendix 2).
[15] CD Projekt Red, 'User Agreement' (Appendix 2).
[16] ibid.

In the Quick summary, the more playful iteration of the assertion of ownership reveals that the player's ability to have 'fun' in fact justifies the game company's assertion of ownership. The contract cages this restriction with a rhetorical question ('will it?') and uses a winking emoticon (notably, the only emoticon to appear in this dataset) which, whilst not strictly text, can be used to 'hint at desirable outcomes or to prod someone to take a particular action'.[17] As the player is an actor engaged in 'fun', they are therefore also idealised as an entity who does not *want* to be an owner. According to the contract, 'play' is not compatible with the comparable seriousness and formality of ownership.

There is – perhaps unsurprisingly – no legal definition of what it means to 'enjoy', 'entertain', have 'fun', or 'play' a game as distinct from 'using' it. But the conscious choice to differentiate between the two in the textual dimension is intriguing. Is this difference significant? 'Use', for example, is more utilitarian in the sense that it tends to be a wider grant in the pursuit of an interaction with a work. If 'play', at its plain meaning, implies only using a game for frivolity or personal enjoyment, does this preclude using the game eg for research purposes, or to monetise as a hobby (eg through streaming)? Combined with the explicit non-commercial designation of the player (explored more fully in Chapter 6), this limitation seems plausible. To *play* with something is a specific interaction, rather than the broader designation of what 'use' encompasses. Curiously, unlike in the *Authority* theme, where the indie designation of the player as play*ful* is a means of rejecting a heavy-handed approach to copyright, in this theme 'play' is instead used as a limiter to describe the quality of the interactions a player can have with a game. It is a personal right to enjoy and experience play *within* the limited space of the game.

B. Player as Non-Reseller

The second component in textually constructing non-ownership is the prevention of downstream transfer of a game. This is the natural corollary of the first component of non-transfer – the player cannot give away what they do not own (*nemo dat quod non habet* in legal parlance). Often, this restriction is buried within a list of prohibited activities such that it does not take the same precedence as the early and stressed format of non-ownership:

> You agree that you will not … License, sublicense, transfer, assign, reproduce, duplicate, copy, sell, resell, distribute or otherwise exploit for commercial purposes, any portion of, use of or access to the Application.[18]

[17] Dictionary.com, 'Winking Face emoji' (*Dictionary.com*, date unknown) https://www.dictionary.com/e/emoji/winking-face-emoji/.
[18] Konami, 'Terms of Use: Metal Gear Solid V: The Phantom Pain' (Appendix 2).

Instead, the effect is more subtle. In combination with other broader restrictions on distribution and sublicensing, the intention is that the player should be the end-point of the transactional chain. According to the contract, the game, once purchased, should be retained by the player indefinitely. The contract obliges, for example, that '[y]ou must be an end user to purchase products from the Store. Resellers are not eligible to purchase'.[19] Presented again as fact, the contract precludes the possibility of 'resellers' to obtain a game in the first instance.[20]

The homogenous characteristic of this construction is such that, with only one exception, each contract examined contains a broad and explicit prohibition of resale of a game. The exception, CD Projekt Red, does not exactly list resale as an affirmative right of the player, but rather does not prohibit it: '[d]on't copy, rent, lend, lease, sublicense, distribute, publicly display any of CD PROJEKT RED games or services'.[21] Only two other contracts provide an *exception* to the broad and explicit prohibition of resale, which is conceptualised differently depending on whether the game exists in a physical or digital carrier:

> You may permanently transfer all of your rights and obligations under this Agreement to another person only by (i) where applicable, physically transferring the original media (eg the CDROM or DVD you purchased), all original packaging, and all User Manual(s) and Documentation distributed with the Software Product[22]
>
> … you may permanently transfer all of your rights and obligations under the License to another person for non-commercial use by physically transferring the original Game Software media (eg the CD-ROM or DVD you purchased) …[23]

While only evidenced in two agreements, the existence of this exception suggests that the connection to a physical disk results in a different type of player – one who has a legitimate entitlement to resell – as opposed to their digital counterparts, whose interest is impliedly less legitimate. A player's connection to the physical chattel (also discussed in Chapter 2) remains important in the contract. Only notably on one occasion does a contract (Sony) explicitly prohibit both physical and digital resale:

> You must not resell either Disc-based Software or Digital Software, unless expressly authorised by us and, if the publisher is another company, additionally by the publisher[24]

For the most part however, the distinction between physical and digital carriers is not explicitly outlined by the contract. Instead, the broad restrictions on resale can be read to indiscriminately apply to both formats. Nintendo, for example, has a

[19] Microsoft, 'Terms of Sale' (Appendix 2).

[20] Noting that it is unclear in this example whether this restriction may be referring to eg purchase of a game by a retailer (commercial actor rather than reseller as natural person(s)), but there is no compelling reason to infer this from the text.

[21] CD Projekt Red, 'User Agreement' (Appendix 2).

[22] Hi-Rez, 'End User License Agreement' (Appendix 2).

[23] PUB G, 'End-User License Agreement' (Appendix 2).

[24] Sony, 'Software Usage Terms' (Appendix 2).

broad prohibition on the transfer of 'Game Software', which it defines as 'the game you have just purchased',[25] regardless of whether physical or digital:

> NINTENDO does not recognize the transfer of the Game Software. Therefore, you may not give, purchase, sell, bargain, barter, market, trade, offer for sale, sell, license, assign or otherwise divest your rights, responsibilities or obligations under the Agreement, either in whole or in part, without the prior written consent of NINTENDO. Any attempt to do so shall be void and of no effect.[26]

The result in this example is paradoxical: on the one hand, by the contract's own definition, the game has been purchased; on the other, there is no recognition of any transfer. Instead, this restriction creates an artificial entanglement between the non-ownership construction of the player (Section I.A above) and their status as non-reseller. The interlinkage ('Therefore') between non-owner and non-reseller concepts reveals that the purpose of creating the initial non-owner status is only in furtherance of the, more extensive and purposeful, restrictions on resale. Iterated here in several variations, the player may not 'sell' (repeated twice), 'give', 'offer for sale', 'market', 'licence', 'assign' or 'otherwise divest [their] rights, responsibilities or obligations' under the catch-all clause. These restrictions go beyond mere prohibition, and instead the contract refuses the *reality* of these transactions: it simply does not recognise any such transaction and declares them, factually, to be 'void and of no effect'. The power conveyed *through* this discourse is therefore absolute, as it obliges the player to reject the evidence of their own eyes: the game they have just purchased has not been transferred, and anything they have done to subsequently transfer it simply does not exist.

It is worthwhile pausing here to consider how this strong exertion of power *through* discourse is somewhat indicative of the absence of power *behind* it, a matter which will be explored further in Section III (but is worth signposting now given the strong presence in the textual dimension). As illustrated in the *Authority* theme, the contract will readily engage with the copyright concepts that it finds helpful to bolster its own position, while obscuring the concepts that apply to the player. Extending this to the question of ownership and resale, the right to legally transfer second-hand physical goods is almost unambiguously legal in copyright law; for digital goods however, this is contentious· and unclear.[27] In part, this is because different rights are implicated where digital goods are transferred – aspects of them are necessarily copied in a technological process (a rights which is retained by the copyright owner), rather than simply distributed like for like

[25] Nintendo, 'End User License Agreement' (Appendix 2).

[26] ibid.

[27] For example, in the EU, resale of pure digital software is legal (Case C-128/11 *UsedSoft v Oracle* EU:C:2012:407), but does not apply to audiovisual works (Case C-263/18 *Nederlands Uitgeversverbond v TomKabinet* EU:C:2019:1111). Video games are considered to contain both of these aspects, as well as being standalone subject-matter (Case C-355/12 *Nintendo Co Ltd v PC Box SRL* EU:C:2014:25). In the US, the answer is apparently more unequivocal that digital files cannot be lawfully resold, but has only been litigated in respect of music (*Capitol Records v ReDigi*, 910 F3d 649 (2d Cir 2018)).

as with a physical carrier. Evidentially, the lack of legal clarity on this issue seeps into the text: there is *less* (legal) power behind the claim that a player does not own a physical copy of a game (it is claimed less in the text), and *more* (legal) power behind the claim that a player does not own a digital copy of a game (it is emphasised repeatedly, throughout). The contract plays on the uncertain status of the legality of digital resale, clearly stating its intention to forbid this. Much as with the techniques historically employed when faced with ongoing legal uncertainty (Chapter 2), the contract attempts to cut through the Gordian knot of messy law by creating a strong construction of the player as a non-reseller in the text. Taking this into the present day, we see that this construction is employed regardless of whether the game is distributed physically or digitally, and regardless of the presence – or absence – of the institutional power of law behind it.

The strong construction of the player as a non-reseller extends also to the restrictions placed on virtual currency and virtual goods within the game (the aforementioned 'tiered' effect). These goods 'are not redeemable for any sum of money or monetary value',[28] or are characterised as being 'non-commercial'.[29] Not only then are virtual goods tied to the idea of the player as the end-point in the transactional chain, but more accurately, the player is prohibited from receiving any subsequent *income* for these goods after the transfer. The result is again paradoxical: while these goods are by their nature transactional, in the sense they have been offered by a company and subsequently bought, this does not extend to the player. Once virtual goods are associated with the player, they are absorbed into the concept of being personal, for private enjoyment and entertainment: specifically not for monetary value. Again then, the designation of the player being invited to 'play' rather than 'use' is significant, as it situates the player as a distinctly non-commercial entity. The player is invited to *have fun* with the copies of virtual goods in games, but not to *use* the proprietary software that underlies them for their own benefit.

As a final remark, unlike the *Authority* theme, where there is a demonstrable 'indie effect' in the softening of the proprietary mindset towards copyright protection and enforcement, there is no fragmentation at industry level when conceptualising the player as a non-reseller. The presence of this theme is consistent throughout the contracts, regardless of a game company's background context. For example, Superhot Team, who has been notable for taking a much more informal approach throughout the contract (detailed in Chapter 4), has a more rigid, formalistic and explicit stance on resale from the outset: '[t]his copy of SUPERHOT … is licensed and not sold'.[30] In contrast to the otherwise informal

[28] Rockstar Games, 'Limited Software Warranty and License Agreement' (Appendix 2).
[29] Konami, 'Terms of Use: Metal Gear Solid V: The Phantom Pain' (Appendix 2).
[30] Superhot Team, 'End User License Agreement' (Appendix 2).

and friendly construction of the contract, the authoritative formulation is reiterated again when preventing downstream transfer:

> Without first obtaining the express written consent of SUPERHOT Team, you may not assign your rights and obligations under this Agreement, or redistribute, encumber, sell, rent, lease, sublicense, or otherwise transfer your rights to the Software Product.[31]

Much of this example replicates the more restrictive legal tropes typical of the dominant triple A discourse explored in *Authority* and is not reflective of the indie ideology towards copyright more generally. Instead, again, the control of the *copy* is conceptualised differently from the reliance on copy*right* for the indie company, making them severable: restrictions on what a player can do with the copy is apparently a power that *can* be legitimately exerted, even in a ludic medium. With no notable indie effect, the consistency of this theme throughout the contracts suggests that this construction of the player, as a non-reseller and non-owner, is textually homogeneous.

C. Player as Pirate

The general construction of non-ownership, and related restrictions on resale, rental, lending etc are justified in the contract by positioning these activities as being closely associated with serious and unlawful acts, such as piracy and fraud. In doing so, the contracts construct resale – which is lawful, but an apparently undesirable behaviour – as being *factually* illegal. There are three notable examples of contracts in which this manifests: Mojang, Microsoft and Nintendo.

The first example, Mojang's contract, otherwise notable for its very permissive and anti-interventionist stance ('If you steal a game there are simply more of them in the world'),[32] explicitly prevents resale or rental of its game under a broad prohibition that can apply to both physical and digital copies. Being, at least historically,[33] part of the indie genre of games, Mojang justifies this position, rather than leaving it as a simple prohibition. The contract explains that prevention of resale is 'important to help us stop piracy and fraud and to protect our Game'.[34] Here, prevention of resale is presented as a natural corollary of preventing piracy and fraud, both serious and unlawful activities, and therefore a legitimate means of protecting the game based on this implied connection. In the context of an otherwise very permissible contract, which takes a more relaxed approach to its copy*right* more generally, this restriction is notable for exhibiting a protectionist stance towards the actual *copy* of a game.

[31] ibid.
[32] R Purchese 'Minecraft Man: "Piracy Is Not a Theft"' (*Eurogamer*, 3 March 2011) https://www.eurogamer.net/articles/2011-03-03-minecraft-man-piracy-is-not-a-theft.
[33] Mojang was subsequently acquired by Microsoft in 2014.
[34] Mojang, 'Minecraft End User License Agreement' (Appendix 2).

In the second example, the contract for Microsoft games similarly equates the resale of gamertags, or purchases of games from 'unauthorised sellers', both of which are prohibited by the contract, as being fraudulent – it is presented under the heading of 'fraud benefits no one'.[35] Again, this creates a close association between resale and deceptive, or unlawful behaviour. By constructing two separate groups – authorised and unauthorised sellers –by default, anyone who is restricted in their entitlement to resell, including the player upon acquiescing to this contract, is acting *fraudulently*. Microsoft is also notable for taking a strong stance on 'accounts-sharing' (ie the practice of using someone else's online account to access a game, similar to 'password sharing' on eg Netflix). These practices are described as 'not a victimless crime – it robs game providers of revenue that funds games and add-ons that people want to play'.[36] The emotive and violent language of 'robbery' creates a close association between the act of the player accessing another person's account and committing a crime.[37] Both the game creators (the 'victims') and the wider community (the 'people [that] want to play') are framed as the casualties in the act of sharing accounts, creating a double moral imperative on the player to remain as the transactional end point.

The third example, Nintendo, presents an interesting case whereby the player is doubly constructed as both a non-owner *and* lawful acquirer, depending on the ultimate purpose of the text itself. In its contract, Nintendo frames the player very explicitly as a licensee and non-owner, who is explicitly prohibited from resale. Indeed, the very first line of Nintendo's contract reads 'THIS SOFTWARE IS LICENSED NOT SOLD',[38] the primacy and emphasis of which suggests 'licenseeship' is an important and essential construction of the player. This protectionist stance is mirrored in its Anti-Piracy Programme, where players are urged to 'use caution when purchasing used games'.[39] Again, by tying to the heading of 'piracy' and 'caution', Nintendo creates a close association between unlawful behaviour, danger, and the resale of used games. In a similar manner to Mojang and Microsoft, the player is first constructed as a non-owner and non-reseller, bolstered by a moral imperative associated with criminality.

However, this discourse changes in Nintendo's Anti-Piracy agreement, where players are instead framed as legitimate, lawful *owners* of copies, not licensees, in the 'battle'[40] against piracy. In the context of this battle, Nintendo claims that it 'depend[s] on legitimate *sales* of their games … in order to survive' (emphasis added).[41] The player is thanked in this agreement for their lawful purchase. The result is of course contradictory; on the one hand, Nintendo emphasises in its

[35] Microsoft, 'Community Standards for Xbox' (Appendix 2).

[36] ibid.

[37] PL Loughlan, '"You Wouldn't Steal a Car": Intellectual Property and the Language of Theft' (2007) 29(10) *European Intellectual Property Review* 401.

[38] Nintendo, 'End User License Agreement' (Appendix 2).

[39] Nintendo, 'Anti-Piracy Programme' (Appendix 2).

[40] ibid, noting again the similarities to language of theft explored in Loughlan (n 35).

[41] ibid.

contract that its games were never sold in the first instance, but in the Anti-Piracy agreement, it is simultaneously admitting that it is reliant on legitimate sales of games, and recognises that the player is an essential contributor to this. The construction of the player as a licensee or lawful owner is therefore strategic depending on the particular business imperative of the text. Where preventing resale is concerned, the player is a non-owner, transactional end-point; where the company's 'survival' is concerned, the player is a valued owner of a Nintendo game in the 'battle' against piracy.

Throughout all these examples, concepts like piracy and fraud are closely aligned to resale. The overall effect and intention is to doubly deter the player from resale in conjunction with the more general prohibition and statement of non-sale through a moral deterrent. However, and notably, none of the contracts offers further explanation about this connection. Unlike the legal tropes of 'if-then' explored in Chapter 4, resale rules have no corresponding enforcement mechanism. Rather, it is a subtle discouragement of the act by aligning it with criminality. In essence, this activity is listed under the heading of piracy and/or fraud, without further justification as to why the two are connected. The reader is instead left to infer this connection for themselves and draw their own conclusions as to why this is the case.

II. Discursive Dimension

As noted in the textual dimension, the contract insists that no ownership of the copy of a game is conferred to the player and that, because of this, no subsequent transfers of the game are permitted. Some contracts stratify this restriction on the lines of physical or digital distribution, and so we might anticipate that this textual construction will change if the method of distribution for the game itself changes. However, despite substantial distributive variability in the dataset of contracts, it is notable that regardless of the differences in distribution, this ultimately has no effect on the textual construction of non-ownership and non-resale. Whether the game is distributed physically, digitally, as a service or through a game key, the same textual narrative persists; nothing is transferred, and nothing can subsequently be transferred by the player.

As illustrated in Chapter 2, historically, games have been distributed in a physical chattel, such as a cartridge or disk (or earlier iterations in eg arcade coin-operated machines), which have been necessary to play or run the game via hardware (eg console or PC). Physical copies of a game can be purchased first or second-hand directly from the game publisher, or through third-party retailers (eg in the UK: Game, in the US: GameStop). However, the sale of physical games is undeniably in decline,[42] and while it is difficult to anticipate

[42] OS Good, 'COVID-19 Pandemic Turns Console Gamers to Digital Sales in Record Numbers' (*Polygon*, 11 August 2020) https://www.polygon.com/2020/8/11/21363951/video-game-sales-digital-online-xbox-one-ps4-publisher-figures-ea-activision-2k-games.

exactly which games in this dataset are more frequently consumed from the physical disk or the digital sale, digital consumption is undeniably becoming increasingly common.

The games in this dataset are distributed in a variety of ways but broadly can be grouped under three mediums: physical disks, digital downloads, and streaming. Games are rarely exclusive to one distributive medium, with the biggest exception – as a rule – being indie titles: from this dataset, *Undertale*, *Superhot*, *Cuphead* and *Outlast* are all digital exclusives.[43] Instead, most titles will rely on more than one method of distribution, and indeed, it is possible for all three to be made available to the player. For example, it is possible to buy Sony's *The Last of Us* on a physical disk, via digital download on the PlayStation Store, or to stream as part of a subscription service on PlayStation Now. However, and regardless of the distribution method employed, the terms of access predicated in the text of the contract do not change in response to this; or rather, regardless of the variety of methods employed in the discursive dimension, the textual dimension remains constant.

Yet, as illustrated in Section I.A above in relation to the application of the legal aspects of this, the distributive medium of a game can still be crucial in determining whether one claims power *behind* the discourse, with the institutional backing of law, or *through* it, by manufacturing its own power in the text. Copyright law does not bolster every claim that a player is a non-owner and non-reseller: resale is almost always allowed in the case of physical objects. But there is uncertainty, if not outright restriction, on the lawful status of digital resale. As such, in the discursive dimension, it may be desirable for a game company to steer the player towards a digital medium, where there may be some valid claim to power *behind* discourse when preventing resale, with the institutional backing of law. For example, in the latest generation of game consoles (at the time of writing, on which many of the games in the dataset can be played),[44] both Microsoft (in respect of its Xbox Series X) and Sony (in respect of its PS5) now offer two alternative models of their consoles: one with a physical disk drive, the other without. The disk drive is effectively monetised, as both consoles cost more to incorporate this feature. As such, without textually spelling it out, there is a deterrent effect at the discursive level, which aims to cement the player as a non-owner and non-reseller by physically removing any lingering problematic (legally ownable and resellable) physical chattels in the method of distribution. By forcing a movement towards all-digital distribution of games, this can be read as intent to claim power *behind* discourse: if the law also supports the prevention of reselling digital copies of games, and this is also the desire of the game company as evidenced in the text, forcing

[43] The lack of physical chattel for indie games is a noted hallmark of the industry (see F Dutton, 'What is Indie?' (*Eurogamer*, 18 April 2012) https://www.eurogamer.net/what-is-indie).

[44] All titles are available for next generation consoles through backwards compatibility or remaster, with the exceptions of: *Arena of Valor*, *Dota 2*, *League of Legends*, *Shadowverse* and *Starcraft II* (all being PC exclusives).

digital distribution models at the discursive level is strategically significant. Constructing the player as a non-owner is explicit in the textual dimension, but more subtly enforced in the discursive.

For games which are bought for a one-off fee in return for permanent possession, the above explanation is plausible (that the push to all-digital distribution at the discursive level is strategic in achieving a particular proprietary ideology or construction of the player as non-owner). However, and alternatively, stronger prohibitions on resale may correlate with newer methods of distribution which more explicitly do not legally confer any ownership rights, such as subscription services. Indeed, some of the games in this dataset are accounts-based and access is determined through ongoing membership of a service, rather than as a game purchased in return for a one-off fee to permanently possess. Valve for example, exclusively releases games on the subscription and accounts-based platform, Steam. Free-to-play titles, such as *Fortnite*, add another complicating vector as they are in fact never 'purchased' in the first instance (though may include subsequent micro-transactions for virtual goods).[45] The use of these games is therefore more akin to a service, and accessing an online account rather than the purchase of a copy of a game as a product.[46] Restrictions on ownership and resale in these cases are indeed more accurately understood as restrictions on the ownership or resale of a personal *account*, tied to a specific player, than a singular game as such. This changes the context of the distributive mechanism because there is less slipperiness around the conceptualisation of sale and subsequent possession of the copy of a game: it is more apparently 'use' in the truest sense, and the player more apparently the recipient of a service than an owner. So where there is explicit discursive framing of the game as a *service*, this can be used to legitimate the textual construction of the player as a non-owner.

However, in illustrating the variety of ways in which games *can* be distributed at the discursive level, the key conclusion from this analysis is that, *regardless* of the physical or digital character of the work, the textual construction of the player does not change. The most common textual constructions of the player as non-owner and non-reseller are drafted so broadly as to apply to *all* distributive types. And while there are some efforts in the discursive dimension to drive players towards an all-digital distribution system and claim power *behind* the discourse by aligning itself with the law, this is not as critical as the power claimed *through* the discourse in the textual dimension that insists the player is, in any case, a non-owner and non-reseller.

[45] See *Epic Games Inc v Apple Inc*, 493 F Supp 3d 817 (9th Cir 2023).

[46] This is more extensively discussed in A Perzanowski and J Schultz, *The End of Ownership: Personal Property in the Digital Economy* (MIT Press, 2016).

III. Sociocultural Dimension

Access is the most homogenous theme throughout the player contract discourse. Textually, the construction of the player as a non-owner and non-reseller does not alter regardless of the background context of the game company, or whether the distribution format changes. Here, we see an example of power *through* the discourse, because this construction is exclusively achieved by the text, rather than relying on the institutionally backed power of the law. Whereas physical resale of a lawfully acquired game is always, indisputably permitted given its tie to the physical chattel, it is consistently contracted out of. The law is not omitted, but deliberately subverted, and in fact inverted; resale is *strategically* framed as being factually unlawful and, by extension, the player as reseller. Resultingly, the construction of the player as a non-owner and non-reseller is perhaps the most artificial, as it has seemingly no justification outside of the text itself.

Instead, framing the contract as a 'licence to access' a game speaks directly to its historical origins, where the purpose was to convert a perceived sale into a licence, and to change the recipient from a consumer to a *licensee* with conditional access-based usage. As this formulation is critical to the operation of the contract, it is perhaps unsurprising that it continues to be a stable and consistent factor across the discourse today. As detailed by Perzanowski and Schultz, the ongoing use of this puzzling and contradictory construction may in fact be a poorly expressed statement of what is otherwise an obvious fact: the contract does not grant the recipient any property rights over the copy*right* of a copy itself.[47] An optimistic speculation is that this is the intention of the expression, rather than to restrict the player's potential personal property rights in the *copy* of the game. However, when looking at the contracts, we see that an optimistic reading is unlikely. Textually, the player is not merely a non-owner, which may be explained by the logic above, but also, very explicitly, a *non-reseller*, even of the physical chattel post-purchase. The contract is explicit in portraying resale as being associated with crime, creating not only a quasi-legal but also morally deterrent effect. The desired outcome suggests that the game company should always have some ongoing right to control the individual *copy* of a game, not only the broader copy*right*. Resultingly the construction of the player suggests they must either indefinitely retain that individual copy or destroy it should they wish to be rid of it. In either case, they are not a consumer in the sense that a consumer owns the thing they purchase; instead, they are the end point of access for that particular copy of a game.

The 'end of ownership' has been noted in many industries,[48] but the emphasis on the corollary of non-resale is perhaps more peculiar to the gaming industry and bears further explanation. And while many other digital formats of copyrightable works will not be able to be resold (technically or legally), this issue is not framed

[47] ibid.
[48] ibid.

in the same way as it is here, closely tied with piracy, fraud and crime. There is no commonsense explanation as to why these two concepts are connected, or why resale is positioned as an obviously harmful activity. Instead, the homogenous characteristic of this discourse must be explained with reference to the broader sociocultural context of the video games industry.

Unlike other industries, the games industry has traditionally placed less blame on piracy – the unlawful acquisition of a game – as an explanatory factor behind declining revenues.[49] Rather, blame has usually been placed on subsequent uses of a game by others, post-legal purchase – including, but not limited to resale. The primary reason for this concern is that game distribution is necessarily straight-to-home: unlike other creative industries, games have historically received no supplementary income through other revenue streams or staggered forms of release. Films, for example, may benefit from initial revenues from a cinematic release, followed by limited rental periods and subsequent home distribution. Effectively, where re-use is concerned, games can be offered on the market shortly after their initial release, with the same quality, for far less than if they were purchased 'first hand' – and with no direct revenues reaching the game company.

Industry rhetoric, and legal action, on this issue began in the early 1980s,[50] following a de facto legal ban of game rentals in Japan, which were first positioned as the culprit of declining profits for the industry.[51] Then chairman of Nintendo America, Howard Lincoln, expressed the reasoning behind the subsequent attempt to ban rentals in America[52] in similarly violent and emotive language as we see influencing present-day discourse:

> [video game rental] is nothing less than commercial rape. I can spend thousands of hours and millions of dollars creating a game. I expect, therefore, to be compensated every time the thing sells … What does the guy who's renting the cartridge contribute?

[49] Again, see the quip by the creator of Minecraft that 'piracy isn't theft': Purchese (n 30). In part, the lack of concern about piracy is because unlawful copying of games has historically been technically difficult to do, with most employing some form of early technical protection measure. See E Erickson. and FP Rodriguez, 'Technological Protection Measures and Digital Preservation: Evidence from Video Games' (Knowledge Rights 21, 2024).

[50] Both the pivotal Nintendo Entertainment System (NES) and Blockbuster were established in 1985 – this may suggest some confluence which would have made game rentals a particularly attractive target for game-based litigation.

[51] *Nintendo of America Inc v Blockbuster LLC*, 746 F2d 112 (1990).

[52] Legislation to ban game and software rentals was proposed to the US Senate in 1989 by an alliance of software companies like Microsoft and the Software Publishers Association, and Nintendo. Games were eventually excluded from the scope of the legislation (The Computer Software Rental Amendments Act 1990) specifically because of the digital rights management protections available in game cartridges which meant that they could not be easily copied (unlike computer software). Litigation nonetheless persisted by video game companies, with Nintendo successfully obtaining a preliminary injunction against Blockbuster for its use of copyrighted material in game packaging and instruction manuals (*Nintendo of America Inc v Blockbuster LLC*, 746 F2d 112 (1990) (settled outside of court)). Rental companies began writing their own bespoke instruction manuals as a result.

> What does he pay in terms of a royalty for the commercial exploitation of copyrighted work? Zip.[53]

While the rental market has declined – witnessed by the significant closure of Blockbuster in 2014 – the industry rhetoric has perhaps naturally extended from rental to resale.[54] Particularly as game lead production costs have become among the most expensive of the entertainment industry, the need to recoup costs through primary sales has accelerated.[55] The language surrounding opposition to game re-use continues to be emotive, with game companies and creators describing the situation as 'disastrous',[56] and something that should be 'actively fought against'.[57] Others express hope that, given resale is relatively limited to physical exchanges, digital distribution will 'stab [the] used game market in the heart'.[58] At the centre of these concerns, the insinuation is that each resale of a game by a player is deprivation of revenue from a hypothetical primary sale: it is 'a critical situation, because *people* are selling multiple times intellectual property' (emphasis added).[59] From this statement, we see again that the construction of the player as a non-reseller within the discourse is *not* a statement of the obvious – that the player does not own the copyright of a game – nor a product of clumsy, over-broad drafting in the contract: it is indeed much more explicitly the intention to retain ongoing control of the individual copy of a game.[60] Readers may also recognise that much of this rhetoric resembles the discourses surrounding piracy and deprivation of revenue in other industries:[61] however, here the direction of the complaint is altered towards a player's *legal* behaviour.

[53] As quoted in D Sheff, *Game Over: Press Start to Continue* (Cyberactive Media Group, 1999) 282.

[54] Some readers may also remember the prominent 'NOT FOR RESALE' tags emblazoned on game cartridges throughout the 1990s, notably on the Sega Genesis *Sonic the Hedgehog*.

[55] Game designer Bleszinksi as quoted in T Cushing, '"Gears of War" Designer: Used Games Must Be Killed So Sustainable Development Can Live' (*Techdirt*, 18 June 2013) https://www.techdirt.com/articles/20130616/20142123500/games-war-designer-cliff-bleszinski-used-games-must-be-killed-order-unsustainable-aaa-development-to-live.shtml.

[56] ISFE, 'French Ruling on Copyright Flies in Face of Established EU Law' (*ISFE*, 20 September 2019) [*archived*] https://web.archive.org/web/20201111192302/https://www.isfe.eu/news/french-ruling-on-copyright-exhaustion-flies-in-face-of-established-eu-law.

[57] Game developer Avellone, as quoted in W Yin-Poole, 'Fallout: New Vegas Dev Hopes Digital Distribution "Stabs Used Game Market in the Heart"' (*Eurogamer*, 13 December 2011) https://www.eurogamer.net/articles/2011-12-13-fallout-new-vegas-dev-hopes-digital-distribution-stabs-used-game-market-in-the-heart.

[58] ibid.

[59] Intat as quoted in M Martin, 'EA: Second-hand Sales Are a "Critical Situation"' (*Gamesindustrybiz*, 28 August 2008) https://www.gamesindustry.biz/articles/ea-second-hand-sales-are-a-critical-situation.

[60] This intention is also expressed through the types of technologies which have subsequently been deployed: see eg a Sony patent which would prevent a disk from playing if it was inserted in any other console than the one it was originally installed on, with the intent to 'prevent … electronic content from being used unlimitedly by successive owners': US Patent Application No 13/611,243, Publication No 2013/0007892 (published 3 January 2013). See also S McIntyre, 'Game Over for First Sale' (2014) 29(1) *Berkeley Technology Law Journal* 1.

[61] Loughlan (n 35).

Another interesting aspect is that, unlike other parts of the discourse, where indie developers differentiate themselves from the mainstream, even indie companies share a hostile sentiment towards resale. Indie companies mimic the dominant, triple A discourse claiming, for example, that the reselling of game keys is more harmful to them than piracy.[62] This perspective, even from indie companies, helps explain the homogeneity of the textual connections of resale to serious crimes such as piracy and fraud. In this industry, reselling is perceived as the real, more serious, or at least equivalent offence:

> In a literal way, when you purchase a game used, you are not a customer … If I am purchasing games in order to reward their creators, and to ensure that more of these ingenious contraptions are produced, I honestly can't figure out how buying a used game was any better than piracy. From the perspective of a developer, they are almost certainly synonymous.[63]

The responsibility to prevent this purported 'disastrous', and 'critical' piratical situation is deflected via the contract onto the player, who is given a moral imperative to act in a way that is desirable both for game companies and, by extension, the broader gaming community. Strategically configuring the player as a non-reseller within the textual and discursive dimension mimics the discourse in the sociocultural dimension and can be used to bolster and support it. In essence, it is not only a complaint that the act of reselling is unethical, but also a *technicality* that resale has never legally been permitted in the first instance through the mechanism of contract, making its breach doubly unethical.

However, there is some limited suggestion that the strategic framing of non-ownership, and its corollary non-resale, is not necessarily a static designation even within the same contractual 'conversation'. Nintendo's Anti-Piracy statement transforms the player from a non-owner into a legitimate *consumer* when faced with the 'battle' against piracy. So while the concept of player as non-owner is highly homogenous, it is not completely static, and can change depending on the business imperative of the game company. In the case of Nintendo, where there is a need to morally deter piratical acts, presenting the player as a welcomed, legitimate customer is perhaps more appealing than the (largely artificial) construct of the player as non-owner and heavily regulated non-reseller.

The malleability of this concept is best illustrated by reference to one of the stronger iterations of the resale restrictions discussed above: Sony's explicit prohibition of resale of *both* physical disks and digital copies of a game. The explicit prohibition of resale of physical disks is striking, not least due to its incompatibility with even the most restrictively interpreted legal rules on resale of copyright works. What is more striking is that Sony, quite famously, have previously and explicitly engaged with the malleability of the resale concept when the framing of the player as an owner of a copy

[62] L Kelion, 'Pirate Our Games, Don't Buy Them from Key Resellers, Say Indies' (*BBC* News, 8 July 2019) https://www.bbc.co.uk/news/technology-48908726.

[63] J Holkins and M Krahulik, 'Words and Their Meanings' (*Penny Arcade*, 25 August 2010).

was strategically beneficial. During the 2012 'console wars' (the competition between video game console manufacturers trying to secure better sales of their new hardware upon release), the initial design of Microsoft's Xbox One caused widespread controversy due to its inclusion of restrictive digital rights management technologies.[64] Amid these controversial design choices, Microsoft gave third-party game companies the ability to determine whether to block or restrict the resale, rental or lending of used games.[65] Physical game disks would only be a means of transferring the initial code onto the hard drive of the Xbox One, and was merely a means of installing a game, but was not necessary to run it. As such, the physical copy of the disk was not tied to ownership of the centrally important game code and, by extension, neither was the possibility to resell or lend the game code without some technical interference with the code, rather than the disk. If a game company elected to allow this code to be technically resold – or indeed borrowed by a friend of the initial player – additional fees would have to be paid upon the repurchase or replay directly to the game publisher. So while resale and lending were technically possible, it could be prohibited, or otherwise heavily restricted subsequent to payment of additional fees. Essentially, Microsoft proposed to make real the textual reality of the transactional relationship envisioned by the contract: games had always been licensed, never sold, and players as licensees were only ever entitled to 'sublicence' where permitted. The new Xbox design merely offered a technological realisation of this fact.

These initial design proposals received resoundingly negative feedback and outcry from game communities,[66] with Microsoft's plans described as 'devastating to consumer rights'.[67] The negative response to Microsoft's controversial plan was subsequently leveraged by its main rival in the console war: Sony, in its promotion of the PlayStation 4. The negative response to the Xbox One was such that Sony's branding strategy for its console became centred around 'not being Microsoft'. Indeed, one of its central claims was that the PlayStation 4 did not include any of the same technical restrictions on resale as the Xbox. During the unveiling of the PlayStation 4 at the gaming exhibition E3, Sony produced a 21-second long promotional 'Used Game Instructional Video',[68] which simply shows someone handing a game to another person in order to 'transfer' it.

In contrast to the controversial and complicated plans of Microsoft, Sony purports that lending and resale of physical disks is not only possible on the PlayStation 4, but easy to do, and encouraged. In mocking Microsoft's plan, Sony

[64] The initial design included an 'always on' microphone system, persistent camera access, and the requirement for a persistent internet connection to permit a server 'check-in' every 24 hours, otherwise access to games would be disabled.

[65] 343 Industries, 'How Games Licensing Works on Xbox One' (*Xbox News*, 6 June 2013) https://news.xbox.com/en-us/2013/06/06/license/.

[66] T Bramwell, 'Microsoft Kills Game Ownership and Expects Us to Smile' (*Eurogamer*, 7 June 2013) https://www.eurogamer.net/articles/2013-06-07-microsoft-kills-game-ownership-and-expects-us-to-smile.

[67] ibid.

[68] PlayStation, 'Official PlayStation Used Game Instructional Video' (*YouTube*, 10 June 2013) https://www.youtube.com/watch?v=kWSIFh8ICaA.

aligned itself as being the more socially responsible company, representing the interests of players, assuring them of their own personal property interest in the physical copy of a game. The outward discourse of mockery creates camaraderie with the player by suggesting that Sony agrees with their disapproval of Microsoft, and indeed that their allegiance is best placed with the PlayStation 4.

Yet, we also see that this veil of outward mockery disguises the reality behind which Sony has operated – it in fact emulates the very system it sought to mock. As discussed above, the first clause of the Sony contract states that 'this product is licensed to you not sold'. And indeed, it is the only contract that makes a separate and conspicuous rule against the resale of physical disks, a critical component of the 'Used Game Instructional Video'. As with the Nintendo example, while the concept of the player as non-owner is very stable in the contract, where there is a strategic business significance (eg to incentivise more primary sales of a console) in presenting the player as a legitimate *consumer* of a copy of a game – its lawful owner – this concept can become malleable. This is a powerful technique, and indeed, even after the forced redesign of the Xbox One saw resale restrictions removed, Sony is still largely viewed as the winner of the previous console war,[69] and was praised for subsequently 'embracing consumer rights'.[70]

IV. Save Point: Chapter Summary

While players have characteristics of consumers in the sense that they buy a product from the game company, the contract emphatically constructs them as non-owners of games, and non-resellers. Of these two aspects, the latter is the most important to a game company, while the former is a functional means of achieving this end. In tandem, they communicate the impression that the player is granted *access* to a game – a temporary, condition-based possession – but not ownership. These constructions further a proprietary ideology towards games – an ideology that insists no game was ever transferred by the company, and so no game is owned to be given away: game property is always retained. In doing so, this constructs a system whereby all primary sales of games are routed through the game company, rather than the reseller, addressing an ongoing (however real or imagined) industry concern. Yet, while highly homogenous, the construction of the player is malleable and can be strategic. Occasionally, the player can be presented as a lawful *consumer* (that is, the owner of a copy of a game) where commercial interests are at stake – in the battle against piracy or the war against a competitor.

[69] 343 Industries, 'Your Feedback Matters – Update on Xbox One' (*Xbox News*, 19 June 2013) https://news.xbox.com/en-us/2013/06/19/update/. Note that – at the time of writing – the initial plans for Nintendo Switch 2's 'game share' are curiously reminiscent of Xbox One's preliminary designs.

[70] T McShea, 'Sony's Triumphant Night' (*Gamespot*, 10 June 2013) https://www.gamespot.com/articles/sonys-triumphant-night/1100-6409715/.

6

Artifice

The idea of the 'creative' player is not new. One of the earliest – and quirkiest – examples is *Castle Smurfenstein*, a Smurf-themed total conversion mod of *Castle Wolfenstein*, which was developed in the early 80s.[1] However, with the emergence and buzz around participatory culture and Web 2.0, player creativity is certainly more *prevalent* than it has ever been. And with the prevalence of UGC, the contract has a new function in mediating the rights-based relationship between the game company and the creative player. In brief, who made and owns what when it is made using material from a game? This chapter shows how the contract draws a fine line between encouraging the kinds of creativity that can extend the value and duration of a game's life cycle, while also constraining the risk of a derivative commercial blockbuster that could divert sales from the game company.

The chapter and theme is titled *Artifice*, suggesting that the contract has elements of fakery, or deception where the creative player is concerned. This is for two reasons: first, because the construction of UGC within the contract, and the justification for its ownership, is highly subjective – a pure fabrication of the text not based in law. The contract sets its own criterion for what is, or is not, UGC, and what can or cannot be owned, quite separately from default copyright rules. Second, the creative player is subject to a differentiated discourse – one that is deceptive because of the language it adopts. Rather than the authoritative and formalistic approach of the mainstream triple A discourse, the creative player is addressed in a manner that is friendly, informal, polite, and encouraging: on the surface, as a *friend* of the game company. However, this outward friendliness disguises the reality of the controversial and often contradictory nature of ongoing control of UGC, presenting it as commonsensical when it is often anything but.

[1] Dead Smurf Software (1996) The first 'official' Castle Smurfenstein Home Page https://www.evl.uic.edu/aej/smurf.html – the mod replaced Nazi antagonists with Smurfs, and changed German voices in to unintelligible Smurf-speak. And indeed, as illustrated in Chapter 1, player creations have even been litigated in relation to the packaging of player-created *Duke Nukem 3D* maps, albeit the player's property interests in this were never explicitly discussed (*Micro Star v FormGen Inc*, 154 F3d 1107 (9th Cir 1998)).

I. Textual Dimension

In the textual dimension of *Artifice*, the player is constructed in a highly contradictory manner. They are defined as a creative subject which is intrinsically linked to originality and uniqueness, but somehow this is not tantamount to authorship in the legal sense, despite sharing similar characteristics (Section A). This contradictory nature, and its (debatable) ability to instil ongoing control by the game company, is disguised by the presence of a differentiated discourse aimed towards the creative player, which is informal, encouraging, and friendly (Section B). As a final facet of creative playership, the textual dimension shows how the player is constructed as a distinctly non-commercial entity, evidencing how UGC is permitted only insofar as it does not disadvantage the game company (Section C).

A. Defining UGC

As shown in Chapter 1, the definition of UGC in copyright – both conceptually and literally – is contentious.[2] Broadly, it refers to a new category of creative *content* which is somehow different from authored works 'proper'. Usually, it is constructed as an 'exception' – a permission to use someone else's work under certain circumstances – rather than an acknowledgement of a copyright in that new content. While we can accept that this term has been widely (imperfectly) accepted into legal, copyright parlance, its translation into the game industry is more fragmented. The analysis that follows shows how contracts define UGC on a sliding scale between an all-encompassing designation for a myriad of derivative creative activities to a rather narrow formulation of player activity. It also – crucially – implies that UGC is something where permission is needed in the first instance.

The majority of contracts define content created by players, either within or outwith the game, as 'User Generated Content',[3] or a variant thereof (eg as an

[2] C Barlow, *Selected Essays on Technology, Creativity, Copyright, and the Future of the Future* (Tachyon Publications, 2008) 1: '[T]he new meaning of the word "content" is plain wrong. In fact, it is intentionally wrong. It's a usage that only arose when the institutions that had fattened on their ability to bottle and distribute the genius of human expression began to realize that their containers were melting away, along with their reason to be in business. They started calling it content at exactly the time it ceased to be.' See also Burgess as quoted in H Jenkins, 'Vernacular Creativity: An Interview with Jean Burgess (Part Two)' (*Confessions of an Aca-Fan*, 8 October 2007) http://henryjenkins.org/blog/2007/10/vernacular_creativity_an_inter_1.html: 'Let me say to begin with that I don't like the term user-generated content very much at all. First we're masses and now we're generators? Users isn't great either, but it's hard to think of a better term for the relationship it describes.'

[3] Valve, 'Steam Subscriber Agreement'; Riot Games, 'Legal Jibber Jabber'; Psyonix, 'End User License Agreement'; Activision, 'Terms of Use'; CD Projekt Red, 'User Agreement and Video Policy'; Bethesda, 'End User Agreement', Zenimax Media, 'Terms of Service', 'Code of Conduct' and 'Video Policy'; Warner Bros, 'End User License Agreement' and 'Terms of Use'; and Bandai Namco, 'Terms of Use' (all Appendix 2).

acronym – UGC).[4] This is in keeping with the legal adoption of the same term and is the most neutral of the variants observed in this dataset. Within this, we might interpret some implication of passivity: 'generated' suggests that a player's content is a by-product of a primary activity, rather than consciously created. By contrast, other contracts which use 'User Created'[5] or 'Player Created'[6] content to describe UGC offer a subtle but distinct acknowledgement of active engagement – of bringing something into existence. Other contracts take a narrower and more restrictive approach to defining UGC. For example, contracts which permit the creation of 'Fan Content'[7] narrow the scope of the player considerably by implicating creativity only as a fan service. This tends to be framed more specifically in relation to works of homage, such as personal fan art or merchandise (eg a t-shirt with a game character),[8] and more subtly a positive endorsement of a game, having its etymological origins in *fanatical* (ie enthusiastic support). The most restrictive approach gives the least autonomy to the creative player by labelling UGC as the more abstract 'Use of the Licensed Items',[9] 'Game Content Usage',[10] or 'Brand and Asset Usage'.[11] Where this framing is used, it limits the player's creativity to a form of risk management for the game's brand (re-use of their content), rather than an acknowledgement of new creative content in its own right.

Regardless of how UGC is defined, the contract tends to use this as an umbrella catch-all term that includes multiple, different kinds of creativity. Commonly, UGC is employed in contracts to include game recordings and streaming on online platforms, game photography, fan art, fan fiction, fan sites and the creation of merchandise (eg hand-crafted items such as t-shirts, prints, buttons etc).[12] Surprisingly, the practice of 'modding' (ie altering the game itself to change its appearance, behaviour etc), while theoretically interesting in copyright scholarship,[13] is mostly *excluded* from permitted UGC activities.[14] Instead, mods tends to be expressly prohibited by broad restrictions on 'modifications' of

[4] EA Games, 'User Agreement'; Rockstar Games, 'Limited Software Warranty and License Agreement' and 'Policy on posting copyrighted Rockstar Games materials'; Sony, 'Software License and Software Usage Terms' (all Appendix 2).

[5] Take2, 'Limited Software Warranty and License Agreement' (Appendix 2).

[6] PUB G, 'End-User License Agreement' and 'Using PLAYERUNKNOWN'S BATTLEGROUNDS in Player-Created Content' (Appendix 2).

[7] Red Barrels, 'Message to YouTubers' (Appendix 2).

[8] Capcom, 'FAQ' (Appendix 2).

[9] Proxima Beta (Tencent), 'Arena of Valor – Terms of Service' (Appendix 2).

[10] Microsoft, 'Game Content Usage Rules' (Appendix 2).

[11] Mojang, 'Brand and Asset Usage Guidelines for Our Games' (Appendix 2).

[12] See A Thomas, 'Merit and Monetisation: A Study of Video Game User-Generated Content Policies' (2023) 12(1) *Internet Policy Review*.

[13] G Lastowka, 'Copyright Law and Video Games: A Brief History of an Interactive Medium' (*SSRN*, 2013) https://papers.ssrn.com/sol3/papers.cfm?abstract_id=2321424.

[14] Only permitted in Superhot Team, 'End User License Agreement'; CD Projekt Red, 'User Agreement'; Mojang, 'End User License Agreement' and 'Brand and Asset Usage Guidelines for Our Games'; and Bethesda, 'Code of Conduct' (all Appendix 2). This is explained further in Thomas (n 12).

a game,[15] and unless explicitly thereafter excused within the contract, remains reserved to the game company. The relative absence of modding may in part be explained by the fact that most games in this dataset include a multiplayer, competitive, online community, where modding can constitute unfair advantage against other players (such as eg an auto-aim mod for first person shooter genres), or are otherwise technically 'untinkerable' where they exist on a remote, cloud-based server.[16] Supporting this suspicion, none of the titles from the eSports dataset, all of which are online and competitive, permit any kind of modding.

Another, notable creative work frequently excluded from the definition of UGC is any use of the original game soundtrack (OST), the bespoke, custom music written for the game, usually by a third-party composer.[17] Where UGC is concerned, contracts treat OSTs as 'not ours to give',[18] or alternatively carefully exclude it from the ambit of, for example, permitted 'video', whilst not explicitly permitting audio.[19] This restriction is fairly consistent at industry level, with even permissive indie creators, such as Toby Fox (who also writes and composes the music for his self-published *Undertale* and *Deltarune*) having separate OST policies that restrict use (usually only to be used in conjunction with gameplay, and not eg as the background music for a product review) and monetisation in game video recordings and streaming.[20] Perhaps most succinctly summarised in CD Projekt Red's fan content policy,[21] 'music licensing is complicated' and the player should be 'careful' about using the OST.[22] The almost *sui generis* status of the OST, and its exclusion from the ambit of UGC, is particularly curious as most contracts will first include a claim to own all 'audio' in the game at the outset, which we would presume *includes* the OST as part of this broad definition. Instead, it seems that where the player's position is concerned, they again become obscurified – the game company can claim ownership, but the extent of this ownership is disguised when applied to the player and their entitlements. As

[15] eg Activision, 'Terms of Use' (Appendix 2): 'you may not … modify … the Product, any updates or any part thereof'.

[16] Bethesda, 'Code of Conduct' (Appendix 2) expressly excludes 'god modding', defined as 'forcing another community member's character into a situation they have not agreed to'.

[17] Notable composers and OSTs from the dataset include Gustavo Santaolalla (Sony, *The Last of Us*), Marcin Przybyłowicz (CD Projekt Red, *The Witcher 3: Wild Hunt*), Toby Fox (*Undertale*, compositions of such complexity as to only be playable through using a computer).

[18] Microsoft, 'Game Content Usage Rules' (Appendix 2).

[19] eg CD Projekt Red, 'Video Policy' (Appendix 2).

[20] See Studio MDHR, 'Message to YouTubers' (Appendix 2), which includes separate guidance for 'Use of the Cuphead Soundtrack'. Toby Fox, despite composing their own music for use in *Undertale* and *Deltarune*, does not permit OST usage outwith strict guidelines maintained by Materia Music Publishing (Materia Music Publishing, 'YouTube FAQ' https://materiamusicpub.com/youtube-faq/).

[21] In the wake of criticisms following the release of its latest title, *Cyberpunk 2077*, CD Projekt Red created an automated feature to 'disable copyrighted music' when creating UGC (see CD Projekt Red, 'Dedicated Cyberpunk 2077 Feature for Content Creators: "Disable Copyrighted Music"' (*Cyberpunk 2077*, 23 November 2020) https://www.cyberpunk.net/en/news/36734/dedicated-cyberpunk-2077-feature-for-content-creators-disable-copyrighted-music).

[22] CD Projekt Red, 'Fan Content Guideline' (Appendix 2).

such, the construction of the player as 'creative' is certainly not unlimited – it is at the discretion of the game company's terms.

Contracts employ one further consistent definition of UGC – that it has to be *original and creative work*. The contract obliges players to include 'your creative input and commentary',[23] 'your own unique content',[24] 'your own, original contribution to the community',[25] or 'your creative spin on our owned content'.[26] Here, it is worthwhile pausing to acknowledge that some of these concepts – particularly 'originality' – have specific, technical meanings in copyright law. The requirement to show originality, usually defined as a creative contribution (again echoed in the UGC requirements above), is one of the prerequisites for acknowledging 'authorship' and a copyright interest in a work.[27] However, game companies treat the requirement for 'originality', 'authorship' and 'copyright' quite distinctly, suggesting that there is either no intention to engage with the legal definitions of these concepts, or that they are being applied flexibly. Riot Games, for example, demands 'original' content from its creative players, but simultaneously refuses to acknowledge any 'works of authorship' based on the game.[28] The intention here appears to be to construct a new creative *player*, and specifically *not* an author in the sense of being a person who has a new copyright interest in the UGC – even though the law might say otherwise.

The obligation to make original UGC also translates to the natural corollary of hostility towards light-touch adaptations of an existing work, whether the proprietary content of the game company, or that of another player. UGC should not 'just rip off or add light commentary to existing content' or 'cannibalise' the content of others.[29] Instead, the purpose of the contract is to '[h]elp foster community and creative expression. Simply duplicating content does neither. You're better than that'.[30] This suggests that the original and creative player is apparently a more legitimate creator ('better') than those who merely 'copy' the work of others, but all are nevertheless captured within the same scope of 'UGC'.

Another key characteristic of UGC definition in the contract is that it is subject to a degree of *ongoing control* by the game company. There is an omnipresent reminder throughout the UGC policies that any UGC is at the behest of, and reliant on the game company's copyright. In this sense, the company's interest in their 'original' copyrighted work does not end where the player's potentially begins, but rather extends. One contract, broadly put ('to be safe'), 'if you include content in your work which can be *interpreted as representative* of Game Content, you're

[23] Nintendo, 'Game Content Guidelines' (Appendix 2).

[24] Mojang, 'Brand and Asset Usage Guidelines for Our Games' (Appendix 2).

[25] Riot Games, 'Legal Jibber Jabber' (Appendix 2).

[26] Ubisoft, 'Video Policy' (Appendix 2).

[27] National states finding commonality for the authorship requirement in the obligations of the Berne Convention.

[28] Riot Games, 'Legal Jibber Jabber' (Appendix 2).

[29] ibid.

[30] Ubisoft, 'Video Policy' (Appendix 2).

using Company-owned IP' (emphasis added).[31] Indeed, the majority of contracts (17) observed within the dataset contain an automatic licence grant *from* the player in favour of the company, in respect of any content that the player generates within the game (eg avatars, player-made maps or items etc) or as derived from the game (eg fan art, video walkthroughs/reviews etc).[32] This means that if a player does generate any copyright interests in their UGC – even though the contract also says this is not possible (not recognising 'works of authorship') – then the game company will benefit from rights to use it. This effectively extends the initial copyright interest in the game itself over any player content created through or within the game. The rights claimed by this licence are often extensive, including broad permissions to 'use' the UGC, to be able to transfer or sub-license that right (usually anywhere in the world), for no compensation, and on an irrevocable or perpetual basis (ie forever). This licence grant is usually expressed by a string of lexically dense and all-encompassing legalese:

> You grant us, from the time of uploading or transmission of Your Content, a worldwide, perpetual, irrevocable, sublicenseable, transferable, assignable, non-exclusive and royalty-free right and license to use, reproduce, distribute, adapt, modify, translate, create derivative works of, publicly perform, publicly display, digitally perform, make, have made, sell, offer for sale and import Your Content, including, all copyrights, trademarks, trade secrets, patents, industrial rights and all other intellectual and proprietary rights related thereto, in any media now known or hereafter developed, for any purpose whatsoever, commercial or otherwise, including, giving Your Content to others, without any compensation to you.[33]

When claiming this entitlement, the contract returns to the same format of the legal genre of discourse which characterises the typical, triple A contract (most apparent in '*Authority*' – see Chapter 4 above). As a single sentence, it is lengthy (98 words long), with dense, technical, legal jargon ('irrevocable', 'non-exclusive') and tropes ('thereto'). The claim is also expressed as a direct command to the player ('*You* grant us'), who is obliged to act. The seriousness of the tone does indeed match the seriousness of the consequence – if the player is an author of a copyright work (the UGC), then they are being asked to give extensive rights to use this without being able to control how it is used, or to ask for compensation from it. And much as with earlier examples of the legal genre in player contracts, the purpose of constructing the text in this way is to claim a particular type of power by invoking the 'magical' precedent of law, and to subsequently exercise that power over another object: here, the player. Because UGC has some causal

[31] PUBG, 'Content Creation Guideline' (Appendix 2).

[32] Of the remainder, two included an attempted assignation of the player's copyright ('attempted' because for assignations to be effective, they typically require a specific form), and of the companies that did not include a licence clause almost half (five) outright prohibited the creation of UGC in the first instance (which would suggest that – if it is prima facie prohibited – there would be no anticipation that it could subsequently be licensed back to the company).

[33] Riot Games, 'Terms of Service' (Appendix 2).

relationship with the game, which is an object of legal property, then the text infers a justification for the ongoing regulation of that UGC.[34]

Pausing for a moment to ponder the *intent* behind this dense and wide-reaching list of licensed permissions, it is worth noting an ongoing debate as to whether these clauses are simply necessary, invisible parts of the UGC sharing process, or are more sinister in nature. Indeed, any copyrights held by the player would be so extensive that they would technically cover the small, transient acts of reproduction which would prevent UGC from being hosted on a game server without their permission. If we presume that this is something the player would like to consent to when they access and make UGC – to share it with other players – then the automatic licence becomes commonsensical.[35] If, on the other hand, the very broad encompassing nature of this licence grant covers more expansive activities – eg using a player's content in for-profit advertising or promotional material created by another company – then we may rightly be more sceptical of the intent behind it. For now, in respect of the textual dimension, it is sufficient to acknowledge that while the player is obligated to make an original creation which is not 'authored', it is predicated on a degree of ongoing *control* of the 'copyright' by the company through an automatic licence grant. It is, indeed, a rather obvious contradiction.

Notably, the same licence grant is not usually reciprocated to the player, and rarely will they be granted an explicit licence to *create* the same UGC that is being gifted back to the game company (found only once in this dataset).[36] Instead, it is common that any permissions to create UGC are bundled into a much less formal 'statement of acquiescence' – an implied promise by the game company that this is allowed. Alternatively, some contracts, such as that of Sony, acknowledge the *possibility* for UGC's existence, in the sense that they include an automatic licence grant from the player in favour of the company, but never otherwise give the player permission to make the UGC in itself.[37] The result is that the player technically has no permission to make UGC, but in any case, if they do, Sony (or equivalent) owns it.

It is tempting to explore at this point the contract's contradictory construction of the creative player from a copyright perspective. The player is both someone who is explicitly granted only a use-based permission to use the company's content, but who is also a unique creator in their own right, who can express originality

[34] As a recent example, in *Resident Evil Village* any screen captures of game footage taken with in-built sharing tools are automatically accompanied by a Capcom watermark and caption. Capcom is notably one of the few games in this dataset which do not have any UGC policy, presumably implying it is not permitted in any way.

[35] See, for example, contrasting opinions in A Perzanowski and J Schultz, *The End of Ownership: Personal Property in the Digital Economy* (MIT Press, 2016) and C Tan, *Regulating Content on Social Media: Copyright, Terms of Service and Technological Features* (UCL Press, 2018).

[36] Riot Games, 'Legal Jibber Jabber' (Appendix 2).

[37] Sony, 'Software License' and 'Software Usage Terms'; Capcom, 'End User License Agreement'; Konami, 'Terms of Use: Metal Gear Solid V: The Phantom Pain'; Proxima Beta (Tencent), 'Arena of Valor – Terms of Service'; Activision, 'Terms of Use'; Wargaming, 'End User Licence Agreement' and 'Game Rules'; Cygames, 'Service Agreement'; Warner Bros, 'End User License Agreement' and 'Terms of Use'; and Bandai Namco, 'Terms of Use' (all Appendix 2).

through repurposing of that content. For the moment, it is worth noting that the licence does not acknowledge this contradictory nature but rather purports that these characteristics can co-exist within the ambit of 'player': whether passive or active, the contract 'encourage[s] everyone'[38] to create.

B. Differentiated Discourse Towards the Creative Player

Supplementary agreements about UGC, particularly video policies and fan art policies, adopt a distinct textual approach when compared against the dominant discourse of the triple A contract. Whereas the triple A contract is characterised by its formality, authoritative tone and complexity, UGC-specific agreements adopt informal, friendly, and less complex language. Colloquialisms are used, with simpler, shorter sentences and indicators of empathy and emotion – rather oppositional to a 'legal', serious document. The opening statements of UGC policies are particularly emotive and informal in encouraging players to be creative:

> We love our players and the awesome stuff they create.[39]
>
> We are humbled every day by your loyalty and passion for Nintendo's games, characters and worlds, and respect that you want to be able to express yourself creatively by sharing your own original videos and images using content from our games.[40]
>
> Everyone at Epic Games is extremely honored by the interest shown by our fans in our games and our company, and we think it's cool that you want to create artwork, websites, and other stuff based on our intellectual property.[41]
>
> We consider ourselves extremely fortunate to have fans actively engaging and creating with our game content.[42]
>
> You wow us. You make us laugh. You inspire our fans, the game community, the Internet, and of course, the entire company.[43]
>
> We know that people like you – gamers, fans, individuals, and enthusiasts – love our games and sometimes want to use things like gameplay footage, screenshots, music, and other elements of our games ('Game Content') to make things like machinima, videos, and other cool things (your 'Item(s)'). We'd like to make that easier to do for fans of our games.[44]

These examples show stark textual differentiations from the typically authoritative voice of the contract by using emotive language ('love', 'extremely honored') and appraisal lexis ('extremely') which contribute to its informal and friendly tone. Colloquialisms transform the formal 'protected content' into 'things' and

[38] CD Projekt Red, 'Video Policy' (Appendix 2).
[39] Riot Games, 'Legal Jibber Jabbber' (Appendix 2).
[40] Nintendo, 'Game Content Guidelines' (Appendix 2).
[41] Epic Games, 'Fan Content Policy' (Appendix 2).
[42] Ubisoft, 'Video Policy' (Appendix 2).
[43] PUBG, 'Content Creation Guideline' (Appendix 2).
[44] Microsoft, 'Game Content Usage Rules' (Appendix 2).

'stuff' – more relatable concepts. Elsewhere, forms of 'internet-speak' are adopted, such as 'TL;DR' (too long; didn't read)[45] as a way of condensing information into friendlier, shorter expressions, or 'defo' to indicate permission (internet shorthand for definitely).[46] This personable and more informal approach is also mirrored at the end of the UGC policy, which thanks the player for their contributions,[47] encourages them to 'create, have fun and be awesome'[48] and even includes a personal signature from the game creator.[49] The combined effect of this textual differentiation lessens the social distance between the game company and player through the 'conversationalisation' of the discourse.[50] Indeed, some UGC policies are framed as questions and responses, which gives the impression of immediacy and mimicking of a conversation with the company, rather than a contract.[51] The creative player is framed not as a mere recipient of the discourse, but an active and valued participant in the conversation.

This lessening of social distance between the player and the company is also achieved by disavowing responsibility for any restrictions on the creation of UGC and placing this instead on 'lawyers'.[52] Riot Games makes for an interesting example of this through its use of hypermediacy. Its UGC policy (entitled 'Legal Jibber Jabber') gives permission for the player to create works based on the game 'by formal decree of the Demacian High court (our legal team)' (Demacia being a kingdom within the world of *League of Legends*). The UGC policy ends by advising that the player simply '[doesn't] upset Corporate Mundo'[53] (a skin in *League of Legends*, presenting a character as a business manager who wields his suitcase in battle). A somewhat meta representation of a suited, gold watch wearing, Corporate Mundo accompanies the UGC policy, with the character offering the player the very contract they are presently reading. Including this picture within the UGC policy is further evidence of a differentiated discourse, accompanying an otherwise formalistic, black and white legal document with colourful, quirky art.[54]

By linking the UGC policy to the whims of Corporate Mundo, rather than the game company, Riot Games disavows responsibility for restrictions on UGC in two ways. First, this framing lessens the seriousness of the contract by connecting it to a character within the game, framing the UGC policy as a broader paratext of the game itself. Corporate Mundo is a cartoonish exaggeration or mockery of a profit-driven business manager, which the company again disassociates

[45] Riot Games, 'Legal Jibber Jabbber' (Appendix 2).
[46] ibid.
[47] Microsoft, 'Game Content Usage Rules' (Appendix 2).
[48] CD Projekt Red, 'Video Policy' (Appendix 2).
[49] Red Barrels, 'Message to YouTubers' (Appendix 2).
[50] P Baker and S Ellege, *Key Terms in Discourse Analysis* (Continuum, 2011) 22.
[51] Observed in FAQ-style policies in Nintendo, 'Game Content Guidelines', Capcom, 'FAQ' and Riot Games, 'Legal Jibber Jabber' (all Appendix 2).
[52] Microsoft, 'Game Content Usage' (Appendix 2).
[53] Riot Games, 'Legal Jibber Jabber' (Appendix 2).
[54] Note that there is only one other example where a policy is accompanied with pictures/art: Sony, 'Software Usage Terms' (Appendix 2).

from – Mundo is offering the terms, not Riot Games.[55] Second, the textual framing disavows responsibility for UGC regulation by creating an 'us and them' narrative. The UGC policy presents the *game company* as being happy with the player creating works in principle – but 'corporate', a supposed separate entity, is not. Similar devices in other UGC policies scapegoat lawyers (or per Wizards of the Coast, the 'law mages')[56] as the entity responsible for enforcing these restrictions:

> This means that if you add to the game universe or expand on the story told in the game with 'lost chapters' or back story or anything like that, distribution of your story or idea may appear in a future game without any compensation to you. (Sorry, but our lawyers tell us we need to do this in order to avoid frivolous lawsuits getting in the way of making more great games.)[57]

Framing the text in this way suggests that the company is more closely aligned with the interests of the player than the antithetical corporate or lawyers. Apologising for these restrictions ('sorry') suggests hesitancy and regret, and also a call for empathy from the player; it's the *lawyers* that are obliging these restrictions and, but for their influence, the company would be acting differently. The attempt to explain or justify these restrictions is also in contrast to the formal, authoritative mainstream contract, which usually does not ever necessitate, nor attempt to justify itself. Instead, by offering explanation, the company attempts to build mutual understanding and camaraderie with the player.

However, the player is, more subtly perhaps, also positioned here as a potential *threat* by merit of their creativity. In the example above, the company suggests that UGC restrictions are necessary in order to avoid 'frivolous lawsuits.' By framing any lawsuit in respect of UGC as 'frivolous', the UGC policy recognises that the player may be entitled to take legal action against them, but suggests this is unworthy of the time or cost of pursuing. This may be doubly emphasised as being an illegitimate pursuit, both in terms of legalities and community interests:

> We want fans to create and share cool things with each other, and we want to remove barriers to sharing. If we spotlight a fan Project or make something that resembles what a fan might have made, we don't want to be sued, so you give us permission to spotlight or share your Project with the world.[58]

Automatic licence grants to share players' works are framed as *fair* because 'we don't want to be sued' (legal threat) but also because any 'barrier[s] to sharing' are a threat to the larger community. This double-framing of illegitimacy immediately problematises any suggestion of enforcement measures by the player, as a creator of that content. This is so even where we may be rightly sceptical as to whether it is fair, or indeed legal, to oblige that a player's copyrighted UGC 'works' should be

[55] Forming part of the universe of *Dungeons and Dragons*, Wizards of the Coast also suggests that enforcement measures will be taken by the 'Demogorgon' (see Wizards of the Coast, 'Fan Content Policy' (Appendix 2)).
[56] ibid.
[57] Microsoft, 'Game Content Usage' (Appendix 2).
[58] Riot Games, 'Legal Jibber Jabber' (Appendix 2).

used without constraint or compensation. Instead, the ongoing control of player creativity is framed as necessary for the company, which is doubly bolstered by an underlying moral deterrent to the player if they challenge these restrictions.

As a side note, while many of these characteristics of informality, friendliness, and lessening of social distance, resemble the differentiated indie discourse noted in '*Authority*', here, there is not an indie effect as such. This is because most indie companies use a more informal register and style as a default throughout their legal documentation. But for companies that otherwise adopt a formalistic style in their contract, particularly triple A companies, this differentiated approach in UGC policies is very stark indeed.[59] The strategic choice to engage with this language is often an attempt to build rapport and lessen social distance between the company and the player by indicating solidarity and a common interest.[60] Certainly, the stance is less authoritative, and suggests the contract is presenting the interests of the company and player as more closely aligned where UGC is concerned. The lawyers are, by contrast, the common enemy.

There are only two, notable exceptions from this differentiated, friendly, and informal discourse. First, and as briefly noted in Section I.A above, larger companies, such as Warner Bros, Sony, and Proxima Beta (subsidiary of Tencent),[61] do not have separate detailed UGC policies, and instead only address UGC insofar as they include an automatic licence grant from the player to the company in respect of their content. In doing so, the company technically does not *add* any restrictions on UGC in the same way more complex agreements negotiate eg commerciality (detailed in Section I.C above), though neither does it explicitly permit its creation. This approach acknowledges creative use as a *possibility*, but does not negotiate it, nor engage in a friendly conversation with the player about it.

The second notable exception relates to Japanese companies, which consistently take a restrictive view of UGC.[62] At the time of the original data collection, two of those companies prohibited *any* UGC, with the remaining three permitting only very limited use of game content (typically for streaming or Let's Plays). Capcom, for example, has only limited policies on the creation of fan sites and the use of characters, and 'one-off' activities on the creation of works for 'school projects or a personal T-shirt'.[63] Japanese contracts are notable in the textual dimension for maintaining a higher degree of rigid formality throughout their documentation than other comparable contracts (eg Cygames addressing the player in

[59] Notably: Epic Games, Microsoft, Nintendo, Riot Games, Rockstar Games, Ubisoft, and Wizards of the Coast (all documents detailed in Appendix 2).

[60] Baker and Ellege (n 50) 22.

[61] Sony, 'Software License' and 'Software Usage Terms'; Capcom, 'End User License Agreement'; Konami, 'Terms of Use: Metal Gear Solid V: The Phantom Pain'; Proxima Beta (Tencent), 'Arena of Valor – Terms of Service'; Activision, 'Terms of Use'; Wargaming, 'End User Licence Agreement' and 'Game Rules'; Cygames, 'Service Agreement'; Warner Bros, 'End User License Agreement' and 'Terms of Use'; and Bandai Namco, 'Terms of Use' (all Appendix 2).

[62] These are: Cygames, Nintendo, Bandai Namco, Capcom, and Konami.

[63] Capcom, 'FAQ' (Appendix 2); note a substantial change in 2021 with the introduction of a new video policy.

the third person as – defined term – 'Customer').[64] Similarly to the approach of larger companies, UGC is only acknowledged implicitly as a derivative asset of the primary, game company-owned materials. Indeed, at the date of the initial research, both Bandai Namco and Konami obliged an exclusive *assignment* of UGC, which was absorbed into the broader definition of 'Content', alongside the proprietary materials of the company.[65] This goes beyond the (more typical, and albeit very extensive) purpose-limited licence to instead claim a wholesale *ownership* of UGC. The legal implications here are very different if the player creates a property which is automatically, wholesale transferred to a game company. This very restrictive attitude towards UGC is mirrored in the authoritative tone of the text, which achieves formality through its brevity. There is no engagement in conversation: the creative player is acknowledged but ultimately absorbed within the proprietary ideology of the company.

C. Player as Non-Commercial

As noted in Chapter 1, the creative player as an *amateur* – that is, someone who is making something for the love of the game, but not the promise of remuneration – is often assumed in copyright. This underlying assumption weaves its way into the discourse of the contract through the widespread prohibition of commercial uses of UGC. Every contract surveyed[66] restricts the use and dissemination of UGC to non-commercial purposes, forming the 'fundamental rule'[67] for player creativity (which must be '[o]ne word: F-R-E-E').[68] 'Non-commercial' is doubly-constructed in the contract as either meaning 'free for others' (eg not behind a paywall, such as Patreon), or a prohibition on the UGC itself generating revenue for the player. The Blizzard contract is an example that blends both:

> For clarity, please note that as long as the website that hosts your Production provides a free method to allow viewers to see the Production, Blizzard Entertainment will not object to your Production being hosted on that site, regardless of the site's 'for pay' premium service plans.[69]
>
> … you may not license a Production you have created to another company for a fee, or for any other form of compensation, without specific written permission from Blizzard Entertainment to do so.[70]

[64] Cygames, 'End User License Agreement' (Appendix 2).

[65] Bandai Namco, 'Terms of Use' and Konami, 'Terms of Use: Metal Gear Solid V: The Phantom Pain' (both Appendix 2). This has been retracted upon consulting the updated materials – but Krafton and Ubisoft now include attempted assignations in their latest documentation.

[66] Arguably, Mojang permits limited commercial activities as a 'carve out' of its broader prohibition on commercialisation, including an allowance to make merchandise up to a certain monetary amount: see Mojang, 'Minecraft End User License Agreement' (Appendix 2).

[67] Blizzard, 'Video Policy' (Appendix 2).

[68] Wizards of the Coast, 'Fan Content Policy' (Appendix 2).

[69] Blizzard, 'Video Policy' (Appendix 2).

[70] ibid.

The non-commercial restriction is often justified by reference to reciprocity in free-to-play models ('Our games are free-to-play, and so must be the Video Content!'),[71] or by invoking the community's interest in accessing content for free: '[y]our Video Content must be free to the public to enjoy, forever';[72] or '[w]e support players who use our intellectual property … to create free fan projects for the benefit of the community'.[73] This framing emphasises that conformity to this restriction is a moral imperative, rather than being driven by any commercial interest on the game company's behalf. It speaks of ideas of openness, freedom, and community harmony, which are central to this invocation. However, this moral imperative is not reciprocated by the company, as evidenced by a closer reading of the automatic licence grant from the player:

> … you agree that we may use, copy, modify, distribute, and make derivative works of your Project in any form, on a royalty-free, non-exclusive, irrevocable, transferable, sub-licensable, worldwide basis, for any purpose and without having to credit you, pay you anything, or obtain your approval.[74]

This automatic licence offers the possibility of a commercial interest in the player's content, albeit just not for the player themselves – it can be sold indefinitely, or used in commercial materials for the game company. This seems to be in disconnect from the claim, made from the same document, that 'free fan projects [are] for the benefit of the *community*' – which also includes, presumably, the player themselves.[75] In sum, the non-commercial condition of UGC is limited only in application to the player themselves, but not the company.

Commerciality is often presented as having a self-evident meaning in the contract ('Free means FREE'),[76] but there is some evidence that the 'fundamental rule' of non-commerciality is more stratified than its plain, everyday meaning, or indeed the definition given in copyright law. At its plain, everyday meaning, we might expect this to both restrict activities relating to commerce (eg that a company should emblazon its website with game UGC) or profit-making of any kind. While there is no static definition of commerciality in copyright law, the definition given by Creative Commons indicates a similarity to the plain meaning, that it is 'in any manner that is primarily intended for or directed toward commercial advantage or private monetary compensation'.[77] The exclusion of commerce and commercial advantage is perhaps fairly self-evident, given that contracts are usually limited to a *personal*, private right to enjoy the game, which would seemingly exclude non-natural persons like other companies. This, it seems, is just confirmation of the same. However, the profit-making dimension of commerciality is more complex.

[71] Hi-Rez, 'Policy for Streaming Videos and VODS' (Appendix 2).
[72] ibid.
[73] Riot Games, 'Legal Jibber Jabber' (Appendix 2).
[74] Riot Games, 'Terms of Use' (Appendix 2).
[75] Riot Games, 'Legal Jibber Jabber' (Appendix 2) (emphasis added).
[76] Wizards of the Coast, 'Fan Content Policy' (Appendix 2).
[77] 'Defining "Noncommercial": A Study of How the Online Population Understands "Noncommercial Use"' (Creative Commons, 2009) 11.

In contrast to both the plain meaning and copyright definition, in the contract, 'non-commercial' differentiates between profit-making commercialisation and *monetisation*.[78] Often, the rules against commerciality are waived in respect of UGC which generates passive ad revenue, or is available on a partner program for videos on online platforms such as YouTube or Twitch:

> The only exceptions to this rule are if you participate in partner programs with YouTube, Justin.tv, Blip.tv, Own3d.tv, or Ustream.tv (the 'Production Websites') whereby a Production Website may pay you for views of a Production if you are accepted into their partner program.[79]
>
> Am I allowed to have advertisements in my Video Content? … Yes, but only if you are doing so as part of an official partner program operated by YouTube, Twitch, or other similar online video publication platform.[80]

In copyright law, these types of monetisation would be within the ambit of commerciality, meaning the use of game content by players could be potentially constrained for these purposes.[81] But monetisation through mechanisms such as passive ad revenue is conceptualised very differently within the contract – it is much broader and surprisingly generous. This contradictory nature is recognised in the UGC policy by Wizards of the Coast:

> Q: You said I can't license my content to third parties for money. Aren't partner programs with YouTube or Twitch technically licenses that I earn money on? Is this allowed?
>
> A: … who let the rules lawyers into the FAQ?[82]

Here we see a return to a gaming idiom repeated throughout this research – the 'rules lawyer'. Here, the contract refers to a person who frustrates the play of a game by following the letter, rather than the spirit of the rules that regulate it. The company suggests that the player is a 'rules lawyer' for noticing the inherent contradiction between preventing commerciality while condoning money-making activities, like passive ad revenue. The company suggests that the spirit of player creativity is not that the player is prevented from making money per se, but rather this cannot be actively solicited: it must be passively generated where any monetary value only comes through the use of that content by others.

As a final note on this aspect, the non-commercial construction of the player is so consistent that it even applies to eSports UGC, which may be more closely tied with a professional player, dependent on exploitation of the game for income. eSports are only explicitly permitted (with conditions, such as limits on prize money offered) by six companies in the dataset, and in almost all cases this is dealt

[78] Thomas (n 12).
[79] Blizzard, 'Video Policy' (Appendix 2).
[80] Hi-Rez, 'Policy for Streaming Videos and VODS' (Appendix 2).
[81] While non-commercial use is not a requirement for limitations and exceptions under the three-step test outlined in the Berne Convention, it can be taken into account when determining/interpreting the second and third steps.
[82] Wizards of the Coast, 'Fan Content Policy' (Appendix 2).

with in a supplementary document which is separate from the UGC policy or primary contract.[83] This suggests that the eSports player is treated with exceptionalism, existing outwith the space of creative content more generally.

Surmising, much like the homogeneous construction of the player as a non-reseller (explored in '*Access*', see Chapter 5 above), non-commerciality is also a highly consistent player characteristic where UGC is concerned. The non-commerciality condition also complements other facets of the player, such as only using a game solely for personal play or enjoyment – it is an inherently *private* grant. In combination, these characteristics make explicit the underlying assumption that the player is constructed as an *amateur*, making UGC only for pleasure in their personal life, and only entitled to derive passive monetary value from their creations without actively soliciting it.

II. Discursive Dimension

Whereas discourses in the '*Authority*' and '*Access*' themes are packaged within a click-wrap document, discourses on UGC are produced and distributed in more disparate ways, and may be scattered across multiple mediums that exist outside of the contract itself. Typically, only the automatic UGC licence grant given by the player in favour of the company is incorporated into a short clause within the contract itself.[84] This is treated as part of the operation or initial conclusion of the contractual relationship but often does not constitute the company's entire policy on UGC.

Instead, in many cases, guidelines on the exploitation of UGC are in a separate document ancillary to the contract. The manner of access is similar, in that they exist within the same virtual space as the contract and tend to be accessible through the same section of the institutional webpage. The contract may refer to this policy but does not necessarily incorporate it in the same way as it does eg a privacy policy, which are usually a necessary pre-condition of accepting the contract itself. As a result, there is some doubt as to whether UGC policies are legally binding in the contractual relationship, or rather are non-binding statements of acquiescence that merely *accompany* the main contractual relationship – a kind of promise that these activities will be allowed. Notably, for such agreements, no click-wrap functionality is included, for which two plausible explanations exist. The first possibility is that assent to the UGC policy, if incorporated by reference through the contract, is also concluded upon agreeing to the primary document. This does not appear to be the case for the majority of contracts surveyed. Alternatively, if the UGC

[83] Namely, Valve, Riot Games, Blizzard, Krafton, Nintendo and EA. Only Valve's rules on eSports tournaments are incorporated within its broader guidelines.

[84] See eg Activision, Bethesda Epic Games, Hi-Rez, PUB G, Riot Games, Rockstar Games, Sony, Ubisoft and Wizards of the Coast (all Appendix 2).

policy is considered a non-legally binding promise and not an agreement, no such demonstration of assent would be required.

Discourses on UGC are also scattered through other, more informal mediums, including social media and other online social spaces. For example, while having no formal UGC policy included within its contract or institutional homepage, Superhot Team confirms in a comment through its Kickstarter page that the creation and monetisation of all video content of its game is permissible: 'sure, anyone can record/edit/monetize any videos of Superhot'.[85] The brevity of the comment deals with the question in an offhand matter. With characteristics of the same conversationalisation as other UGC policies, this communication is formed through question and response, and a more proximate means of communicating directly with the player. This is also a rare example of the player being an active participant in shaping the direction of their construction (but for the question being asked, this activity may never have been permitted).

Toby Fox, creator of indie titles *Undertale* and *Deltarune*, also makes for an interesting study of the distribution of UGC discourse. Fox has previously responded directly to player queries through his Twitter (X) account to communicate his own preferences as to how game content should be used:

> if you see someone selling unofficial undertale merch at a con, contact convention staff about it. dont make me fly there and yell at them [sic]
>
> Q: can i sell undertale stuff at an anime con
>
> A: 1. No
>
> 2. UNDERTALES NOT EVEN AN ANIME

Evidenced here are many of the same textual approaches as analysed in the differentiated textual discourse towards the creative player, including brevity and informality, but on this occasion through a different medium. There is a restriction ('if you see someone selling unofficial undertale merch at a con, contact convention staff about it') but this is caged by a friendlier or humorous 'enforcement' mechanism ('dont make me fly there and yell at them'). The discourse format also changes at the textual dimension as appropriate for the genre of discourse expected on social media. It is succinct, informal and humorous, without formal grammar (eg lowercase 'i', no apostrophe in 'dont' or 'undertales'). It satirises more formal, enumerated forms of restrictions (beginning the list alphabetically, then changing to numerically). Again, the player becomes closer in proximity to the company (or in this case, the individual) through their participation in the UGC conversation and sharing of the same language: internet-speak. Fox would later use his Tumblr account to inform players of his 'Changing Policy on Fan Merch'.[86] This static page

[85] Superhot Team, 'Superhot' (*Kickstarter*, 2015) https://www.kickstarter.com/projects/375798653/superhot.

[86] Official Undertale Blog, 'Changing Policy on Fan Merch' (*Tumblr*, 21 February 2016) https://undertale.tumblr.com/post/139726155020/changing-policy-on-fan-merch.

is a more consolidated version of the restrictions, and is less ephemeral than X, but still exists on a separate and less official space than comparative policies. The *Undertale/Deltarune* website also encourages players to contact Fox directly via email if they have a query about using game content for a 'class project, performance etc' rather than offering a generalised policy.[87] Again, the possibility of a conversation is invited.

This is a responsive approach, indicative of a more intimate company-player relationship where the policy is being treated as a conversation, rather than as a static, unilateral document. A more functional possibility is that this is reflective of the fact that indie games may be made by smaller companies (or in the case of Toby Fox above, an individual person), who can communicate their wishes more directly and responsively than those made in a larger, corporate structure.[88] In such cases, responsive mediums like social media are a more adaptable approach than the formalisation of a static policy. The lessening of the social distance between the company and player is therefore both functional *and* ideological. The choice to use this discursive medium encourages direct contact with the company, which is both pragmatic and responsive for the indie company, as well as a rejection of the formalised, static policies more typical of the triple A publisher (in line with the indie countercultural ideology explored in '*Authority*', see Chapter 4).

With so many different mediums used to communicate discourse in UGC, it is too disparate to quantify meaningfully. However, with observations limited to this particular dataset, this difference in discursive approach may offer a limited explanation of the differentiated discourse in the textual dimension – ie it may explain why the language is 'friendlier'. To the extent that different distribution methods necessarily imply different textual approaches, such as social media, there may be some justification for adopting a style or register of writing which is more informal, friendly, or humorous appropriate to that medium. What is more puzzling is where this friendly and informal approach exists alongside, and in close approximation to, a formal and authoritative contract.[89] Where the otherwise formal and authoritative discourse differentiates in its style and register towards the creative player *specifically*, it implicitly acknowledges that they are not as weak as their more passive counterparts. They are not being commanded, but encouraged and welcomed. Something has changed where the creative player is concerned: as the following section will explore, perhaps they are viewed as more powerful, essentially as a co-creator, extending the value of the game past its normal life cycle. As such, speaking to one's co-creator encourages the kind of conversationalisation observed in these contracts, as the company requires their support, collaboration, and good will.

[87] T Fox, 'FAQ' (*Deltarune*, date unknown) https://www.deltarune.com/help/.

[88] A notable exception being Capcom, which encourages direct email (Capcom, 'FAQ' (Appendix 2)).

[89] Notably: Epic Games, Microsoft, Nintendo, Riot Games, Rockstar Games, Ubisoft and Wizards of the Coast (all documents detailed in Appendix 2).

III. Sociocultural Dimension

Discourses surrounding the creative player are very different in their textual and discursive approach than the mainstream discourse. In the context of the otherwise formal and authoritative quasi-legal relationship envisioned by the contract, UGC policies tend towards a friendlier, humorous, polite, and encouraging discourse. The effect of this differentiated approach is to reduce social distance between the company and the player and to develop a rapport. Heavy-handed uses of power are less obvious here than in '*Authority*' and '*Access*' (see Chapters 4 and 5, respectively), with a change in register and style that indicates a less powerful stance by the company. Indeed, any restrictions are instead caged as being the fault of lawyers/corporate or justified explicitly as an object of necessity ('we need to do this'), rather than an arbitrary rule which is commanded. Where the creative player is concerned, the once powerful company is presented as comparatively subservient under the rule of a legal/corporate 'other'. By contrast, the player, textually and discursively, is outwardly positioned as being more (perhaps unexpectedly) powerful, involved in a reciprocal conversation with the company, as a near co-creator, an equal, extending the world of the game. This positive role is seemingly acknowledged by the company, which is friendly, outwardly encouraging, and grateful for this work.

In demystifying this discourse, the contract and accompanying UGC policies must be understood with reference to the broader sociocultural context in which they are situated. In the game industry, the creative player is perhaps more accurately understood as a participant within a player *industry*, rather than a community. The most obvious example is the professional eSports player, who commodifies their UGC, in the form of game recordings and streaming, in competitive tournaments and competitions. This UGC is packaged and traded between different teams, player associations, tournament hosts, and game companies themselves: in 2020, Google reportedly paid US$ 160 million to Activision Blizzard for rights to broadcast the Overwatch League, Call of Duty League, and Hearthstone.[90] Even outwith the context of competitive gaming, game recording streaming personalities (or influencers), such as PewDiePie, Markiplier, or Jacksepticeye, are followed by millions, and earn millions in return. These personalities have been notable for bringing previously obscure games to unprecedented popularity. For example, Psyonix sold five million copies of its then little-known *Rocket League* after becoming one of the fifth most-watched games on Twitch;[91] many obscure indie titles, without the benefit of large marketing budgets, have found success through the game streaming economy, including *Among Us*, *Fall Guys*, and *Getting Over*

[90] K Partleton, 'Report: Google Paid 160 Million USD for Activision Blizzard Esports Streaming Rights' (*PocketGamer.biz*, 18 February 2020) https://www.pocketgamer.biz/google-activision-blizzard-deal-worth-160-million-usd/.

[91] A Brooks, 'Rocket League's Live Streaming Performance' (*Stream Hatchet*, 30 August 2023) https://streamhatchet.com/blog/rocket-leagues-live-streaming-performance/.

It. Modding, while less present in this dataset, is not the sole remit of the bizarre (even though that may be better publicised),[92] but is now increasingly commonly used to patch, improve (eg appearance, controls, handling) and debug a game post-release. In part due to long lead and development times, it is not uncommon for games to be released without being fully polished and functional, and indeed, there are notable games in this dataset have been substantially modded by players to improve their base functionality: *The Elder Scrolls V: Skyrim, Batman: Arkham City* and *Cyberpunk 2077* were all slated upon release for their poor performance. Here, the players who mod these games to make them more playable are an extension of the game company itself, acting as a kind of quality assurance industry.

Given the potential value of player creativity to the game company, on the face of it, the contract supports these activities. It in fact offers a more *liberal* regime for players than the default law of copyright, which may not be as accommodating for the range of uses illustrated here. It is not clear, for example, that a video recording of a substantial part of a game (or in many cases, the entirety of a game) would be eligible to benefit from a copyright exception in many jurisdictions.[93] A typical game recording may have elements of criticism and review, because the player may comment on which aspects of the game they enjoy or dislike. However, this does not usually comprise a large part of any such recording, so finds little solace in any such exception or copyright defence. Other creative player activities, such as the creation of merchandise, fan sites, or mods[94] find even less legal support, or rather face substantial legal uncertainty, under the copyright regime. Instead, the contract constructs the possibility for permitted uses of UGC that fall *outwith* default copyright exceptions or limitations – it is more permissive. The contract goes even further to construct non-commerciality as a more liberal community standard which permits monetisation of some content, something which copyright would prima facie prohibit. As such, it is tempting to view the contract's treatment of UGC as a more player-friendly regime than copyright itself.

However, and approaching this finding from a necessarily critical angle (being a fundamental component of the methodology adopted), power is not absent here, despite its outwardly disarming presentation. The type of style and register switching evidenced in the contract is in fact indicative of a *more* powerful speaker, not less. By selecting or altering linguistic elements due to the social context or conversational setting, it is the prerogative of a *powerful* speaker to determine the tone of conversation; for example, in a job interview, it is the interviewer who

[92] While too plentiful to mention, see J Wolens, 'Weird, Niche Mods Make PC Gaming Great, and These Ones Prove It' (*Yahoo!Tech*, 1 February 2025) https://tech.yahoo.com/general/articles/weird-niche-mods-pc-gaming-111200827.html, including for example *Dark Souls 2* 'Australia' mod, where the game perspective is simply flipped upside-down.

[93] Except perhaps as a 'transformative use' in the US, though this has been untested: see D Hagen, 'Fair Use, Fair Play: Video Game Performances and "Let's Plays" as Transformative Use' (2018) 13(3) *Washington Journal of Law, Technology and Arts* 245.

[94] Detailed further in A Thomas, 'Contested Game Spaces: Romance Modding and Copyright' (2024) 7(2) *Interactive Entertainment Law Review* 55.

sets the tone as formal or informal, rather than the interviewee. Likewise, it is the game company, not the player, who has determined to take this more friendly and informal approach. In doing so, the outward presentation of friendliness and encouragement ultimately disguises the reality of the aspects of the contract that may be disagreeable to the player. The player, for example, may not be pleased that they cannot commercialise what they perceive as their own independent creation (that they have made efforts to make 'original' and 'unique'), but the contract reassures them that this is necessary; that it is only imposed because of 'corporate'; that the game company is humbled by the wonderful creation; and in any case the player should not be a 'rules lawyer' if they notice a discrepancy. The player may likewise be unhappy if their work can then be sold to other companies and commercialised in an advert or marketing campaign, but they are reassured that if they make UGC available 'freely' that this is in the 'best' interests of the community. The cumulative effect is to present the disagreeable aspects of UGC as being commonsensical and reasonable – part of a conversation between friends with their best interests at heart – and in doing so naturalising acquiescence to this by the player. The player is not only framed as being a *recipient of the copyrighted work* rather than an author-proper, but as someone whose work can be legitimately controlled by the game company. Independent creation becomes absorbed into the broader proprietary ideology being perpetuated here – creativity is permitted, not assumed – a matter which is disguised behind a friendly approach.

In justifying this criticism, it is important to acknowledge the fragmentation of distribution methods outlined in the discursive dimension. This fragmentation across different types of communicative mediums, such as social media, leads to the temptation for another Occam's razor argument; that is, that different mediums of communication result in necessary differences in text appropriate to their genre. Technically, many of the UGC policies surveyed here are not incorporated within the contract as such but rather are ancillary to the primary conclusion of the contractual relationship. UGC is both interesting and risky to the player, and so UGC policies may be more likely to be consulted than the contract itself. Resultingly, the deliberate intention to make UGC policies more readable by using friendly, plain, short, and jargon-free language may be a natural response to anticipated high levels of readership. Certainly, addressing questions on UGC via social media platforms implies a different stance of formality related to the medium of communication, as opposed to a conscious choice to switch tone or register to manufacture camaraderie. Alternatively, if the player is truly valued as a co-creator in the process of extending a game's world past its release date (or eg as a promotional tool for a lesser-known game), then communicating in a clear and friendly manner with an 'equal' is entirely plausible. This may either be because of the 'co-creator' status of many professional players, for whom there is often mutual benefit in a fair, clear, UGC system. In the indie context, the players creating UGC may be the same players who were responsible for funding its creation or manufacturing its subsequent success: in this case, it is not possible for the game company to have a bad relationship with the player, who in such a scenario is more akin to their investor.

However, this argument becomes less persuasive when we examine the broader context within which the UGC policy is created. If UGC is very important, or presents a significant risk such that it must be addressed separately from the initial contractual relationship, why adopt a *less* formal approach which, when adopted elsewhere in the contract, is intended for its accuracy through the invocation of the technical specificity of the law? If UGC only became a consideration after the conclusion of the initial contract, the company is not prohibited from amending the agreement to include such an addition. Indeed, contracts are updated frequently, and appear to be live documents (noted in Chapter 3). Why then create a UGC policy separately if the primary agreement can simply be amended? If, instead, clearer, plainer communication is preferred, why be selective only in respect of UGC, and not the entirety of the agreement? It is more obvious, for example, that indie titles adopt a plainer language throughout their contractual relationship, rather than for selective aspects. In sum, where the formality of the contract and informality of the UGC policy co-exist, this Occam's razor argument is less plausible.

The alternative explanation is that the deliberate choice to engage in friendly and informal language masks the reality of what is permitted to the player: creativity, but heavily conditioned, and only to the extent it may benefit the game company. The dramatic switch in language, register, and tone, and particularly elements of politeness and humour, signal that the company wishes to avoid disharmony and build rapport to achieve agreement on the subject discussed. This, in itself, is indicative that what is being discussed is contentious and, indeed, the logic behind conceptualising the creative player as a 'content generator' at all is debatable if they are, by the company's own definition, creating things of authorial 'originality'.[95] By framing UGC policies in a friendly and informal manner, the effect is to naturalise and normalise the assumption that UGC is an object that *can*, and *should*, be controlled, not by the creator (in this case the player) but by the enabler of its creation (the game company). Framing the creative player in this way legitimates the dominant proprietary ideology of the game company – that, in any and all creative interactions with a game, *their* copyright will attach, and the player is always subservient to this.

Part of this problem is exacerbated by the fact that there is no good conceptual vocabulary to describe the creative revolution that has allowed players to participate in the co-creation of a game-work. UGC is an awkward creation that clings to the rhetoric of 'us and them', rightsholders and users, game companies and players, despite a fundamental breakdown in this distinction in the participatory era, and

[95] Issues around the implications of the word 'generated' have also been noted in generative AI discussions: see MD Murray, 'AI Pirated my Art and Birthed Infringing Works, and Other Metaphors that Confound Copyright Law' (*SSRN*, 28 March 2025) https://papers.ssrn.com/sol3/papers.cfm?abstract_id=5116714.

the interactive medium. If UGC was instead described as 'the content *you create*', there would presumably be more active contestation and questions of why *any* third party should regulate what has been created other than its author (here, the player). Instead, the contract treats creativity as a spectrum that can be moderated, rather than a yes/no question. Attaching 'player' or 'user' to the notion of creativity within the contract is therefore an artificial construct that justifies this control: creativity as an exception granted by the enabler, rather an entitlement of the player as an author.

Creativity by the player is, in any case, subservient to the more homogenous construction of the player as a non-commercial entity. More accurately, the 'player' or 'user' component of UGC acts as a proxy for 'amateur' in UGC policies. The 'professional' eSports player is, by contrast, largely absent from this discourse, and is directed to a closed environment elsewhere. The suggestion that the player is an amateur is an implicit assumption in copyright law which is made explicit through the contract's limitation of commercial activities. This amateur construct bolsters the subversion of authorship elsewhere in the contract. Ultimately, the conceptualisation of the creative player is only permitted insofar as it makes good business sense to do so (eg free 'marketing' material by streamers), and this determination tends to be tied to capital (preventing eg competing game merchandise).

The importance of the strategic configuration of player creativity for commercial interests can in part be illustrated by the puzzling, restrictive approach of Japanese companies in the dataset. Initially, when looking for an explanation for this more restrictive approach in the sociocultural dimension, this finding is difficult to explain. The Japanese companies observed here vary in size, and genre of game, but all share the same restrictive view of player creativity. Further, and paradoxically, as Japan is widely understood to be the home of fan culture and fandom, this would assume a more permissive, rather than restrictive, view of user creativity – which would make this finding even more surprising. In reframing the commonality between all Japanese companies observed here we can see that they also share the oldest dates of founding (Nintendo being by far the oldest established in the dataset, established in 1889). Most have roots in arcade games, with well-established characters, game series and OSTs: Nintendo is responsible for *Mario, Pokemon, Legend of Zelda*, amongst many others; major Konami titles include the *Metal Gear Solid* series and *Silent Hill* series; Bandai Namco's predecessor Namco created *Pac-Man*; Capcom is responsible for series such as *Street Fighter* and *Resident Evil*. The richness of the assets from these well-established game series in terms of merchandising probably has more value than any other company in the dataset.[96] A more in-depth analysis would be needed to confirm this suspicion but, in any case, it seems that the restrictive view of UGC is more

[96] Of most note is Nintendo, whose held intellectual property assets would prevent the company from going bankrupt for some time. See M Cundy, 'Is Nintendo Doomed? Not Likely. Just Take a Look at How Much Money It's Got in the Bank' (*GamesRadar*, 13 February 2012) https://www.gamesradar.com/nintendo-doomed-not-likely-just-take-look-how-much-money-its-got-bank/.

closely correlated with the length of establishment of the branding and the value of the intellectual property of a game franchise viewed *holistically*, rather than its country of origin. The value of *property*, in sum, is a more important determinant of how UGC will be restricted, because it demands a proprietary mindset.

IV. Save Point: Chapter Summary

The creative player is constructed in the contract through '*Artifice*', a veneer of fakery. First, because the definition of what the creative player is allowed to make – UGC – is constructed strategically and selectively by the game company. By crafting a definition of what is *allowed* to be made, the company changes player creativity into an excused infringement of its copyright, rather than an acknowledgement that creativity is, in any case, allowed. And second, because the creative player is subject to a differentiated discourse which is outwardly conversational, informal and polite, this can be deceptive about the reality of what is permitted, and the potential curtailing of the real, comparable rights of the player.

The *Artifice* theme also shows how the creative player is, ostensibly, treated like a *friend*, or a welcome *co-creator* of the game company in both textual and discursive dimensions. Their creative contributions are indeed valuable to the game company in extending the economic lifespan of the game, but only insofar as it is not allowed to create a competing commercial enterprise. In this sense, while the player is constructed as a friend, there is also the impression that this is in an effort to curtail a potentially dangerous variable within the community: that is, any potential legal challenge or litigation on the use of, or ownership of, UGC. This is indeed a real fear, as the legal grounds of UGC are fundamentally unstable. And in this sense, we might be sympathetic to the function of contracts which attempt to delineate and establish rules about a nascent, developing concept. At the same time, we can rightly be critical of the proprietary ideology which attempts to extend the reach of company copyright to any and all creative interactions with a game.

Conclusion: The Final Boss

This book began with the metaphor of the rules lawyer: a figure who reads game rules closely, insists on the meaning of precise language, and exposes their limitations. While rules lawyering is not generally considered a desirable trait, I have embraced this identity for the purposes of this research, taking the terms of play to their logical extremes and interrogating their ideological underpinnings. This is not intended to be a cynical exercise, but rather one of critical inquiry: if we must play by these rules, then the rules deserve scrutiny.

Through 'rules lawyering', we can see that the player is not a natural, inevitable or stable legal subject. Rather, the player is a product of a contractual imagination: an ideal designed to reflect and reinforce industry priorities. And like the 'perfect' Vitruvian man on the front cover, the 'perfect' player also only exists on paper. Indeed, throughout this research, it is clear that the player does not influence the discourse of the contract – they cannot change or shape their terms – but rather they are influenced by it. In turn, the contract tells us less about the reality of the player, and more about the hopes, fears and strategies of the entity doing the idealising: namely, the game company. Often, these ideals centre around presenting a strong, proprietary and protectionist view of games-as-copyrightable-software, insisting on the legal power behind that claim, and reinforcing this through the discourse of the contract.

I. Key Findings

In the first theme – *Authority* – copyright law is invoked as a contractual weapon (in the spirit of this 'boss fight'). Emphatically, the player is positioned as a *user of proprietary (game) software*, in a strictly *legal* relationship with the game company. This impression is created in the text through the frequent citation of law, and the adoption of legalistic tropes: it is a Very Serious Matter written by Very Serious People. However, the implications of this legal relationship are different at industry level. Triple A companies use legal tropes to frame players as potential infringers to be disciplined, and who are subject to a plethora of legal restrictions. To the triple A company, the player is a comparatively weak subject who can be lawfully controlled. But beneath this, the player is also a vaguely threatening figure – one who implicitly is antithetical to commercial copyright interests and would deliberately disrupt them. By contrast, indie companies might engage with the format of the legal relationship – they use contracts, but they evidence a distaste of copyright, or rather what copyright is *thought* to represent when filtered through the dominant triple A discourse: profit-driven production and merciless ownership and enforcement. Instead, they invite the player to join them in a shared space of 'play', using the contract to mock the dominant, triple A discourse, signalling their differing creative values while simultaneously engaging with the legal rules that make this possible. But whether triple A or indie, the player is assumed to be *oppositional* to copyright: either a potential infringer, or someone who doesn't like the implication that they are. In both cases, *Authority* is also highly selective, speaking loudly where the law suits the priorities of the company, and quietly (or not at all) where it does not.

The second theme – *Access* – is about gatekeeping ownership, both to the game itself and to the broader *property* of the game as an object of copyright. The theme evidences a homogenised, seemingly universally agreed upon construction of the player: whether games are sold on disks, downloaded, or streamed, the text of the contract insists that the player is merely the temporary custodian of a game, and is emphatically *not* the owner. While perplexing on the face of it, this construction is in furtherance of the more purposeful restrictions on resale of games, which is presented as the 'imaginary dragon' of the games industry, blamed for declining revenues. Here, the text of the contract is a powerful use of discourse, justifying this construction without any reference to law, but rather through repetition, and suggestive ties to illegal, criminal behaviours. By constructing the player as a non-reseller (a kind of transactional end point) they are simultaneously given consumerist qualities – because they buy a copy of a game – but are strategically excluded from many of the *benefits* of being a consumer. These benefits are in fact framed as undesirable for the player – in the ideal world of the game company, the player would not *want* to own a copy of a game or resell it because it is harmful for the ecosystem of the game industry, of which the player is part. And by emphasising the player's role as a temporary custodian and transient user of a game, the proprietary ideology of the game company is furthered.

The final theme – *Artifice* – disguises control of player creativity behind friendly language. In *Artifice*, the player is constructed through a differentiated discourse that is outwardly informal, friendly, and encouraging to the player who creates UGC: a sharp contrast from the formal, legalistic tropes adopted throughout the dominant discourse that precedes it. This type of 'tone switching' distorts the seriousness of what is being implicated in the outward friendliness: creativity, but heavily constrained. Players are only permitted to be 'content creators', but are emphatically not authors. They are permitted to create only in non-commercial ways, ultimately only allowing promotional, non-threatening re-uses of game content. In doing so, the protectionist, proprietary view of games is furthered by transforming player creativity into a permission granted by the game company, artificially dressing up limits as freedoms.

These three facets make it clear what the player is not: they are not an owner, not a consumer, and not an author. We might instead conclude they are an empty vessel, filled with whatever qualities best serve the company's ideological and economic goals in each moment: a vaguely piratical threat, a non-reseller, a maker of 'great stuff'. None of these constructs are natural or inevitable; the player is, as designed by copyright, a very neutral vessel upon which these more colourful characteristics have been applied by the external forces of contract. And strategically, the contract applies these characteristics in such a way as to best perpetuate the industry needs of the time. The player then, as a neutral vessel, can be shaped by the contract not only to realise the rights of the game company, but also to achieve particular ideologies about how the world *should* look or how the player *should* behave. And throughout, this is often in furtherance of a strong, proprietary vision of games-as-software.

This industry imperative – presenting games as unqualifiedly copyrightable, protectable products – is evident even in the historical narrative explored in Chapter 2. And having reviewed the findings, we see that the historical constructions of the player have not actually disappeared over time, but rather have been incorporated and amalgamated into the player of today. The need for a *legal* relationship with the player, manifested through the industry need for copyright enforcement in the early 1980s, is still present. As is the transient and selective treatment of *consumership*, which disappeared almost as soon as it was introduced in the 1990s. The most recent variable of player creativity from the web 2.0 era, in itself an echo of the quasi-programmer role assumed of the player in the 1970s, is also prevalent. These historical facets of the player co-exist and build upon each other temporally – an absorption of characteristics, rather than a replacement.

A final observation of the findings is how the legitimacy and negotiation of power varies throughout each theme. Beginning with *Authority*, the symbolic invocation and interaction with law evidences power *behind* the discourse, which is presented as the strongest and most legitimated justification for the contract's existence – it exists because the law says it can. In *Access*, power is instead shown *through* the discourse, as the crucial construction of the player as a non-reseller exists only through its justification in the text. The artificial nature of this construction makes it more contestable, hence its occasionally bizarre and heavy-handed framing – an imperative to doubt the evidence of your own eyes when you buy a copy of a game, and believe the contract instead. Finally, in *Artifice*, the lack of power, whether because the game company is weaker (on uncertain legal ground) or the player more powerful (an author in their own right), is disguised behind a friendly and informal discourse which aims to build rapport and disguise the disagreeable. In this final theme, any legitimacy of power whether behind or through the discourse is contestable, and so is deliberately hidden.

II. Implications: Beyond the Game

Much of this research deliberately presupposes the importance and justification of games and the player as an object of study (recalling the position to not 'plead their significance'). But when considering the implications of these findings, and their life after the book, there are several which extend beyond the study of the player and, indeed, the game industry.

First, there is a methodological provocation. Contracts might look like dry boilerplate, but when read with CDA, they become cultural artefacts showing how language does not merely describe the world, but can also bring it into being. As stated above, the strong, protectionist views of games-as-copyrightable-software is not inevitable nor universally accepted, but rather has been artificially imparted on the player by a limited number of very identifiable actors in the triple A sector. In this respect, studying language through 'rules lawyering' is less about cynically exploiting legal loopholes, and more about revealing how power hides in plain sight, disguised through a black-and-white click-wrap text box whose acceptance has become wholly normalised.

The second implication is about our conceptual vocabulary, and the tensions and limitations of words and their meanings in copyright scholarship and policy. A key preposition of this research is that language is ultimately neutral, but that we should interrogate who wields it and for what purpose. So, for example, the terms 'player' and 'UGC' may appear natural and self-evident, but they obscure as much as they reveal, while normalising and embedding unhelpful assumptions. Players who buy a copy of a game are, in law, *consumers*. Players who create something original may, in law, be *authors*. But once wrapped in the language of contractual discourse, both become 'players' – a label that strips away competing entitlements, with the deprivation of the associated benefits. Precision in language matters, and the way that contracts wield this as an exercise in power can remind us why.

The third implication is a more fundamental interrogation of copyright doctrine, which while promising balance between rightsholders and users, has largely given unchecked discretion to private contracts which can tip that balance. Especially through the historical narrative of the player contract in Chapter 2 we see that these legal tools are not unqualified necessities, but rather adaptive responses to industry anxieties – whether about piracy, resale, or player creativity. The evidence for contractual overreach or override may well inform policy debates surrounding user rights: indeed, there are several indicators here that the 'balance' is tipped unfavourably towards rightsholders in the games industry. But these contractual anxieties are also, on reflection, a response to sometimes genuine uncertainties in copyright doctrine. And rather than offering an implication on whether copyright overreach or override is defensible in these cases, the more apt implication would be to encourage copyright scholars to look inward to understand *what* anxiety the contract is responding to and whether it can be remedied. UGC policies, for example, while imperfect, arguably exist as they are often the only meaningful tool to permit user creativity without the continuous *implication* of infringement in most jurisdictions. And legal definitions which have been confusedly or inconsistently interpreted in the doctrine (eg 'non-commercial') are affirmatively defined – however contestably, but more precisely – in contract. Importantly, this should not be read as an indictment of the many problematic player contracts which have been observed in this research; but if we want to challenge the power wielded through contract, it may well be copyright itself, rather than its contractual afterlife, that requires reform.

The final implication is a wider cultural warning. Powerful actors can leverage their copyright, and use contracts to speak their power into being, shaping the narratives and norms around our use of creative content. If contracts can effectively construct the perfect player, then they can do the same in other domains: the perfect 'listener' on Spotify; the perfect viewer on Netflix. The most salient example at the time of writing is, of course, the perfect 'user' of an AI system; for where there is ongoing legal uncertainty, contracts will almost certainly be wielded to construct the narrative of the perceived business needs of the most powerful economic actors on the market. In sum, the stakes here extend *beyond* games: whenever we tick the '(read and) agree' checkbox we step into a narrative written by someone else – one that normalises our roles, entitlements and exclusions, and presents them as common sense.

III. Final Save Point

I cannot claim to have 'discovered' the player in copyright: the player is not a natural or self-evident legal subject. Rather, this book has been about showing how the player can be subjectively, strategically, and selectively constructed through contracts to actualise perceived business needs of powerful economic actors in the game industry. The result is a confusing amalgamation of characteristics which can exist simultaneously – the player is a suspect pirate, a loyal fan, a consumer (but not really), and a creator but not an author. This instability is deliberate in its design: keeping the player undefined, as an empty vessel, means it can be adapted when and where it is needed.

This is, however, not an inevitable conclusion. This book began with the idea that games should be fun, while contracts rarely are. But 'rules lawyering' the terms of play shows that the distance between them is smaller than our first impression. If law insists on taking games seriously, then perhaps players might return the favour by treating the law playfully; the player should press at its limits, expose its bugs, and demand a patch. Because if rules lawyers know anything, it's that every rule can be argued with – and every rule can be re-written.

Appendix 1

Extract of Player Contract Appended to Pitfall II *Programme Manual (1985) (Activision/Tandy Software)*

https://colorcomputerarchive.com/repo/Documents/Manuals/Games/Pitfall%20II%20(Tandy).pdf (accessed 11 November 2025)

LIMITED WARRANTY

...

SOFTWARE LICENSE

RADIO SHACK grants to CUSTOMER a non-exclusive, paid-up license to use the Tandy Software on **one** computer, subject to the following provisions:

A. Except as otherwise provided in the Software License, applicable copyright laws shall apply to the Software.
B. Title to the medium on which the software is recorded is transferred to CUSTOMER, but not title to the Software.
C. CUSTOMER shall not use, make, manufacture, or reproduce copies of Software except for use on **one** computer and as is specifically provided in this Software License. Customer is expressly prohibited from disassembling the Software.
D. CUSTOMER is permitted to make additional copies of the Software **only** for backup or archival purposes or if additional copies are required in the operation of **one** computer with the software, but only to the extent the Software allows a backup copy to be made.
E. All copyright notices shall be retained on all copies of the Software.

Appendix 2

Dataset of Player Contracts

Contracts last accessed and confirmed live on 11 November 2025 (except where otherwise indicated).

Game title	Rightsholder	Country of origin	Industry category	Dataset	Sources
Dota 2	Valve (founded 1996)	US	Platform	eSports	Valve, 'Steam Subscriber Agreement' https://store.steampowered.com/subscriber_agreement/ Valve, 'Valve Video Policy' https://store.steampowered.com/video_policy
Fortnite	Epic Games (founded 1991)	US	Triple A	eSports	Epic Games, 'Fortnite End User License Agreement' https://www.epicgames.com/fortnite/en-US/eula Epic Games, 'Fan Content Policy' https://www.epicgames.com/site/en-US/fan-art-policy
League of Legends	Riot Games (founded 2006)	US	Triple A	eSports	Riot Games, 'League of Legends Terms of Use' https://www.riotgames.com/en/terms-of-service Riot Games, 'Legal Jibber Jabber' https://www.riotgames.com/en/legal

Starcraft II	Blizzard (founded 1991)	US	Triple A	eSports	Blizzard, 'Custom Game Acceptable Use Policy' https://www.blizzard.com/en-gb/legal/d98bbabd-9e50-49f2-81b9-b27120a2bbf1/custom-game-acceptable-use-policy Blizzard, 'End User License Agreement' https://www.blizzard.com/en-gb/legal/08b946df-660a-40e4-a072-1fbde65173b1/blizzard-end-user-license-agreement Blizzard, 'Terms and Conditions of Fan Art Submissions to Blizzard Entertainment' https://www.blizzard.com/en-gb/legal/a03da66c-273f-4a11-b18c-869db5b53688/terms-and-conditions-of-fan-art-submissions-to-blizzard-entertainment Blizzard, 'Video Policy' https://www.blizzard.com/en-gb/legal/2068564f-f427-4c1c-8664-c107c90b34d5/blizzard-video-policy
PlayerUnknown's Battlegrounds	PUB G Corporation (founded 2018)	South Korea	Triple A	eSports	PUB G, 'Terms of Service' https://pubg.com/en/clause/term_of_service/label_playstation/latest PUB G, 'Content Creation Guideline' https://www.pubg.com/en/clause/content_creation_guideline/label_steam/latest
Arena of Valor	Proxima Beta (subsidiary of Tencent) (founded 2003)	China	Triple A	eSports	Proxima Beta, 'End User License Agreement' https://www.arenaofvalor.com/terms.html
Rainbow Six Siege	Ubisoft (founded 1986)	France	Triple A	eSports	Ubisoft, 'End User License Agreement' https://legal.ubi.com/eula/en-GB Ubisoft, 'Terms of Use' https://legal.ubi.com/termsofuse/en-GB Ubisoft, 'Video Policy' https://www.ubisoft.com/en-us/videopolicy.html

(continued)

(Continued)

Game title	Rightsholder	Country of origin	Industry category	Dataset	Sources
Rocket League	Psyonix (founded 2000)	US	Indie	eSports	Psyonix, 'End User License Agreement' https://www.psyonix.com/eula/ Psyonix, 'Terms of Use' https://www.psyonix.com/tou/
SMITE	Hi-Rez Studios (founded 2005)	US	Indie	eSports	Hi-Rez, 'SMITE EULA' https://www.hirezstudios.com/legal Hi-Rez, 'Hi-Rez Studios Policy for Streaming Videos and VODS (videos-on-demand)' https://www.hirezstudios.com/_files/ugd/126c6a_33d643407b2245a3850f5a59ae764e44.pdf Hi-Rez, 'FAQs' https://www.hirezstudios.com/legal
Call of Duty: Black Ops 4	Activision (since merged with Blizzard) (founded 1979)	US	Triple A	eSports	Activision, 'Terms of use' https://www.activision.com/uk/en/legal/terms-of-use
Halo 5: Guardians	Microsoft (Game Studios founded 2000)	US	Platform	eSports	Microsoft, 'Terms of Sale' https://www.microsoft.com/en-gb/storedocs/terms-of-sale Microsoft, 'Community Standards for Xbox' https://www.xbox.com/en-US/legal/community-standards Microsoft, 'Game Content Usage Rules' https://www.xbox.com/en-us/developers/rules Microsoft, 'Services Agreement' https://www.microsoft.com/en-gb/servicesagreement#serviceslist

Magic: The Gathering Arena	Wizards of the Coast (founded 1990)	US	Triple A	eSports	Wizards of the Coast, 'Magic Online End User License Agreement and Software License' https://store.steampowered.com/eula/2141910_eula_0 Wizards of the Coast, 'Fan Content Policy' https://company.wizards.com/en/legal/fancontentpolicy Wizards of the Coast, 'Code of Conduct & Community Guidelines' https://company.wizards.com/legal/code-conduct
World of Tanks	Wargaming (founded 1998)	Belarus	Triple A	eSports	Wargaming, 'End User Licence Agreement' https://legal.eu.wargaming.net/eula/?_ga=2.226753625.519148912.1591803691-1999682024.1591803690 Wargaming, 'Game Rules' https://legal.eu.wargaming.net/en/game-rules/ Wargaming, 'Player Content Policy' https://legal.wargaming.net/en/user-documents/content-policies/player-content-policy/view
Apex Legends	EA Games (founded 1982)	US	Platform	eSports	EA, 'EA's content policy' https://help.ea.com/en/articles/security-and-rules/ea-content-policy/ EA, 'Electronic Arts User Agreement' https://tos.ea.com/legalapp/WEBTERMS/US/en/PC/
Shadowverse	Cygames (founded 2011)	Japan	Triple A	eSports	Cygames, 'Content Guidelines' https://shadowverse-wb.com/en/guideline/ Cygames, 'Service Agreement' https://shadowverse.com/terms.php

(continued)

(Continued)

Game title	Rightsholder	Country of origin	Industry category	Dataset	Sources
The Witcher 3: Wild Hunt	CD Projekt Red (founded 1994)	Poland	Triple A	Video game	CD Projekt Red, 'User Agreement' https://regulations.cdprojektred.com/en/user_agreement CD Projekt Red, 'Fan Content Guideline' https://www.cdprojektred.com/en/fan-content CD Projekt Red, 'Video Policy' https://support.cdprojektred.com/en/witcher-3/playstation/content-policies/issue/830/video-policy
The Elder Scrolls V: Skyrim	Bethesda (founded 1986)	US	Triple A	Video game	Bethesda, 'End User Agreement (EULA)' https://bethesda.net/data/eula/en.html Bethesda, 'Zenimax Media Terms of Service' https://bethesda.net/en/document/terms-of-service Bethesda, 'Code of Conduct' https://bethesda.net/en/document/code-of-conduct latest version retrieved 1 December 2020 Bethesda, 'Video Policy' https://bethesda.net/en/article/3XrnHrB0iAesac8844yeuo/bethesda-video-policy
Red Dead Redemption II	Rockstar Games (founded 1998)	US	Triple A	Video game	Rockstar Games, 'Limited Software Warranty and License Agreement' [*archived*] https://web.archive.org/web/20210530214354/https://www.rockstargames.com/eula Rockstar Games, 'Terms & Conditions' https://www.rockstargames.com/legal

					Rockstar Games, 'Policy on Posting Copyrighted Rockstar Games Material' https://support.rockstargames.com/articles/200153756/Policy-on-posting-copyrighted-Rockstar-Games-material
The Last of Us	Sony Interactive Entertainment (founded 1993)	US	Platform	Video game	Sony, 'Software Product License Agreement' https://www.playstation.com/en-us/legal/softwarelicense/ Sony, 'Software Usage Terms' https://www.playstation.com/en-gb/legal/software-usage-terms/
Batman: Arkham City	Warner Brothers Interactive Entertainment (founded 2004)	US	Triple A	Video game	WB Games Inc, 'End User License Agreement' https://legal.wbgames.com/wbgames-legal/epic/eula/eula_epic_en_NZ.html WB Games Inc, 'Terms of Use' https://policies.warnerbros.com/terms/en-us/html/terms_en-us_1.2.0.html
The Legend of Zelda: Breath of the Wild	Nintendo (founded 1889)	Japan	Triple A	Video game	Nintendo, 'End User License Agreement' https://www.nintendo.com/sg/support/switch/eula/usage_policy.html?srsltid=AfmBOopHUhYYuCNvD7WmJswiWxY6u14_xsrHUJwC8_o_PIUgQYKwOvv Nintendo, 'Intellectual Property' https://www.nintendo.co.uk/Legal-information/Intellectual-Property/Intellectual-Property-Policy-625951.html Nintendo, 'Nintendo Game Content Guidelines for Online Video & Image Sharing Platforms' https://www.nintendo.co.jp/networkservice_guideline/en/index.html

(continued)

(Continued)

Game title	Rightsholder	Country of origin	Industry category	Dataset	Sources
					Nintendo, 'Nintendo's Intellectual Property Enforcement Program' (formerly Anti-Piracy Programme) https://www.nintendo.com/en-gb/Legal-information/Nintendo-s-Intellectual-Property-Enforcement-Program/Nintendo-s-Intellectual-Property-Enforcement-Program-732261.html
Minecraft	Mojang (founded 2009)	Sweden	Indie	Video game	Mojang, 'Minecraft End User License Agreement' https://account.mojang.com/documents/minecraft_eula Mojang, 'Minecraft Usage Guidelines' https://www.minecraft.net/en-us/usage-guidelines
Borderlands 2	Take2 (founded 1993)	US	Triple A	Video game	Take2, 'Limited Software Warranty and License Agreement' [*archived*] https://web.archive.org/web/20210616021823/https://www.take2games.com/eula/ Take2, 'Take-Two Terms of Service' https://www.take2games.com/legal
Dark Souls III	Bandai Namco (founded 2006 – merger of two earlier companies, Bandai 1960 and Namco 1955)	Japan	Triple A	Video game	Bandai Namco, 'Terms of Use' https://en.bandainamcoent.eu/terms-of-use Bandai Namco, 'Entertainment Video Policy' https://www.bandainamcoent.co.jp/english/videopolicy/ Bandai Namco, 'Content Creator Guidelines' https://www.bandainamcoent.com/legal/community-events/content-creator-guidelines

Resident Evil 2 (Remake)	Capcom (founded 1979)	Japan	Triple A	Video game	Capcom, 'End User License Agreement' https://game.capcom.com/eula/eng.html Capcom, 'FAQ' https://capcom-europe.com/faq/ Capcom, 'Video Policy' https://www.capcomusa.com/video-policy/
Superhot	Superhot Team (n/a – active since 2016)	Poland	Indie	Video game	Superhot Team, 'End User License Agreement' https://superhotgame.com/eula/
Undertale	Toby Fox (n/a – active since 2009)	US	Indie	Video game	Toby Fox and YoYo Games, 'Undertale EULA' https://store.steampowered.com/eula/391540_eula_0
Cuphead	Studio MDHR (n/a – active since 2017)	Canada	Indie	Video game	Studio MDHR, 'Cuphead Video Streaming Policy' http://studiomdhr.com/video-streaming-policy/
Metal Gear Solid V: The Phantom Pain	Konami (founded 1969)	Japan	Triple A	Video game	Konami, 'Terms of Use: Metal Gear Solid V: The Phantom Pain' https://www.konami.com/mg/mgs5/tpp/_common_all/eula/tppps3web/eula/eula.en.html Konami, 'Copyrights, Career Opportunities & Goodies' https://eu-support.konami.com/hc/en-gb/articles/9648771731479-Copyrights-Career-Opportunities-Goodies
Outlast	Red Barrels (founded 2011)	Canada	Indie	Video game	Red Barrels, 'Message to YouTubers' [*archived*] https://web.archive.org/web/20210920205601/https://redbarrelsgames.com/contact/

BIBLIOGRAPHY

Books

Althusser, L, *Lenin and Philosophy and Other Essays* (New Left Books, 1971)

Aplin, T, *Copyright Law in the Digital Society: The Challenges of Multimedia* (Hart Publishing, 2005)

Baker, P and Ellege, S, *Key Terms in Discourse Analysis* (Continuum, 2011)

Bourdieu, P, *Language and Symbolic Power* (Harvard University Press, 1991)

Bushnell, P, *Tragic Time in Drama, Film and Videogames* (Palgrave MacMillan, 2016)

Chapdelaine, P, *Copyright User Rights: Contracts and the Erosion of Property* (Oxford University Press, 2017)

Cohen, J, *Configuring the Networked Self* (Yale University Press, 2012)

Fairclough, N, *Discourse and Social Change* (Polity Press, 1992)

—— *Critical Discourse Analysis* (Longman, 1995)

—— *Language and Power*, 2nd edn (Longman, 2001)

Foucault, M, *Discipline and Punish* (Penguin, 1979)

Gramsci, A, translated by Q Hoare and G Nowell-Smith, *Selections from Prison Notebooks* (Lawrence and Wishart, 1971)

Guibault, L, *Copyright Exceptions and Contracts. An Analysis of the Contractual Overridability of Limitations on Copyright* (Kluwer Law International, 2002)

Habermas, J, translated by T McCarthy, *The Theory of Communicative Action: Reason and the Rationalization of Society* (Heinemann, 1984)

Halliday, M, *Language as a Social Semiotic: The Social Interpretation of Language and Meaning* (Edward Arnold Ltd, 1978)

Kaplan, JP, *Linguistics and Law* (Routledge, 2019)

Kent, SL, *The Ultimate History of Video Games: The Story Behind the Craze that Touched our Lives and Changed the World* (Prima Publishing, 2001)

Lessig, L, *Code: And Other Laws of Cyberspace, Version 2.0* (Basic Books, 2006)

—— *Remix: Making Art and Commerce Thrive in the Hybrid Economy* (Penguin Press, 2008)

Mailland, J, *The Game That Never Ends: How Lawyers Shape the Videogame Industry* (MIT Press, 2024)

McDonagh, L, *Performing Copyright: Law, Theatre and Authorship* (Hart Publishing, 2021)

Meese, J, *Authors, Users and Pirates: Copyright Law and Subjectivity* (MIT Press, 2018)

Murray, JH, *Hamlet on the Holodeck* (MIT Press, 1997)

Perzanowski, A and Schultz, J, *The End of Ownership: Personal Property in the Digital Economy* (MIT Press, 2016)

Radin, MJ, Boilerplate: *The Fine Print, Vanishing Rights, and the Rule of Law* (Princeton University Press, 2013)

Senftleben, M, *Copyright, Limitations and the Three-Step Test* (Wolters Kluwer, 2004)

Sheff, D, *Game Over: Press Start to Continue* (Cyberactive Media Group, 1999)

Simone, DT, *Copyright and Collective Authorship: Locating the Authors of Collaborative Work* (Cambridge University Press, 2019)

Swalwell, M, *Homebrew Gaming and the Beginnings of Vernacular Digitality* (MIT Press, 2021)

Tan, C, *Regulating Content on Social Media: Copyright, Terms of Service and Technological Features* (UCL Press, 2018)

Weber, M, *Wirtschaft und Gessellschaft* (JCB Mohr, 1925)

Contributions to edited books

Barlow, JP, 'Introduction' in C Doctorow, *Selected Essays on Technology, Creativity, Copyright, and the Future of the Future* (Tachyon Publications, 2008)

Campos-Pardillos, MA, 'End-User Agreements in Videogames: Plain English at Work in an Ideal Setting' in A Ensslin and I Balteiro (eds), *Approaches to Videogame Discourse: Lexis, Interaction, Textuality* (Bloomsbury, 2019)

van Dijk, TA, 'Principles of Critical Discourse Analysis' in M Wetherell, S Taylor and S Yates (eds), *Discourse Theory and Practice: A Reader* (Sage, 2001)

—— 'Multidisciplinary CDA: A Plea for Diversity' in R Wodak and M Meyer (eds), *Methods of Critical Discourse Analysis* (Sage, 2001)

—— 'Socio-cognitive Discourse Studies' in J Flowerdew and J Richardson (eds), *The Routledge Handbook of Critical Discourse Studies* (Routledge, 2017)

Dinwoodie, GB and Gangjee, D, 'The Image of the Consumer in European Trade Mark Law' in D Leczykiewicz and S Weatherill (eds), *The Image(s) of the Consumer in EU Law* (Hart Publishing, 2015)

Elkin-Koren, N, 'Governing Access to Users-Generated-Content: The Changing Nature of Private Ordering in Digital Networks' in E Brousseau, M Marzouki and C Meadel (eds), *Governance, Regulations and Powers on the Internet* (Cambridge University Press, 2009)

Finegan, E, 'Discourses in the Language of the Law' in M Handford and JP Gee (eds), *The Routledge Handbook for Discourse Analysis* (Routledge, 2012)

Foucault, M, 'The Order of Discourse' in M Shapiro (ed), *Language and Politics* (New York University Press, 1984)

Hancock, M, 'Playing It By the Book: Instructing and Constructing the Player in the Videogame Manual Paratext' in A Ensslin and I Balteiro (eds), *Approaches to Videogame Discourse* (Bloomsbury, 2019)

Hultunen, R, 'The Grammar and Structure of Legal Texts' in LM Solan and PM Tiersma (eds), *The Oxford Handbook of Language and Law* (Oxford University Press, 2012)

Iljadica, M, 'User Generated Content and its Authors' in T Aplin (ed), *Research Handbook on Intellectual Property and Digital Technologies* (Edward Elgar, 2020)

Niemi-Kiesilainen, J, Honkatukia, P, and Ruuskanen, M, 'Legal Texts as Discourses' in A Gunnarsson, E Svensson and M Davies (eds), *Exploiting the Limits of Law* (Ashgate, 2007)

Reisigi, M, 'The Discourse-Historical Approach (DHA)' in J Flowerdew and JE Richardson (eds), *The Routledge Handbook of Critical Discourse Studies* (Routledge, 2017)

Articles and working papers

Aronsson-Storrier, A, 'Copyright Exceptions and Contract in the UK: The Impact of Recent Amendments' (2016) 6(1) *Queen Mary Journal of Intellectual Property* 111

Bakos, Y, Marotta-Wurgler, F, and Trossen, DR, 'Does Anyone Read the Fine Print? Testing a Law and Economics Approach to Standard Form Contracts' (2009) Working Papers 09-04, NET Institute

Barker, T, 'Unplayable Games: Time and Digital Culture' (2023) 2 *Kunsttexte*

Boyden, B, 'Games and Other Uncopyrightable Systems' (2011) 18 *George Mason Law Review* 439

Burk, D, 'Owning eSports: Proprietary Rights in Professional Computer Gaming' (2013) 161 *University of Pennsylvania Law Review* 1535

Chow, SY, 'A Snapshot of Online Contracting Two Decades After ProCD v Zeidenberg' (2017) 73(1) *The Business Lawyer* 267

Cohen, J, 'Lochner in Cyberspace: The New Economic Orthodoxy of Rights Management' (2019) 97(2) *Michigan Law Review* 462

Craig, C, 'Reconstructing the Author-Self: Some Feminist Lessons for Copyright Law' (2007) 15(2) *Journal of Gender, Social Policy and the Law* 207

Deng, Z and Li, Y, 'Players' Rights to Game Mods: Towards a More Balanced Copyright Regime' (2021) 43 *Computer Law & Security Review* 105634

Derclaye, E and Favale, M, 'Copyright and Contract Law: Regulating User Contracts: The State of the Art and a Research Agenda' (2010) 18(1) *Journal of Intellectual Property Law & Practice* 65

Edwards, L et al, 'Discourse, Justification and Critique: Towards a Legitimate Digital Copyright Regime?' (2015) 21(1) *International Journal of Cultural Policy* 60

Erickson, K, 'User Illusion: Ideological Construction of "User-generated Content" in the EC Consultation on Copyright' (2014) 3(4) *Internet Policy Review*

Fasciana, S, 'The Gaming Theatre Company: Players, Gameplay, Performance and the Law' (2022) 5(2) *Interactive Entertainment Law Review* 80

Favale, M, Kretschmer, M, and Torremans, P, 'Who is Steering the Jurisprudence of the European Court of Justice? The Influence of Member State Submissions on Copyright Law' (2020) 83(4) *Modern Law Review* 831

Fiesler, C, Lampe, C, and Bruckman, AS, 'Reality and Perception of Copyright Terms of Service for Online Content Creation' (2016) CSCW' 16 Proceedings of the 19th ACM Conference on Computer-Supported Cooperative Work and Social Computing

Gasser, U, 'iTunes: How Copyright, Contract, and Technology Shape the Business of Digital Media – A Case Study' (2004) Berkman Center for Internet and Society at Harvard Law School Research Publication No 2004-07

Geiger, C and Jutte, BJ, 'Copyright as an Access Right: Concretizing Positive Obligations for Rightsholders to Ensure the Exercise of User Rights' (2024) 73(11) *GRUR International* 1019

Gervais, D, 'The Tangled Web of UGC: Making Copyright Sense of User-Generated Content' (2009) 11(4) *Vanderbilt Journal of Entertainment and Technology Law* 841

Ginsburg, J, '"Une Chose Publique"? The Author's Domain and the Public Domain in Early British, French and US Copyright Law' (2006) 65(3) *Cambridge Law Review* 636

Good, NS et al, 'Noticing Notice: A Large-Scale Experiment on the Timing of Software License agreements' (2007) CHI'07: Proceedings of the SIGCHI Conference on Human Factors in Computing Systems

—— 'Stopping Spyware at the Gate: A User Study of Privacy, Notice and Spyware' (2005) SOUPS' 05: Proceedings of the 2005 Symposium on Usable privacy and security

Griffin, J, 'The Interface between Copyright and Contract: Suggestions for the Future' (2011) 2(1) *European Journal of Law and Technology*

Grøndal, L, 'DRM and Contract Terms' (2006) 2(12) *Indicare*

Grossklags, J and Good, NS, 'Empirical Studies on Software Notices to Inform Policy Makers and Usability Designers' (2007) International Conference on Financial Cryptography and Data Security

Hagen, D, 'Fair Use, Fair Play: Video Game Performances and "Let's Plays" as Transformative Use' (2018) 13(3) *Washington Journal of Law, Technology and Arts* 245

Helberger, N and Hugenholtz, B, 'No Place Like Home for Making a Copy: Private Copying in European Copyright Law and Consumer Law' (2007) 22(3) *Berkley Technology Law Journal* 1061

Heymann, LA, 'The Public's Domain in Trademark Law: A First Amendment Theory of the Consumer' (2009) 43(3) *Georgia Law Review* 651

Hollis, K, 'A Critical Discourse Analysis of the Intellectual property Chapter of the TPP: Confirming What the Critics Fear' (2017) 6(1) *Communication*

Kalimo, H, Meyer, T and Mylly, T, 'Of Values and Legitimacy – Discourse Analytical Insights on the Copyright Case Law of the Court of Justice of the European Union' (2018) 81(2) *Modern Law Review* 282

Katzenbach, C, Herweg, S and van Roessel, L, 'Copies, Clones and Genre Building: Discourses on Imitation and Innovation in Digital Games' (2016) 10 *International Journal of Communication* 838

Keogh, B, 'From Aggressively Formalised to Intensely In/formalised: Accounting for a Wider Range of Videogame Development Practice' (2019) 12(1) *Creative Industries Journal* 838

Kretschmer, M, 'Software as Text and Machine: The Legal Capture of Digital Innovation' (2003) 1 *Journal of Information, Law and Technology*

Landsman, V and Stremersch, S, 'Multihoming in Two-Sided Markets: An Empirical Inquiry in the Video Game Console Industry' (2011) 75(6) *Journal of Marketing* 1024

Lemley, M, 'Intellectual Property and Shrinkwrap Licenses' (1995) 68 *Southern California Law Review* 1239

Lintaman, D, 'Unusual Canvasses: Resolving Copyright Infringement through the Lens of Community Customs' (2020) 3(1) *Interactive Entertainment Law Review* 3

Litman, J, 'Lawful Personal Use' (2007) 85(7) *Texas Law Review* 1871

—— 'Readers' Copyright' (2011) 58 *Journal of the Copyright Society of the USA* 325

Loughlan, PL, '"You Wouldn't Steal a Car": Intellectual Property and the Language of Theft' (2007) 29(10) *European Intellectual Property Review* 401

Marcus, TD, 'Fostering Creativity in Virtual Worlds: Easing the Restrictiveness of Copyright for User-Created Content' (2008) 55 *Journal of the Copyright Society of the USA* 67

Marotta-Wurgler, F, 'What's in a Standard Form Contract? An Empirical Analysis of Software License Agreements' (2007) 4(4) *Journal of Empirical Legal Studies* 677

Martinez, E, Mollica, F and Gibson, E, 'Even Laypeople use Legalese' (2024) 121(35) *Proceedings of the National Academy of Sciences*

McIntyre, S, 'Game Over for First Sale' (2014) 29(1) *Berkeley Technology Law Journal* 1

Mezei, P and Harkai, I, 'End-User Flexibilities in Digital Copyright Law – An Empirical Analysis of End-user License Agreements' (2022) 5(1) *Interactive Entertainment Law Review* 2

Miller, DC, 'Determining Ownership in Virtual Worlds: Copyright and License Agreements' (2003) 22 *Review Litigation* 435

Nartey, M and Huang, H, 'Situated Identities in the Discourse of Insurance: A Comparative Critical Discourse Analysis of Chinese and British Contracts' (2018) 6(2) *Language, Discourse and Society* 119

National Commission on New Technological Uses of Copyrighted Works, 'Final Report on the National Commission on New Technological Uses of Copyrighted Works' (1981) 3(53) *Computer Law Journal*

Nichols, J, 'Painting through Pixels: The Case for a Copyright in Videogame Play' (2007) 30(101) *Columbia Journal of Law and the Arts* 117

Obar, JA and Oeldorf-Hirsch, A, 'The Biggest Lie on the Internet: Ignoring the Privacy Policies and Terms of Service Policies of Social Networking Services' (2008) 23(1) *Information, Communication and Society* 128

—— 'The Clickwrap: A Political Economic Mechanism for Manufacturing Consent on Social Media' (2018) 4(3) *Social Media and Society*

Phillips, T '"Don't Clone My Indie Game, Bro": Informal Cultures of Videogame Regulation in the Independent Sector' (2015) 24(2) *Cultural Trends* 143

Pitet, CL, 'The Problem with Money Now, Terms Later: ProCD, Inc v Zeidenberg and the Enforceability of Shrinkwrap Software Licences' (1997) 31(1) *Loyola of Los Angeles Law Review* 325

Rendas, T, 'Are Copyright-Permitted Uses "Exceptions", "Limitations" or "User Rights"? The Special Case of Article 17 CDSM Directive' (2022) 17(1) *Journal of Intellectual Property Law & Practice* 54

Reuveni, E, 'On Virtual Worlds: Copyright and Contract Law at the Dawn of the Virtual Age' (2007) 82 *Indiana Law Journal* 261

Roquilly, C, 'Control Over Virtual Worlds by Game Companies: Issues and Recommendations' (2011) 35(3) *MITS Quarterly* 653

Samuelson, P, 'Why Copyright Law Excludes Systems and Processes from the Scope of its Protection' (2007) 85(7) *Texas Law Review* 1921

—— 'The Uneasy Case for Software Copyrights Revisited' (2011) 79(6) *The George Washington Law Review* 1746

Smith, C, 'Weaponizing Copyright' (2021) 35(1) *Harvard Journal of Law & Technology* 193

Sullivan, CA, 'The Puzzling Persistence of Unenforceable Contract Terms' (2009) 70 *Ohio State Law Journal* 1127
Synodinou, TE, 'Lawfulness for Users in European Copyright Law: Acquis and Perspectives' (2019) 10 *Journal of Intellectual Property, Information Technology and Electronic Commerce Law* 20
Thomas, A, 'A Question of (e)Sports: An Answer from Copyright' (2020) 15(12) *Journal of Intellectual Property Law & Practice* 960
—— 'Merit and Monetisation: A Study of Video Game User-Generated Content Policies' (2023) 12(1) *Internet Policy Review*
—— 'Contested Game Spaces: Romance Modding and Copyright' (2024) 7(2) *Interactive Entertainment Law Review* 55
Thomas, A et al, 'Competition in the Cloud Gaming Market: Proposing the Innovation-Creativity Dichotomy' (2025) 9(1) *Interactive Entertainment Law Review* 1
Wang, JC, 'ProCD, Inc v Zeidenberg and Article 2B: Finally, the Validation of Shrink-Wrap Licenses' (1998) 16 *Journal of Computer and Information Law* 439
Widdowson, HG, 'Discourse Analysis: A Critical View' (1995) 4(3) *Language and Literature* 157
—— 'Reply to Fairclough: Discourse and Interpretation: Conjectures and Refutations' (1996) 5(1) *Language and Literature* 57

Policy documents

European Commission, Communication from the Commission to the Council, the European Parliament and the European Economic and Social Committee (2007) Empowering consumers, enhancing their welfare, effectively protecting them. EU Consumer Policy strategy 2007–2013, COM(2007)99, Brussels

Reports

Danna, R, Martinelli, A and Nuvolari, A, 'Interim Report on Negative Space of EU Creative Industries' (ReCreating Europe, 2021)
'Defining "Noncommercial": A Study of How the Online Population Understands "Noncommercial Use"' (Creative Commons, 2009)
Erickson, K and Rodriguez, F, 'Technological Protection Measures and Digital Preservation: Evidence from Video Games' (Knowledge Rights 21, 2024)
Erickson, K and Stobo, V, 'Survey on Technological Protection Measures: Impacts for Researchers, Libraries and Archives' (Knowledge Rights 21, 2024)
Kretschmer, M et al, 'The Relationship Between Copyright and Contract Law' (UK Strategic Advisory Board for Intellectual Property Policy, 2010)
OECD, 'Participative Web and User-Created Content: Web 2.0, Wikis and Social Networking' (OECD, 2007)
Ramos, A et al, 'The Legal Status of Video Games: Comparative Analysis in National Approaches'(WIPO, 2013)
Trialle, JP et al, 'Study on the Application of Directive 2001/29/EC on Copyright and Related Rights in the Information Society (the "InfoSoc Directive")' (European Commission, 2013)
Xalabarder, R, 'Study on Copyright Limitations and Exceptions for Educational Activities in North America, Europe, Caucasus. Central Asia and Israel' (WIPO, 2009)

Online resources (all last accessed 11 November 2025)

3DO, 'Army Men 3D' (*Internet Archive*, 28 May 2013) https://archive.org/details/Army_Men_3D_1999_3DO_US_SLUS-00491/page/n9/mode/2up

343 Industries, 'How Games Licensing Works on Xbox One' (*Xbox News*, 6 June 2013) https://news.xbox.com/en-us/2013/06/06/license/

—— 'Your Feedback Matters – Update on Xbox One' (*Xbox News*, 19 June 2013) https://news.xbox.com/en-us/2013/06/19/update/

Scott Adams Inc, 'Adventureland' (Color Computer Archive, 1981) https://colorcomputerarchive.com/repo/Documents/Manuals/Games/Scott%20Adams%20Adventure%2001%20(Adventureland)(1981)(Adventure%20International).pdf

Alexander, J, 'Super Seducer Dev under Fire after DMCA Takedown Hits YouTuber, Twitter Fight' (*Polygon* 28 February 2018) https://www.polygon.com/2018/2/28/17058040/super-seducer-iampattyjack-dmca-takedown

'Apple Media Services Terms and Conditions' (*Apple*, 16 September 2020) https://www.apple.com/uk/legal/internet-services/itunes/uk/terms.html

Asselestine, B, 'Freeing an Old Game' (*Free Software Magazine*, 12 March 2007) http://freesoftwaremagazine.com/articles/freeing_an_old_game_moria/

Atari Compendium, 'Scan of Electronic Games Magazine' https://www.ataricompendium.com/faq/faq_vcs_electronic_games_6-82_atari_activision_lawsuit_settled.jpg

Bethesda, 'Fallout 76 EULA' (*Bethesda*, date unknown) https://bethesda.net/en/eulas/fallout-76

Bonk, L, 'Shadow of Mordor's Innovative Nemesis System Is Locked Behind a Patent until 2036' (*EnGadget*, 26 February 2025) https://www.engadget.com/gaming/shadow-of-mordors-innovative-nemesis-system-is-locked-behind-a-patent-until-2036-195437208.html

Bramwell, T, 'Microsoft Kills Game Ownership and Expects Us to Smile' (*Eurogamer*, 7 June 2013) https://www.eurogamer.net/articles/2013-06-07-microsoft-kills-game-ownership-and-expects-us-to-smile

Brooks, A, 'Rocket League's Live Streaming Performance' (*Stream Hatchet*, 30 August 2023) https://streamhatchet.com/blog/rocket-leagues-live-streaming-performance/

Cairngorms National Park, 'Cairngorms Minecraft Project' (*Cairngorms National Park*, date unknown) https://cairngorms.co.uk/caring-future/education/learning/minecraft/

CD Projekt Red, 'Dedicated Cyberpunk 2077 Feature for Content Creators: 'Disable Copyrighted Music' (*Cyberpunk 2077*, 23 November 2020) https://www.cyberpunk.net/en/news/36734/dedicated-cyberpunk-2077-feature-for-content-creators-disable-copyrighted-music

—— 'The Witcher 3: Wild Hunt' (*Steam*, 18 May 2015) https://store.steampowered.com/app/292030/The_Witcher_3_Wild_Hunt/

Craddock, R, 'Nintendo Issues Mass DMCA Takedown, 379 Fan-Games Forcibly Removed' (*NintendoLife*, 6 January 2021) https://www.nintendolife.com/news/2021/01/nintendo_issues_mass_dmca_takedown_379_fan-made_games_forcibly_removed

Creative Computing 'Creative Computing Magazine (May 1978) Volume 04 Number 03' (*Internet Archive*, 18 January 2013) https://archive.org/details/creativecomputing-1978-05/page/n139/mode/2up

Cundy, M, 'Is Nintendo Doomed? Not Likely. Just Take a Look at How Much Money It's Got in the Bank' (*GamesRadar*, 13 February 2012) https://www.gamesradar.com/nintendo-doomed-not-likely-just-take-look-how-much-money-its-got-bank/

Cushing, T, '"Gears of War" Designer: Used Games Must Be Killed So Sustainable Development Can Live' (*Techdirt*, 18 June 2013) https://www.techdirt.com/articles/20130616/20142123500/games-war-designer-cliff-bleszinski-used-games-must-be-killed-order-unsustainable-aaa-development-to-live.shtml

Dead Smurf Software (1996) The first 'official' Castle Smurfenstein Home Page https://www.evl.uic.edu/aej/smurf.html

Dictionary.com, 'Winking Face emoji' (*Dictionary.com*, date unknown) https://www.dictionary.com/e/emoji/winking-face-emoji/

Dietz, J, 'Highest-Scoring Games of the 2010s' (*Metacritic*, 4 January 2020) [*archived*] https://web.archive.org/web/20191211033941/https://www.metacritic.com/feature/best-videogames-of-the-decade-2010s

Djnym, 'RoguelikeRestorationProject: license.txt' (*Github*, 2011) https://github.com/RoguelikeRestorationProject/urogue/blob/master/LICENSE.TXT

Dutton, F, 'What is Indie?' (*Eurogamer*, 18 April 2012) https://www.eurogamer.net/what-is-indie

Fahey, M, 'Ubisoft Does Away With Tree-Killing Instruction Manuals' (*Kotaku*, 19 April 2010) [*archived*] https://web.archive.org/web/20210729215057/https://kotaku.com/ubisoft-does-away-with-tree-killing-instruction-manuals-5520261

Fox, T, Deltarune (*Deltarune*, date unknown) https://www.deltarune.com

—— 'FAQ' (*Deltarune*, date unknown) https://www.deltarune.com/help/

Free Moria, 'Moria Non-Free License' https://free-moria.sourceforge.net/moria-non-free-license.txt

Friedman, Z, 'Stop Falling For This Facebook Scam' (*Forbes*, 19 August 2019) https://www.forbes.com/sites/zackfriedman/2019/08/19/facebook-scam/?sh=5efafd01a4cf

GameCentral, 'Triple-A Games Are Killing Gaming' (*Metro*, 5 April 2020) https://metro.co.uk/2020/04/05/triple-games-killing-gaming-readers-feature-12506993/

Good, OS, 'COVID-19 Pandemic Turns Console Gamers to Digital Sales in Record Numbers' (*Polygon*, 11 August 2020) https://www.polygon.com/2020/8/11/21363951/video-game-sales-digital-online-xbox-one-ps4-publisher-figures-ea-activision-2k-games

'GTA V Player Takes "Street" Photography Using In-game Camera Phone' (*Independent*, 2013) https://www.independent.co.uk/voices/iv-drip/gta-v-player-takes-street-photography-using-game-camera-phone-8879370.html

Holkins, M and Krahulik, J, 'Words and Their Meanings' (*Penny Arcade*, 25 August 2010) [*archived*] https://web.archive.org/web/20201109040508/https://www.penny-arcade.com/news/post/2010/8/25

Humongous Inc, 'Backyard Football 09' https://dn790007.ca.archive.org/0/items/NintendoDSManuals/BackyardFootball09usab.pdf

Ibrahim, M, 'Firewatch Creators Can Target PewDiePie with DMCA Takedowns, and It's Perfectly Legal' (*Polygon*, 12 September 2017) https://www.polygon.com/2017/9/12/16295412/pewdiepie-campo-santo-firewatch-dmca-legal-abuse

Ignatova, I, 'A £24b Market: Why Do Game Studios Pay Influencers' (*80.lv*, 15 August 2024) https://80.lv/articles/a-usd24b-market-why-do-game-studios-pay-influencers

ISFE, 'French Ruling on Copyright Flies in Face of Established EU Law' (*ISFE*, 20 September 2019) [*archived*] https://web.archive.org/web/20201111192302/https://www.isfe.eu/news/french-ruling-on-copyright-exhaustion-flies-in-face-of-established-eu-law

Jenkins, H, 'Vernacular Creativity: An Interview with Jean Burgess (Part Two)' (*Confessions of an Aca-Fan*, 8 October 2007) http://henryjenkins.org/blog/2007/10/vernacular_creativity_an_inter_1.html

Kelion, L, 'Pirate Our Games, Don't Buy Them from Key Resellers, Say Indies' (*BBC* News, 8 July 2019) https://www.bbc.co.uk/news/technology-48908726

Know Your Meme, 'Leeroy Jenkins' https://knowyourmeme.com/memes/leeroy-jenkins

Lastowka, G, 'Minecraft as Web 2.0: Amateur Creativity & Digital Games' (*SSRN*, 5 October 2011) https://papers.ssrn.com/sol3/papers.cfm?abstract_id=1939241

—— 'Copyright Law and Video Games: A Brief History of an Interactive Medium' (*SSRN*, 2013) https://papers.ssrn.com/sol3/papers.cfm?abstract_id=2321424

—— 'The Player-Authors Project' (*SSRN*, 2013) https://papers.ssrn.com/sol3/papers.cfm?abstract_id=2361758

Martin, M, 'EA: Second-hand Sales Are a "Critical Situation"' (*Gamesindustrybiz*, 28 August 2008) https://www.gamesindustry.biz/articles/ea-second-hand-sales-are-a-critical-situation

Materia Music Publishing, 'YouTube FAQ' (Materia Music Publishing, date unknown) https://materiamusicpub.com/youtube-faq/

McShea, T, 'Sony's Triumphant Night' (*Gamespot*, 10 June 2013) https://www.gamespot.com/articles/sonys-triumphant-night/1100-6409715/

Metacritic, 'Games' (*Metacritic*, date unknown) https://www.metacritic.com/game

Microsoft, 'Microsoft Services Agreement' (*Microsoft*, 1 April 2021) https://www.xbox.com/en-GB/legal/XboxComTOU

Midway Manufacturing Company 'Arcade Game Manual: Midway's Pac-Man Parts and Operating' (*Internet Archive*, 4 January 2011) https://archive.org/details/ArcadeGameManualMidwaysPac-manPartsAndOperating/mode/2up

Midway Games 'Mortal Kombat: Armageddon – Manual' (*Games Database*, date unknown) https://www.gamesdatabase.org/Media/SYSTEM/Sony_Playstation_2/Manual/formated/Mortal_Kombat-_Armageddon_-_2007_-_Midway_Games.pdf

Minecraft Middle Earth, 'Minecraft Middle Earth' https://www.mcmiddleearth.com/

Mojang, 'Minecraft: Education Edition' (*Mojang*, date unknown) https://education.minecraft.net/en-us/homepage

Murray, MD, 'AI Pirated my Art and Birthed Infringing Works, and Other Metaphors that Confound Copyright Law' (*SSRN*, 28 March 2025) https://papers.ssrn.com/sol3/papers.cfm?abstract_id=5116714

Neverwinter Nights Wiki 'End-User License Agreement' https://nwn.fandom.com/wiki/End-User_License_Agreement

Origin Systems 'Ultima III: Exodus Manual' (*Internet Archive*, 11 October 2018) https://archive.org/details/c64man_ultima3/mode/1up

Orland, K, 'Posting Persona 5 Spoilers Could Get You Hit With Account Suspension' (*Ars Technica*, 4 May 2017) https://arstechnica.com/gaming/2017/04/atlus-threatens-takedown-of-persona-5-spoiler-videos/

Partleton, K, 'Report: Google Paid 160 Million USD for Activision Blizzard Esports Streaming Rights' (*PocketGamer.biz*, 18 February 2020) https://www.pocketgamer.biz/google-activision-blizzard-deal-worth-160-million-usd/

PC Games, 'The Best Cyberpunk 2077 Mods' (*PC Games*, date unknown) https://www.pcgamesn.com/cyberpunk-2077/mods-best

PC Matic Cybersecurity, '4 Years Later – PC Pitstop EULA Experiment Still the Buzz' (*Tech Talk*, 14 December 2009) https://techtalk.pcpitstop.com/2009/12/14/4-years-later-pc-pitstop-eula-experiment-still-the-buzz/

Perez, M, 'Top-Earning Video Gamers: The Ten Highest-Paid Players Pocketed More Than $120 Million in 2019' (*Forbes*, 2020) https://www.forbes.com/sites/mattperez/2020/01/29/top-earning-video-gamers-the-ten-highest-paid-players-pocketed-more-than-120-million-in-2019/

Pidaparthy, U, 'What You Should Know about iTunes' 56-page Legal Rerms' (*CNN*, 6 May 2011) [*archived*] https://web.archive.org/web/20110509075256/http://edition.cnn.com/2011/TECH/web/05/06/itunes.terms/

PlayStation, 'Official PlayStation Used Game Instructional Video' (*YouTube*, 10 June 2013) https://www.youtube.com/watch?v=kWSIFh8ICaA

Purchese, R, 'Minecraft Man: "Piracy is Not a Theft"' (*Eurogamer*, 3 March 2011) https://www.eurogamer.net/articles/2011-03-03-minecraft-man-piracy-is-not-a-theft

Quinn, 'The Eerie Art of Anti-piracy Screens' (*Medium* 15 May 2024) https://medium.com/counter-arts/the-eerie-art-of-anti-piracy-screens-d92efc433b1f

Ranker, 'How Do Rankings Work?' (*Ranker*, date unknown) [*archived*] https://web.archive.org/web/20211122141043/https://blog.ranker.com/faqs

Reed, M, 'The Atari Anti-Piracy Advertisement' (*Matthew Reed's TRS-80.org*, 2007) http://www.trs-80.org/atari-anti-piracy-advertisement/

Rubin, PQ, 'A Brief History of DRM in Video Games' (*Prompting Culture*, 11 November 2024) https://promptingculture.substack.com/p/a-brief-history-of-drm-in-video-games

Salvador, P, 'Survey of the Video Game Reissue Market in the United States' (*Zenodo*, 10 July 2023) https://zenodo.org/records/8161056

Sirani, J, 'Top 10 Best-Selling Video Games of All Time' (*IGN*, 9 February 2021) https://www.ign.com/articles/2019/04/19/top-10-best-selling-video-games-of-all-time
'SL Modifies Terms of Service and EULA (Sort of)' (*The Alphaville Herald* 6 October 2004) http://alphavilleherald.com/2004/10/sl_modifies_ter.html
Smith, C, '7,500 Online Shoppers Accidentally Sold Their Souls to Gamestation' (*Huffpost*, 25 May 2011) https://www.huffingtonpost.co.uk/entry/gamestation-grabs-soulso_n_541549
Sony, 'Software Usage Terms' (*Sony*, October 2022) https://www.playstation.com/en-gb/legal/software-usage-terms/
Statista 'Games – Worldwide' (*Statista*, 2025) https://www.statista.com/outlook/amo/media/games/worldwide
Steam, 'Deltarune' (*Steam*, 2021) https://store.steampowered.com/app/1671210/DELTARUNE/
Superhot Fandom, 'End User License Agreement' (*Superhot Fandom*, date unknown) https://superhot.fandom.com/wiki/End_User_License_Agreement
Superhot Team, 'Superhot' (*Kickstarter*, 2015) https://www.kickstarter.com/projects/375798653/super-hot
Tandy 'Pitfall II Programme Manual' [1985] (*Color Computer Archive*, date unknown) https://color-computerarchive.com/repo/Documents/Manuals/Games/Pitfall%20II%20(Tandy).pdf
Tassi, P, 'After "The Last of Us Part 2" Insanity, Metacritic Has Changed User Score Submissions' (*Forbes*, 18 July 2020) https://www.forbes.com/sites/paultassi/2020/07/18/after-the-last-of-us-part-2-insanity-metacritic-has-changed-user-score-submissions/?sh=57f869617e6f
TermsFeed, 'EULA Generator' (*TermsFeed*, date unknown) https://www.termsfeed.com/eula-generator/
The Acropolitan, 'Sentence Length Has Declined 75% in the Past 500 Years' (*Medium*, 29 August 2017) https://medium.com/@theacropolitan/sentence-length-has-declined-75-in-the-past-500-years-2e40f80f589f
Thomas, A, 'The First Software Licensing Agreement and its Relationship with Copyright Law' (*CREATe*, 14 November 2018) https://www.create.ac.uk/blog/2018/11/14/the-first-software-licensing-agreement-and-its-relationship-with-copyright-law/
—— 'The Copyright User: A Socio-legal Enquiry' (University of Glasgow, 26 May 2022) https://theses.gla.ac.uk/82902/
tl;drLegal, 'Software Licenses in Plain English' (*tl;drLegal*, date unknown) https://tldrlegal.com/
ToS;DR, 'Terms of Service; Didn't Read' (ToS;DR, date unknown) https://tosdr.org/
Townsend, K, 'The Best Video Games of the 2010s, Ranked' (*Ranker*, 22 October 2020) https://www.ranker.com/list/best-video-games-2010s/kyle-townsend
Valve, 'Steam Subscriber Agreement' (*Steam*, date unknown) https://store.steampowered.com/subscriber_agreement/
Wales, M, 'Player Takes Impressive Stab at Recreating Cult Corridor Horror PT in Media Molecule's Dreams' (*Eurogamer*, 23 January 2019) https://www.eurogamer.net/articles/2019-01-21-player-takes-impressive-stab-at-recreating-cult-corridor-horror-pt-in-media-molecules-dreams
Willings, A, 'Best Selling Games List of 2010s is Surprising for its Lack of Surprises' (*Pocket Lint*, 20 January 2020) https://www.pocket-lint.com/games/news/150785-best-selling-games-of-the-last-decade
Wolens, J, 'Weird, Niche Mods Make PC Gaming Great, and These Ones Prove It' (*Yahoo!Tech*, 1 February 2025) https://tech.yahoo.com/general/articles/weird-niche-mods-pc-gaming-111200827.html
Yin-Poole, W, 'Fallout: New Vegas Dev Hopes Digital Distribution "Stabs Used Game Market in the Heart"' (*Eurogamer*, 13 December 2011) https://www.eurogamer.net/articles/2011-12-13-fallout-new-vegas-dev-hopes-digital-distribution-stabs-used-game-market-in-the-heart
You Can Play, 'Overview' https://www.copyrightevidence.org/ycp/overview
ZombieAli, 'Thomas the Tank Engine over Mr X' (*Nexus Mods*, 3 March 2019) https://www.nexusmods.com/residentevil22019/mods/62

GLOSSARY

CDA	Acronym for 'Critical Discourse Analysis'.
Indie	Slang or shorthand for 'independent' games. Referring to types of games created by individuals or smaller development teams, typically with less financial support than larger publishers.
Mods	Slang or shorthand for 'modifications' to games.
Triple A	Sometimes referred to as AAA. Referring to types of games that are typically characterised by their large budgets, large development teams, and extensive marketing. They may be understood as the equivalent of the Hollywood blockbuster in the gaming world.
UGC	Acronym for 'user-generated content'.

INDEX

www.ingramcontent.com/pod-product-compliance
Ingram Content Group UK Ltd.
Pitfield, Milton Keynes, MK11 3LW, UK
UKHW020817290926
15470UKWH00003B/1215